Plants in the Service of Man

BY THE SAME AUTHOR

Soil and Civilization
Vineyards in England
Pleasure from Plants
From the Wasteland
Dionysus
The English Garden
Irish Gardens
The Gardener's Bedside Book
A History of Gardens and Gardening
Capability Brown and Humphry Repton

Plants in the Service of Man

10,000 YEARS OF DOMESTICATION

Edward Hyams

J. M. Dent & Sons Ltd, London

For IAN BOWLER

IN THE HOPE THAT HE'LL LIKE IT

First published 1971

© Text, Edward Hyams, 1971

Made in Great Britain at the
Aldine Press, Letchworth, Hertfordshire
for J. M. Dent & Sons Ltd
Aldine House, Bedford Street, London

ISBN 0 460 03917 2

Contents

Illustrations

Introduction

The things man has made out of every conceivable kind of inanimate material, since he first began to be a maker and so became man, are studied, illustrated and discussed in thousands of books read by tens of millions of people. But the artefacts on which the whole splendid fabric of civilization has been reared have been neglected by historians of mankind's career as a creator. It is curious, this; for until we had so improved as to transform, to re-create, the plants we live on, we could not accomplish much else.

Farming, the fundamental craft of any civilization, began with plants as nature had made them. It is obvious, but never sufficiently clearly *visualized*, that the first wheat deliberately grown was from a sowing of wild seed; the first cultivated apple-tree, grape-vine, cotton-bush or date-palm were identical with those growing in the wild, just as the first hammer was a stone picked up off the ground, the first needle a thorn or a fishbone, the first knife a fractured flint or a sharp-edged oyster-shell. And just as man soon began to shape those inanimate objects into better tools than they constituted when he first picked them up, so did he begin to shape living plants to the same end—to improve their usefulness to himself.

It is easy to see why only a very few authors have tried to tell the story of the making of cultivated plants: the beginning of the story is so ancient that there are no 'documents', or only a very few provided by archaeology; still more discouraging, one cannot, like the historian of art, architecture or science, introduce into the narrative remarkable men

known by name and character and achievement. The making
of cultivated plant-races is a work of many, many generations, each one adding a little, and although that is a moving
idea, it cannot very well be dramatized. There is yet another
thing which has led to the neglect of this subject by laymen:
it has never occurred to a surprisingly large number of intelligent and educated people that our cultivated plants *are*
man-made. They seem to think of them as bounty from
nature; and so they are, and so is the lump of stone still to be
shaped by the mason or the sculptor.

Of course, there are wild wheats, wild apples, wild cabbage
still to be found if you seek them, as there are still stones
which could be used as hammers, oyster-shells as knives, fish-
bones as needles. But in the case of many species there exists
in the wild state no plant equivalent to the cultigen, or even
clearly ancestral to it. Maize, pea-nuts, coconut palms are
cases in point. Very many of the plants we have made are
dependent on us for survival, would become extinct within
a few decades if not cared for by men; we have, in fact,
created living plants which, in the context of wild nature, are
unfit. Maize again is a good example. Even where obvious
ancestors still do exist, the differences between them and the
plants we have made of them as raw material are startling.
The wild grape-vine of Eurasia, *Vitis vinifera sylvestris*, is
dioecious and has one- or two-ounce bunches of fruit the size
of peas. But of this we have made approximately three
thousand different cultivars, some of which have fifteen-
pound bunches of grapes as big as plums, and all of which
are hermaphrodite. The yield of grain from a cultivated
cereal plant is at least a hundred times that from its wild
ancestor.

The making of plants for our use is a never-finished work.
But how was all that has already been done, done at all
without the modern plant-maker's tool—genetics? Acade-
mician N. I. Vavilov, who made one of the greatest contributions to the foundation of scientific plant-breeding, the

practical use of genetics, says that plant-making was an art
before it became a science. Observation of plant behaviour,
common sense, flashes of insight, did the work we now do
by reference to half a dozen mutually aiding sciences. And
people using these methods, the methods of the artist, accomplished marvels and made living masterpieces.

Thousands of years before Darwin's insight revealed the
workings of natural selection, and before the genes had been
discovered and, in part, understood, men were manipulating
plants *as if* they understood how selection of living plants could
reshape them, *as if* they had knowledge of the working of the
chromosomes. And so effective was this empiricism in practice
that until very recently the fact that we now know more or
less what we are doing when we exploit the genetical endow-
ment of a species, instead of just doing it in the dark, has
made surprisingly little difference. Our new knowledge is
beginning to be used effectively, but only just.

When, in the remote past, a plant species was first brought
into cultivation, the natural selection of characters from
among all those potential in its genes to bring out by natural
forces those favouring survival in the wild was replaced by
artificial, ultimately intelligent, selection of characters useful
to man. In the special conditions of cultivation, with the
plants protected from competition and favoured by artificially
good conditions, those plants could, as it were, afford to give
expression to characters which had become recessive because
they did not serve the purpose of the species in its wild
conditions. Mutants, instead of dying as unfit, might be
noted, protected, propagated. But different mutations,
different expressions of the genetical potential of the species,
might emerge in different places where the same kind of
plant was being grown by men; or one community might
favour and foster one mutation rather than another. Thus
local races of the species in cultivation were established, in
some cases numbered by thousands. And when some social
or political change in the communities of men brought two

or more of those long isolated races together, then crossing
might occur, qualities of the parent plants be transcended, or
hitherto hidden qualities potential in the genetical make-up
emerge. Let me here quote a passage from Vavilov's writings,
though it is repeated in the text later:

The world's *chef d'œuvre* of plant-breeding is to be found on
the island of Sakurajima in southern Japan: a radish one *pud*
in weight [15 to 17 kgs or about 34 lb.]. On the same island,
under conditions similar to those in which it thrives, are a
wild radish and a cultivated radish, each related to the same
botanical species, which form only small roots. It would be
vain then to ask how the wonderful giant has been produced;
no one knows . . . But one thing is certain, the giant forms
were the consequence of skilful selection of extreme variants
by unknown breeders many ages ago.

Another way in which man reshapes plants by controlling
their evolutionary potential is by the bringing together from
remote habitats species of a single genus, which, but for that
interference, could never have cross-bred to produce hybrid
offspring. Species of a genus, separated in nature by a whole
continent or a great ocean, can provide for each other the key
to a sort of genetical lock which, being opened, enables the
genus to realize more of its potential characters. In the orchid
family it has even been possible to cross-breed not merely
species but genera. There are rare instances of this succeeding in other plant families; and as the science of genetical
engineering should make that sort of thing more widely
possible, the prospects for new, almost entirely artificial,
plants are extraordinary.

Which means, of course, that our job of plant-making is
by no means finished. It is probably unlikely that there are
still wild species to be domesticated which would be of any
great importance, although there are certainly many which
would be useful. But until recently the work of plant-making
has been unsystematic, unco-ordinated, a hit-and-miss

business. I cannot do better than conclude this introduction with another short quotation from Vavilov (1940):

We are now entering an epoch of differential ecological, physiological, and genetic classification. It is an immense work. The ocean of knowledge is practically untouched by biologists. It requires the joint labours of many different specialists—physiologists, cytologists, geneticists, systematists, and biochemists. It requires the international spirit, the coöperative work of investigators throughout the whole world. . . . We do not doubt that the new systematics will bring us to a new and better understanding of evolution, to a great increase in the possibilities of governing the processes of evolution, and to great improvement in our cultivated plants and breeds of animals. It will bring us logically to the next step: integration and synthesis.

1

The noble grasses

Although the arts and crafts were beautifully practised while men, or at least some of them, were still hunters and food-gatherers, that is to say before the invention of agriculture and stock-raising, civilization begins with farming. This does not mean that it begins at the same time as farming; far from it. It means that it could not have begun at all without the invention of farming. For alphabets are invented, cities are built, religions, philosophies and sciences are developed from speculation about the environment and the human condition, sophisticated war is waged, political systems are founded and elaborated, books are written and plays performed, industries are devised, perfected and carried on, clothes are made more complex and attractive, pictures are painted and music is composed—all by men and women who are free of the need to go out every day and find food to eat. This freedom is impossible if every man and woman has to go every day hunting, or gathering seeds, berries and shell-fish in order to keep alive; or even if every man in the community has to do so for a household of some kind. Freedom to practise the arts of civilization is the principal benefit of a system of food-getting whereby one man's work will feed not only himself and family but a number of other men and their families as well. Agriculture is that system, and the efficiency with which it is practised can best be measured by calculating the number of people adequately fed by one man's work.

Man is one of the relatively small number of omnivorous animals. In this as in other respects his success as a species is a product of his failure to specialize, or, rather, of his specialization in not specializing. Men can live on a wholly vegetable diet, on fish (including shell-fish), on meat (including the meat of his own kind), even on insect grubs. But it is a true saying that all flesh is grass: whether we eat it directly in the form of leaves and roots, seeds and fruits, or indirectly by eating the flesh of creatures which live on those things, we are living entirely on the green plant which has, what we have not, the power to convert into organic tissue the minerals of which flesh is made.

By far the most important vegetable foods are quite literally grasses, that is to say, members of the family *Gramineae*. That family of green plants not only provides the bulk of the pasture on which all kinds of cattle are fed; it also includes those noble species of grasses we call cereals. Without the exceptional power possessed by grasses to grow again more vigorously than ever after being eaten almost down to the roots, a large number of animal species, including nearly all the farm animals, could not have evolved at all. It is possible to argue that the astounding success of *homo sapiens* as a species is ultimately due to the power possessed by grass to grow again after being eaten down by animals. However, in the present context we are interested less in the fodder grasses than in the cereal grasses: wheat, barley, millet, oats, maize and rice.

At the base of every one of mankind's great societies, of all the original civilizations, is a cereal grass. In the west of the Old World, civilization was founded on wheat and barley; some Far-Eastern civilizations were founded on rice. It was the cultivation of one of these grains which, more than any other factor, made it possible for one man or one woman to support several or many households instead of only one, and so to free a majority of any population to do other work, the work which made what we call civilization.

So at the very origin of civilization is the man or woman who first thought of cultivating grain instead of going out to gather it where it grew wild.

If we try to discover where, when and by whom the cereal grains were domesticated, there is no point in looking outside the regions where such grains grow wild. And there is one thing which archaeologists have discovered and which also serves as a guide: the earliest cereals to be cultivated were *einkorn* and *emmer* wheats, and barley. As to how this great step forward came to be taken, there can be no difficulty. Even if we suppose that men at the hunting stage of economy had not yet realized that plants grow from seed after their kind, they would very soon have had the discovery forced upon them when they started to gather and store seeds as food. In fairly warm, damp conditions the seeds themselves would, by germinating, have taught the gatherers a simple lesson in biology. It would be a mistake to suppose the men of the Stone Ages to have been less able to learn from observation than we are. They were makers of tools, weapons, traps, boats, basket-ware, and in due course of pottery; they were even painters of pictures. The lesson taught by the germinating seed once learnt, it was a fairly obvious step from that to scratching a piece of land and burying the seed; or to treading the seed into the mud near the shore of a lake, or into the alluvium deposited beside a river by a retreating flood. So simple and obvious are these operations that there is no need to postulate a single discovery of the idea and practice by a unique genius, or to assume that the practice of agriculture spread from a single original centre all over the world. It is surely much more likely that the discovery was made several times, by different people in places remote from each other but where conditions were equally favourable.

So the seeds of some of the larger grasses were, in some parts of the world and to some communities of Stone-Age man, as important, as an article of food, to men as to birds. And such seeds were harvested, and even ground into flour, during many centuries, probably thousands of years, before the invention of agriculture. At El Natuf, on Mount Carmel, archaeologists found reaping tools dating as early as

6000 BC, made by setting a row of small, sharp flints into a wooden or bone shaft, the flint teeth showing the characteristic scratching caused by reaping straw. These proto-sickles were used for reaping wild wheat and barley. Similar tools have been found associated with Neolithic communities over a wide area, notably at Merinde in the Nile Delta and at Tepe Gawra in the Tigris alluvium.

The genus to which belongs the grass we call wheat is *Triticum*. There are several species, but many kinds to which specific names have in the past been given were really man-made, a fact of which they exhibit unmistakable genetical signs. This in itself is a sure evidence of great antiquity in cultivation.

What Vavilov called the Near-Eastern Centre of Origin of Cultivated Plants includes all Asia Minor, Transcaucasia, Iran and parts of Turkmenistan. *Emmer* and *einkorn* are not the only wheats native over wide and different areas in that part of the world; also found there are upwards of nine ancient cultivars—that is plants modified by cultivation to which specific names have been given. Some archaeologists hold that the first wheat to be cultivated was *einkorn*; if this was so, then domestication first occurred somewhere between the southern Balkans and Armenia, for that is the habitat of *einkorn* wheat as a wild plant. But it does not seem to me clear that *einkorn* preceded *emmer*, which is native to the region in which urban civilization first developed. Even at Jarmo, in Kurdistan, on a site dated 4750 BC—the home of a people practising very primitive agriculture, for the wheat grains found there show unmistakable signs of being a cultivar—wheat is an *emmer*, not an *einkorn*. Barley found on that site shows the same signs of being a cultivar, not the wild barley. And the very earliest site where any kind of activity which can possibly be called farming was carried on seems to have been in the neighbourhood of Jericho; and there again it was an *emmer* wheat and not an *einkorn* that was in use.

How does the revealing change in a wild plant brought into cultivation occur? We are here discussing a time long before the idea of cross-breeding plants deliberately had occurred to anyone.

Plants are variable. The individuals which compose a species are not by any means identical; they are merely very similar, and 'species' has been defined by at least one cautious botanist as a group of individuals which differ from each other only less than they differ from individuals of the same genus outside that species. In nature, however, variability is kept more or less within narrow limits because cross-pollination is random, and in a given habitat no selection occurs. There are, of course, exceptions to this rule. For example, a plant species may spread uphill into altitudes at which cold begins to affect it. The individuals within that species vary in their resistance to cold; the less resistant individuals will be killed, leaving only the more resistant. In that case plants of the species in question at the new higher altitude habitat will receive pollen only from individuals which, like themselves, are resistant to cold. Natural selection for cold-resistance has occurred, and the resultant seedlings will include individuals even more resistant to cold than were their parents. A sub-species, which may, if it differs enough, develop into a new species of the original plant, has been created, confined to a higher altitude than the typical species.

Man, when he cultivates a plant, deliberately operates a more rigorous and above all much quicker selection. Wanting certain attributes he retains those plants which show them, rejects those which do not. So, in the segregation of cultivation, cultivars emerge, deliberately selected, inbred varieties unknown in the wild. Without going into genetics, it is a question of bringing out combinations and permutations of genetical characters which were always potential in the species but which natural selection did not bring out because the conditions did not exist which would have called for them in order to fulfil the purpose of the species—survival. Of course, one ought not to use words like 'purpose' in this context. But perhaps we may do so for once, to make the point, and even agree that the attribute 'life' implies purpose, though it be blind, deaf, dumb and unconscious.

The segregation process takes time; if we come upon a place where the number of differing cultivated 'races' of a particular species of economic plant is much greater than is found in any other place, we are fairly safe in arguing that the cultivation of that species is older there than elsewhere. Using that kind of evidence we conclude that of the two places where the cultivation of cereals is most ancient, the Tigris-Euphrates region is even older, as a farming country, than Egypt. But there is not much in it; and it may be that a country lying between them, namely Syria and Palestine, is the land of agricultural origin, of the domestication of wheat and barley.

I have referred to the presence of reaping tools on very ancient sites in that part of the world, and also in the Nile Delta and in Tepe Gawra in Mesopotamia. In the Egyptian Fayum a site excavated by Miss Caton-Thompson and Miss Gardner yielded silos of clay, straw and reeds, in which grains of *emmer* wheat, barley and flax were found. It is probable that it was on the borders of the ancient lakes of the Fayum, and in the Nile mud, that cereals were first cultivated in Egypt, about 7,000 years ago. And that farming with wheat and barley began in Mesopotamia at about the same time or possibly rather earlier. Of all the cultivated plants only these two were old enough as such to be written by the Egyptians in ideograms, and not merely in the later phonetic writing.

As for the very first deliberate planting of grain in that part of the world, what we may call the very act of domestication, it would seem most likely to have occurred in Palestine or Syria about 8,000 years ago.

The grains on which the civilization of the Far East were

founded were millet and rice. But although millet—or rather
the millets, for the word is used to describe plants not only of
different species but also of different genera—has retained
some small importance, it is only a forerunner; it cannot be
compared with rice as an efficient transformer of mineral
substances into tissue suitable as food for animals, including
man. The domestication of both grains comes much later
than that of wheat and barley; and although both grains must
have been harvested in the wild for thousands of years before
they were cultivated, the idea of domesticating them must
have been a result of the much earlier domestication of wheat
and barley. At least there is no doubt that this was so in the
case of rice. Millets occur wild in China, India and Africa:
an early and independent domestication of millet is possible
for north China but, to say the least, unlikely. Another
millet was cultivated by very early farmers in the Balkans
(Starcevo-Körös Culture) by people who also had *einkorn*
wheat. As a millet was wild in that region it was doubtless
taken into cultivation after the people had received domesticated wheat, and the idea of cultivating it, from migrant
farmers from the Near East.

Where millet was the original cereal crop, but the climate
and conditions made the growing of rice possible, rice tended
to displace millet, for its food yield is enormously greater and
better. But the question is, where does this process begin?
The wild rice botanically nearest to the cultivar *Oryza sativa*
is *Oryza fatua*, which is considered to be its wild ancestor.
O. fatua is found wild in India, notably in the Gangetic plain
but also right through south-east Asia to Java, so that from
the point of view of availability of material, rice could have
been domesticated anywhere within that vast region of the
world. What one has to look for is a people within that region
who were at a cultural level to accomplish the act of
domestication, say about a thousand years before we find
rice being widely grown—still, of course, in prehistory.
There does not, however, seem to have been such a people.

This would appear to mean that the idea of planting and deliberately cultivating rice, its domestication, came from outside.

The conclusions of archaeology touching the eastward spread of the craft of agriculture from the western Asian centre of origin are briefly as follows. In the fourth millennium BC there were village settlements based on wheat-growing as far from those centres as the south-eastern littoral of the Caspian Sea (Tepe Hissar; Namasga Tepe). It seems that these, as it were, secondary centres of primitive farming may even date from the fifth millennium BC. Now two things tend to force emigration on very early farmers, excepting in the few cases where some natural phenomenon, such as the Nile flood, annually renews the soil. They are pressure of population on land, caused by rapid population increase, a result of relative plenty; and, before the invention of manuring, soil exhaustion. One or both of these causes resulted in colonies of migrants moving eastward from those south Caspian settlements. That eastward drift reached Baluchistan and finally the Indus Valley, and much later spread all over India. The migrants presumably carried their own seed-corn, and the first 'farms' in India were probably wheatfields. But where *Oryza fatua* had long been harvested in the wild as, incidentally, it still is in some places, it would very soon have been taken into cultivation like wheat. It seems, then, most likely that rice was first domesticated in India, probably early in the third millennium BC.

Later in that millennium there began another eastward drift, through Indo-China, and this time the colonists were rice farmers. It is possible that wet rice was first grown in that region. And at last, perhaps about 2000 BC, domesticated rice reached the Yangtse Valley and spread all over south-east Asia. It was certainly the possession of rice as a cultivar that gave a powerful new impulse to the growth of Chinese cultures in and about Kansu; and that it was on rice rather than millet that the great urban civilization of south China was built.

Turning to the Americas: the evidence is conflicting as to where and when *Zea mays*, the grain on which the Central and South American civilizations were built, was domesticated. It is a question of deciding whether that great creative act occurred in the south, and its results were conveyed to the north by diffusion, or occurred in Mexico or somewhere in the isthmus south of Mexico, and was conveyed to the Andean peoples by diffusion. It could be, of course, that domestication occurred independently in those two centres of ancient civilization, but that is not very probable.

We do not even know for sure whether the idea of farming plants occurred independently in the Americas, among some food-gathering people who had reached the Neolithic stage of culture, or whether it reached the Americas with immigrants from north-east Asia. The latter hypothesis is a perfectly possible and even likely one, for although the first migrants from Asia, those who began and continued the peopling of America, until that time empty of men, entered the continent from the extreme north-west a great while before the invention of farming in the Old World, apparently there were many and later waves of migrants, and there seems to be nothing much against the theory that some of these were later than 6000 BC. But there does seem to me to be one reason why the hypothesis of an independent invention of farming in America is the more likely one: would not migrant farmers from Asia, however primitive, have brought seed-corn with them? And if so, would not one or more of the Old-World corns have become established in the American flora? At the time of the Columbian discovery of America none of the Old-World crops was found in cultivation either in Central or in South America; nor, to my knowledge, were any of the Old-World grains or any economic plants ever found as weeds in the Americas until long after the Discovery.

In the second place, American agriculture did not begin with maize. (For that matter we cannot be sure that Old-World agriculture actually began with wheat.) In the valleys of the western watershed of the Andes, and in Mexico, the first cultivated crops were beans of the genus *Phaeseolus* (all the 'haricot' beans, as distinct from broad beans, are confined in nature to America), and some gourds or squashes. I find it a little difficult to accept the date (6500 BC) attributed to remains of beans and gourds found in an excavation site in a cave at Ocampo in Mexico, and said to be *cultivated* varieties. However, there is at least no doubt that beans and gourds are earlier in cultivation than maize in the Americas; and you cannot found a great urban civilization on those crops: the food yield per man-hour-acre is not good enough to enable farmers of those plants to build up the large surpluses of wealth which liberate some members of the community from the task of food production.

Three decades ago two brilliant American research workers, P. C. Mangelsdorf and R. G. Reeves, seemed to have discovered the origin of Indian corn, that is to say, *Zea mays*. They showed first that there is no such thing as a naked-seeded maize, such as the cultivated plant, known in nature; but they also demonstrated that a certain pod-corn, what I may perhaps call a maize with tunicated seeds, can and does, by a single gene mutation, give rise to a maize with naked seeds, in fact a primitive *Zea mays*. But this mutant, however often it may occur, cannot, with its unprotected seeds, survive in the wild to establish a new species; it is too vulnerable. Even cultivated maize on abandoned sites lasts only one or two generations and then disappears. On the other hand, naked-seeded corns are an advantage to the farmer; they do not have to be threshed free of the chaff. So here we have the origin of maize: a naked-seeded mutant of pod-corn selected in cultivation. The problem then becomes, where was the pod-corn first domesticated and cultivated?

The accepted criteria established by Vavilov and other workers led Mangelsdorf and Reeves to believe that Peru, rather than, for example, Guatemala or Mexico, was the oldest habitat of cultivated corn. On the other hand, no wild

corn was ever found in that region, and domestication can
only occur in the region where the wild plant is to be found in
abundance. This was explained away, not quite satisfactorily,
by the argument that so intensively was Peru cultivated for
thousands of years, from the beginning of urban civilization
in the great seaboard nations to the end of the Inca Empire
in the sixteenth century, that pod-corn, a troublesome weed
once maize proper had been segregated, was eliminated. It
seems very unlikely that the ancient Peruvians, with the
Stone-Age methods and tools at their disposal, could have
eliminated an endemic plant, but there it is. Another difficulty was that, whereas the most ancient potters of the region
made representations of maize cobs in plenty, the researchers
could find not a single representation of pod-corn. At last,
however, they seemed to be vindicated when one turned up,
in the Peabody Museum at Yale University. Mangelsdorf
and Reeves concluded that domestication of pod-corn
occurred somewhere in the lowlands now shared between
Paraguay, south-west Brazil and south-east Bolivia. No date
was attributable to the event, but it can hardly have been
later than about 4000 BC.

Then new evidence came to light: pod-corn pollen grains
were found in a boring 200 feet below Mexico City, suggesting that this corn was a native of that region as long as 60,000
years ago. As that was before the last glacial epoch, it does not
seem to be worth much, for there seems no evidence that it
survived into the present interglacial. Much more con-
clusive, excavations at Bat Cave in New Mexico yielded not
only cobs of corn but also an artefact which had been not
quite reliably dated 3500 BC.

No firm conclusion is yet possible. All we can safely say is
that the domestication of maize, on which the civilization of
the Andes (culminating in the great Inca Empire) and the
Maya, Olmec, Toltec and Aztec civilizations were built, and
which has transformed a large part of the farming economy
of the Old World, occurred either in the Paraguayan-

Brazilian-Bolivian lowlands, or in the Valley of Mexico, or in New Mexico, between 4500 and 3500 BC.

So much for the four grasses—wheat, barley, rice and maize—which lie at the origin of mankind's ascent and upon which world-wide technological civilization still rests. Two other cereal grasses have been of importance, since they have been used as substitutes for the major ones in climates and conditions which, before deliberate breeding of grains for specific conditions was possible, were too harsh for those four. So these two, rye and oats, have, like the millets, a secondary but still very considerable role in the history of civilization. It is not possible to place and date their domestication in the present state of our knowledge of the past; and it is not likely to become possible.

The domestication of oats must have occurred within historical times: they are not mentioned in the Bible and there is no word for oats in Sanskrit. In the Far East the first mention in literature of a variety of oats (*Avena sativa nuda*) occurs in a Chinese history of the period from AD 618 to 907. It is true that the *bromos* of the ancient Greeks means oats; but there is no evidence that they were ever cultivated by that people; and they were certainly not grown by the Romans, who knew oats (*avena*) as a weed of cultivation. But Pliny implies that the Germans cultivated oats when he says that they lived on oatmeal. And the physician Galen, in his *De Alimentis* (AD 131), says that oats were abundant in Mysia, Asia Minor, grown as fodder for horses, but used in years of scarcity to make bread. Oat grains, moreover, have been found in excavations of Bronze-Age sites in northern Europe; but they are doubtless wild oats. What probably happened was that north Europeans brought in contact with farming techniques domesticated the oats as cereals which would ripen even in a short, wet summer, which the better grains at that time would not.

In this case habitat is no guide as to where that event occurred for the first time. But if, as De Candolle suggested, oats were domesticated as a result of being found as a weed in wheatfields, then not northern Europe but the south Balkans or south Russia is a probable place.

For rye the case is a little less obscure, because the rule of greatest abundance of varieties can be applied. Only in Asia Minor and Transcaucasia are there cultivated ryes in what Vavilov describes as 'amazing diversity of forms'. Cultivation must first have been tried somewhere within that region of the world. And since rye, again, occurs very commonly as a weed in wheatfields, it was doubtless some intelligent wheat-farmer who, taking seeds from that source, tried it as a crop. As to the date, rye was another late-comer: *Secale cereale* has no name in Hebrew or in Sanskrit and it has never been found on any really ancient archaeological site. There is no evidence for its ancient cultivation in China or Japan, and it was unknown to the ancient Greeks. Pliny and Galen mention it, the first as a crop grown north of the Alps, the other as a grain cultivated in Thrace and Macedonia.

On the whole, philological and historical evidence suggests that rye was first domesticated somewhere in the north of Asia Minor, and towards the east, not much earlier than, say, 300 BC.

2

The wine-vines

Since bread and wine go together, and since both have been for thousands of years, and all over the western half of the world, not only of enormous economic importance but also of such social significance that they have become religious symbols, it will be logical to deal with the subject of the wine-vines after dealing with that of the bread-grains. And although such archaeological evidence as we have seems to indicate that farming begins with wheat, that is by no means sure. It is at least possible that some fruit-plants may have been cultivated even before the cereal grasses, and that the grape-vines were among them.

During the Tertiary epoch a proto-*Vitis* became established in the flora of north and north-east Asia and north-west America, at that time still joined together and enjoying a warm climate. As the climate of the northern hemisphere cooled, vines on the northern side of the habitat did not survive, while those on the southern side did, so that very slowly the whole habitat became more southerly, that movement being checked only when the southerly side of the habitat became too warm for the genus. In the Old World the movement was repeatedly checked, however, by the roughly east-to-west disposition of mountain barriers; cold and poor soil and absence of trees at high altitudes prevented the vines from moving any farther south in Central Asia, though in the Far East they got much farther, and more or less tropical species emerged. In America, where the mountain barriers run roughly north to south, the *Vites* moved farther south than in Central Asia before being checked.

This difference between the disposition of the Old- and New-World mountain barriers had an important result for the vines. In the Americas a large number of species established themselves, adapted to different climates and conditions; in the Old World only a single species survived in the western half of the habitat, that is Eurasia, although a number, still fewer than in the Americas, survived in the eastern half, the Far East. The single Eurasian species, in an enormous number of varieties and later cultivars, became the vine of history. This species, *Vitis vinifera sylvestris*, whose evolution can be traced in a series of many fossil species, became established and stable long before the Neolithic revolution by which man, from being a hunter and food-gatherer, became a farmer. This grape-vine's habitat was vast, extending from Transcaucasia through Asia Minor into western Europe.

Wine and vine first appear on record in association with man in the earliest Mesopotamian urban cultures, those of Kish, Lagash, Ur and Babylon. Yet there is no evidence that the wild wine-vine was ever a native of Mesopotamia or Egypt, where it also appears, though as a cultivated plant, in the earliest records. There is not much point in seeking the place of its original domestication, where the wild plant was entirely unknown. On the other hand, the more or less traceable line of diffusion of viticulture does point to a Mesopotamian or at least west Asian centre of origin. That line of diffusion is worth a glance; it will be best to trace it backwards in time.

Viticulture (the art of cultivating the grape-vine), wine and the plant itself, *Vitis vinifera* in an enormous number of cultivars grouped by botanists as *Vitis vinifera sativa*, were introduced to the Americas by European man in the sixteenth century; to southern Africa by European man in the seventeenth century; and to Australasia by European man in the nineteenth century. They were, that is to say, unknown in those parts of the world before those dates, so that we need

look for the trace only in European and Asiatic parts of the
world, if in Europe for this purpose we include north Africa.
But we can narrow the field at once, for it is a matter of history
that although there are many *Vites* within the territory of the
ancient Far-Eastern civilizations, they were not cultivated
until after the introduction of *Vitis vinifera.* As it happens,
that introduction is also a matter of history: about the year
128 BC the Emperor Wu of the Han Dynasty sent a special
envoy, General Chan k'ien, to Iran with orders to seek out a
people called Yue-chi and to make with them an alliance
against the troublesome Turkish people called the Hiung-nu.

In the course of a protracted mission General Chan k'ien
found himself in many Iranian countries, including Sog-
diana, Fergana and Bactria. Those countries were not
unknown to the Chinese Empire, whose merchants traded
with them; but they were very little visited by Chinese, and
had not been visited at all by anyone of the General's
standing. His own work there was concerned with introducing to China, for her cavalry regiments, horses very greatly
superior to the Mongol ponies which they had to make the
best of until that time; for it was important that the Chinese
imperial army should be better mounted than the Huns.
Among the things which made a great impression on Chan
k'ien were the vineyards and wines of Fergana. There was no
wine of the grape in China, nor was the wine-vine known
there. He considered that it would be a very good thing if
they were introduced to the Empire, and he accordingly sent
seeds of the vines to the Emperor Wu, who had the first
Chinese vineyard planted about 120 BC. So, once again, the
trace leads back to the Eurasian heartland. By the way, it was
at exactly the same time that Chan k'ien sent the first seeds of
alfalfa to China, realizing that the fine Iranian horses he had
been sending home would need this superior fodder crop.

Let us turn again to western Europe, one of the native
lands of the wild vine. The antiquity of the cultivated vine in
the east makes it clear that domestication had been accom-

plished before the Neolithic revolution—that is, before anything that can properly be called farming—started in
western Europe. If we exclude Greece, then the introduction
of viticulture to Europe occurred just within historical times
or at furthest at the very end of the prehistoric epoch. Of the
most ancient Italian civilizations, both the Etruscan in the
north and the Greek in the south, had a sophisticated viticulture which they taught to the Latins. Since we know very
little about the Etruscans, except that they came from the
East, they cannot help us; but there is no question that Greek
colonists brought their vines with them to Sicily and southern
Italy, and to Provence. Before the seventh century BC there
was no viticulture west of Greece; and geneticists have even
found it possible to distinguish between vineyard-vines of
later, wild European origin and the more ancient, introduced
cultivars.

Might not viticulture have been native to ancient Greece,
or at least to Crete? It seems not. Although the introduction
is prehistoric and conjectural, it is capable of being recalled.
In the first place, the word *oinos* is not Greek; it is a loan
word, the Semitic *yain* or *wain*. But the point in time with
which we are concerned excludes the possibility of the
ancient Jews having been the originators of viticulture;
nomad herdsmen are not plantation-crop farmers. However,
the language of the Phoenicians, of Tyre and Sidon, was also
Semitic.

During the first millennium BC the vine and wine were
closely associated with the cult of Dionysus. The oldest
Dionysiac myths and shrines, and the greatest number of
those myths, are Thracian in origin. Mysa, the port in
Thrace from which came the wine for the Greek troops
during the Trojan War, was in Thrace. It was in Thrace that
Odysseus received from Euanthes, the son of Dionysus, the
wine which he used to stupefy and so overcome the Cyclops.
Herodotus says of the Thracian Satres, a mountain people:
'But these Satres, as far as our knowledge goes, have never

yet been subject to any man; they alone of all the Thracians have ever been and are to this day free . . . *It is they who possess the place of divination sacred to Dionysus.*' (My italics.)

It seems at least very probable that vine and wine came into Greece by way of Thrace; and that the Thracians, or at least the Satres, were a colony of the Mysians across the water in Asia Minor. The trace leads back again to that part of the world. As for Crete, trade with the ancient Phoenician, or pre-Phoenician, perhaps Byblian, cities would have resulted in the introduction of viticulture; first came wine, later the vine and the art of cultivating it.

Assuming that plantation-agriculture probably began in Mesopotamia—where likewise the first systematic irrigation was developed (at least so far as we know), not by the proto-Sumerians coming in from the north-east but by the Semites from the south-west—we should at this point be inclined to decide that viticulture must have started here, were it not for the difficulty, already mentioned, that the vine was not native there, and is a woodland, foothills plant.

To the north of Mesopotamia were people, possibly akin to the Sumerians, less advanced technologically than the people to their south, and who, like the wild vines, inhabited the ancient countries of Armenia, Georgia and Azerbaijan. It seems that in the plain between the Tigris and the Euphrates there was orderly village life based on agriculture not later than 5500 BC; and that quite probably this culture was earlier. By the middle of the fourth millennium BC great cities such as Kish of the Sumerians and Ur of the Chaldees were flourishing. It is reasonable to suppose that by, say, 4000 BC, and perhaps a good deal earlier, the hill people to the north had learnt something about farming from their southern neighbours and were practising a settled agriculture in the fertile valleys.

Here, then, we have by 4000 BC at latest a people suffi-ciently advanced to have learnt to bring wild plants into cultivation—that is, to domesticate them—living in a part of the world where *Vitis vinifera sylvestris* was abundant. What is more, it seems quite likely that this is the only part of the world which fulfils our conditions.

One of the principal authorities on the genetics and history of the grape-vines, Dr E. Levadoux, wrote [1]:

The vine is a plant which reacts remarkably to its environment. The study of those reactions is in some sort the foundation of traditional viticulture. We know, for example, that even modifying the manner of pruning the vine considerably alters the quantity and the quality of the vintage; and it has proved possible to establish mathematical relationships between the modifications in the cultivation of vineyards, and their results in terms of production.

(My own translation.)

So the early plantation farmer of ancient Armenia, when he moved vines from their hilly, woodland habitat into some fertile valley exposed to the sun, had chosen a plant well able to adapt itself to change in conditions and to survive novice attempts at domestication. There is another point: the *Vites* are more prone to bud-mutation than are most fruit plants. From time to time a branch would grow bearing grapes of a different size, shape or colour, even a different flavour (e.g. the muscat flavour must have been a mutant) from those borne on the rest of the plant. Sometimes these would have been superior grapes. The farmer would have tried to grow this new variety by propagation from cuttings. For that method of propagation is very ancient indeed, as is proved by the fact that hundreds, perhaps thousands, of varieties originating in such mutations as I have described survived. Probably it seemed natural to primitive farmers to stick a piece of live plant into the ground and expect it to grow; and it happens that vine cuttings strike root very readily. Thus, in time, many different cultivars were established, vines unknown among the wild *Vites* populations but growing ever more common in cultivation.

[1] *La Sélection et l'hybridation chez la vigne.* Montpellier, 1951.

The most obvious and one of the most striking examples of the transformation of the vine, not by natural selection but by deliberate selection in the course of domestication, is the development of hermaphroditism. In the wild, *Vitis vinifera* is a dioecious plant, that is to say that the male flowers are generally borne on one plant, the female flowers on another. Suppose a primitive farmer planted a vineyard consisting of a hundred vines dug up in the wild, or raised plants from seeds from wild grapes: the chances are that his vineyard would contain fifty female vines bearing fruit, and fifty male ones bearing no fruit. Obviously, the figures are only true as an average of many thousands of such vineyards, but they would have been of that order. However, a small proportion of wild vines have hermaphrodite, or some hermaphrodite, flowers; if one or two of these were transplanted into our primitive vineyard, they would have drawn attention to themselves by carrying larger crops of grapes than the female vines, since the pollen needed to fertilize the flowers would not have to come from another plant.

The farmer would throw away those vines which bore no fruit. The female plants remaining would have made an even poorer showing by comparison with the hermaphrodite plants, being deprived of a source of pollen. The peasant, propagating new vines only from the most fruitful in his vineyard, would unwittingly be favouring hermaphroditism. In a few seasons the vine population of his vineyard would be entirely hermaphrodite; moreover, if he then started raising new plants from seed taken from his vineyard grapes, not only would 87·5 per cent of the seedlings be hermaphrodite but, the process being repeated over many years, the degree of hermaphroditism (proportion of hermaphrodite to unisexual flowers) would constantly increase. In short, the dioecious *Vitis vinifera sylvestris* was transformed into the hermaphrodite *V. vinifera sativa*.

To sum up, somewhere in Transcaucasia, perhaps in ancient Armenia, where wild vines were abundant in

Palaeolithic times, a people accustomed to gathering grapes
from the wild vines in the woods, as the colonists of North
America did in the seventeenth century and we ourselves
still gather blackberries, discovered that grapes left too long
in a crock produced a liquor which, being drunk, made the
drinker intoxicated. Wine was discovered, probably between
10000 and 8000 BC. Having learnt farming from their
southern and more advanced neighbours between 6000 and
4000 BC, this people, or their successors in the region, being
by then in the Neolithic phase, began to plant grape-vines.
By segregation and selection they transformed them into
hermaphrodite plants.

With the extension of viticulture to the south, under conditions of the intensive irrigated agriculture of the ancient
oases, there were created for the grape conditions of isolation
which, combined with repeated sowings of seeds and the
selection of bud mutations, facilitated the accumulation of
recessive characters. The first stage of such selection gave, in
regions bordering the Caspian Sea, wine and table varieties
which are found to this day in Daghestan, Azerbaijan and
Turkmenistan . . . [1]

From this region wine, viticulture and even the vines
themselves were carried into Mesopotamia, down into
Phoenicia, thence into Egypt; into Crete and Thrace, and
from both those places into Greece. From Greece they were
carried to southern Italy and the south of France in the
seventh and sixth centuries BC at latest; from France into
Germany and England not later than 100 BC; from Europe to
America in the sixteenth century AD, and thereafter into all
the lands where the vine would grow.

That is not, however, the end of the story of the domestication of the *Vites*.

When Europeans discovered the New World, it was found
to have grape-vines—many species—of its own. If the Vin-
land of the sagas is more or less historical, that discovery was

[1] Negrul, 1938.

actually first made by Vikings about AD 1001, but we are concerned only with the Columbian discovery. The native American vines were at first not used; viticulture was introduced into America by importing European vines. That introduction succeeded in Mexico, and later in several parts of South America, and then, too, in California. But north of Mexico and east of the Rockies it failed time and time again. For a reason which was not understood until the nineteenth century, all *Vitis vinifera* plants, of whatever variety or provenance in the Old World, very soon died. The reason was the presence of an aphis, *Phylloxera vastatrix*, parasitic on American native vines which, having evolved with it, were resistant to it. This aphis, attacking the roots of Old-World vines which had no resistance, killed them. It will be recalled that when *Phylloxera* at last succeeded in establishing itself on the European side of the Atlantic, it very nearly wiped out Old-World viticulture.

Repeated failures with European vines led the Americans to turn to their native ones. As a matter of history, domestication of these had been suggested a number of times even before it became clear that the European vines would not survive in North America east of the Rockies. John Hawkins, the navigator and pioneer slaver, is said to have been the first to suggest this. In 1616 Lord Delaware made the same suggestion in a letter to the directors of the Virginia Company in London. He wrote from Jamestown:

In every brake and hedge, and not far from our pallisade gates, we have thousands of goodly vines, running along and cleaving to every tree, which yield a plentiful grape in their kind. Let me appeal then to knowledge if these natural vines were planted, dressed and ordered by skilled vinearoons whether we might not make a perfect grape and fruitful vintage in short time.[1]

Perhaps the first practically successful domestication of the native American vines was accomplished by a colony of

[1] Hyams, 1949.

Germans from the Rhineland established by Governor
Alexander Spotswood in Spotsylvania County, Virginia, in
1710. We do not know for a fact that the vineyard planted by
those Germans was of native (*?Vitis rotundifolia*) grapes. But
the very fact that it was a success may well mean that this
was so, although *Phylloxera* did not always find a new plantation of Old-World vines for a year or two. The Governor's
white and red 'Rapidan' wines became quite famous. There
were other pioneers: the Swedes settled at Wilmington in
1630 made wine every year from the wild grapes of their
woods, and they may have tried to domesticate them. William
Penn also had the idea, and in a letter to the Society of Free
Traders (1683) he describes some of the native vines and
grapes and wonders whether it would not be better to plant
them than French vines. He allowed his French *vigneron*,
André Doz, to persuade him to use French vines, with the
usual result—failure.

It was left to Thomas Jefferson to be first to try domestication of an American species on a really considerable scale.
This he did at Monticello. Today, of course, the considerable
wine-growing industry of the north-eastern United States,
and Canada, relies chiefly on cultivars of American vines, or
on French-American, German-American or Italo-American
hybrids.

3

The Prunus fruits

The group of fruit-trees whose fruits are what botanists call *drupes*—a drupe is a fruit with a fleshy pericarp and a hard kernel—and which fruit-trade people call 'stone-fruits', all belong to a single genus: *Prunus*. This is a member of the family *Rosaceae*, and it is confined in nature to the northern hemisphere.

Prunus cultivars were all relatively late-comers to Roman horticulture, and, again, to western European horticulture in its turn. Cato, in his *De re rustica*, mentions the plum only once. But the implied scarcity of plum-trees in Roman gardens and orchards had clearly been rectified by Virgil's time, for the poet writes of them as a commonplace. This may well have been in part due to the fact that the grafting of plum varieties onto common blackthorn had become the practice. Even so, the agronomist Columella, the greatest of the Roman authors of gardening and farming textbooks, who based a part of his works on those of his Carthaginian predecessor Mago, seems still to have known only three kinds of plums. But some forty years later Pliny lists a very large number of varieties in cultivation. From Roman gardens and orchards those plums spread all over the western parts of the Empire, that is to say all over Europe; the usual process of segregation and selection creating new, local cultivars all the time. That much is clear, but where did the Romans themselves get their plums? By domesticating the wild plums of their own country; or from some more anciently civilized parts of their Empire?

All the cultivated plums of the western world belong to

two species: *Prunus domestica* and *P. insititia*. The wild form of the first seems to have been native to west Asia; the second, closely related, species is the bullace of our own woods and hedges.

It has often happened that when a people received a cultivated fruit-plant from some more advanced neighbouring people, that introduction drew their attention to the possibility of cultivating a similar fruit with which they were familiar as part of the wild flora of their own territory, and which they were, perhaps, accustomed to gather in the woods. It seems likely that this occurred in the case of the plums. The already domesticated Asian plums were introduced into Greece and Italy, and as they spread throughout the west their very existence led to the domestication of the European plum, and to the emergence of cultivars intermediate between the species, such as the damsons.

There is a little evidence, but it is perhaps enough, that the Latins did have the plum from a Greek source, doubtless from the Greek colonies to their south, Naples or Sicily. Those colonies would originally have had the cultivated plums from the motherland, as our own colonies in America and Australasia had them from Britain, and as the Greeks of Italy had the olive and the vine from home. The evidence that the plums reached the Latins from Greece, by whatever route, is in their name: *prunus* is a loan-word, a corruption of the Greek *proumnon*, which originally meant the wild plum but was later used to mean any kind of plum. It is a safe rule that if a community uses a foreign name for a commodity, that commodity is of foreign origin and comes from the country where the language of its name is spoken: chocolate (Aztec), tea (Chinese) and coffee (Arabic) are good examples. This brings us, then, to the provisional conclusion that the plum was not originally domesticated in Italy, but may have been domesticated in Greece.

Proumnon is not the only and perhaps not the commonest word for plum in ancient Greek. There was also a word used only for the cultivated plum, *kokkymelon*. Victor Heyn, the German philologist, found that the first use of this word in writing is to be found in a quotation by Pollux of a text by Aristolochus who was writing about 700 BC. *Melon* is a word meaning apple; but it also means simply fruit in a much more general sense, or, with a descriptive affix, some specific fruit. One can compare our own use of apple in the same way, e.g. in custard-apple, or even the French *pomme-de-terre*. This word *melon* is Greek; but the other half of the word for the cultivated plum, *kokky*, is an oriental word, evidence that the Greeks had their cultivated plums from Asia. That is as far back as we can take this particular story: and the probability is that the plum was first domesticated in Syria, or possibly farther east, e.g. in Iran, before, but perhaps not long before, 1000 BC.

Because its habitat is much more specific, it is rather easier to trace the career of another stone-fruit, the peach. In Latin—not merely botanical Latin—its name was *Prunus persica*, which at once places its point of origin as far as the Latins, that is the Romans, were concerned, in Iran. There is no evidence at all for the peach in ancient Greek gardens or orchards, so that evidently the Romans had it directly from the east, and not by way of Greece or any Greek colony. Also, it was a late-comer in Italy, for it was not planted there at all until well into the first century AD.

Yet, despite its Persian name, the peach cannot possibly have been domesticated in Iran. For it is not and never has been native there. It is true that the peach is now only known in cultivation, but wild plants close to it have been found in China, and nowhere else. Moreover, the closely related and perhaps ancestral *Prunus davidiana* is also native there but nowhere else. Now China under the Han Dynasty was exchanging useful plants and animals with Iran in the second century BC and probably much earlier. (I am referring here to deliberate exchanges, not to diffusion by drift.) There can, then, be no doubt that the peach was first domesticated in China, but there is no evidence as to when this happened.

From Italy the peach spread quite rapidly all over western Europe as far north as Germany and Britain, and by Pliny's time there was already a distinctively French 'race' of peaches (which Pliny calls 'Gallic'). We can judge how the peach must have behaved during this diffusion by its behaviour in America. Adaptable and very variable, *P. persica*, taken to North America in the sixteenth century, was so widely planted by the Red Indians as well as by colonists that in the seventeenth century, finding it growing in numbers and very flourishing in places where no white man had been before, some explorers assumed the peach to be a native American plant.

Another *Prunus*, *P. armeniaca*, has an extremely curious nomenclatural history, which helps in tracing its course during domestication. This fruit is called in Italian *alberococco* or *albiœco*; in French *abricot*; in German *aprikosa* and in English *apricot*. The first question is, whence did those countries receive that alien name? They received it, with the fruit itself, from Spain between the twelfth (Italy) and the sixteenth (England) centuries. The Spanish name is *albaiquoque* and there is no doubt about its source, which is Arabic—the fruit is called *al-barquq* in Arabic. Apricots were cultivated in Moorish Spain before AD 1000; but this does not mean that it was first cultivated there, or anywhere within the Dar-al-Islam.

There are two centres where apricot cultivars are exceptionally numerous and diverse, some of them primitive: Central Asia (comprising for this purpose Punjab, Kashmir, Afghanistan, Uzbekistan and neighbouring Soviet republics) and north (temperate) China. But the wild apricot has not been found anywhere in Central Asia; it has been found (by Bretschneider) in only one part of the world—China. This would seem to mean that the fruit was domesticated in north China, that some Arabic-speaking people had it from the

Chinese, and that we had it from the Arabs. But the matter is not nearly so simple.

Al-barquq is analysed by philologists as follows: *al* is the article; *barquq* is a corruption of a latinized Greek word, *praicokkia*. If the Arabs had the name of the tree from the Latins, they must have had the tree itself also from the same source. But if the Romans and the Greeks had the fruit, why did we have to get it, so very much later, from the Arabs? The answer seems to be that in the Roman Empire it never moved north-west at all, probably because its introduction was so late that the northern and western parts of the Empire were being barbarized at the time. The Greek original of *praicokkia* is *prokokion*. This can best be expounded, in our context, by pointing out that the flowering of the apricot is, indeed, *precocious*. So we are back to Greece. But Dioscorides (first century AD) says a curious thing: 'We Greeks call them [i.e. apricots] *Armeniaca* but the Romans *praicokia* . . .' It looks, then, as if the Greeks had this fruit from ancient Armenia. And, since it has been found wild only in China, we are back at those Sino-Iranian exchanges during or before the Han Dynasty. As for fixing a rough date for the first domestication, it is not possible, but perhaps 1000 BC is not putting it too early.

Two species of cherries, *Prunus avium*, giving rise to sweet-fruited cultivars, and *P. cerasus*, giving rise to sour-fruited cherries, are native to western Europe, including England. If there ever was an early European domestication of these, the resultant cultivars gave way to better ones introduced from western Asia. It is possible that one group of cultivars—the 'Duke' cherries which are hybrids between the two species— which were still very widely grown until recently and still are grown, does originate in a European domestication.

The principal facts about the introduction of the west Asian cultivated cherry-trees into Europe are as follows. The Romans introduced the trees to northern Italy, Gaul and Britain between AD 90 and 120. That the introduction was made so late in the Empire's history seems odd and is, in fact, significant. The Romans themselves had had these cultivated cherries for only a few decades, having obtained a number of varieties from western Asia about AD 70; the tradition is that the wealthy epicure Lucullus brought the first trees to Rome from that campaign in Asia during which he defeated the forces of King Mithridates. Both the cherry species are found wild in different parts of Asia Minor; they are unknown east of the Caucasus.

If the story of the introduction by Lucullus be true, it is curious that Plutarch, in his *Life* of Lucullus, does not mention it. But it is nevertheless clear that the introduction was made at about this time, because whereas Cato, in his *De re rustica*, never mentions this fruit, Varro, in his work of the same title, mentions it once, and all later authors on matters of rural economy, frequently. The story of the Lucullan introduction is from Pliny; but there is a difficulty.

If the Pontic cherries were *Prunus cerasus* cultivars, they were sour. The Italians were used to eating sweet wild cherries from *P. avium*. There is another source of information: Athenaeus quotes one Diphilus of Siphnus on the subject of sweet cherries, and 'Milesian' cherries from the west Asian provinces of the kingdom of Lysimachus; there seems little doubt that these derivatives of *P. avium* were introduced into Italy before or about AD 100.

In the process of segregation and selection already described, more and more varieties emerged locally as new cherry cultivars were distributed all over the empire. By Pliny's time a large number of local varieties were distinguished, varieties which had emerged in provinces as remote as Portugal. So it is easy enough to follow the history forward in time; what is much more difficult is to work backwards. All we have up to now is that both sour and sweet cultivated cherry-trees were introduced into the west from Pontus about the end of the first century AD, and that the wild cherries are native there.

Very likely it was in Pontus that the cherries were first introduced, for it has been shown (by Heyn among others) that far from the fruit taking its commonest name from the town of Cerasus, whence Lucullus is supposed to have brought the trees for his famous garden, it was the town which took its name from the fruit-trees which flourished all round it. It appears that *kerasos* is an Asia Minor Greek corruption of *kraneia* and referred originally to the close-grained hardness of cherry-tree timber. It does, on the whole, seem likely that if a cultivated and improved cherry was older than Cerasus itself, then Pontus was the place of domestication, although there may very well have been other, local, domestications of the fruit elsewhere and later. As for the date, there is no real evidence of any kind; perhaps we can safely say that the cherry is the youngest of the *Prunus* fruits in cultivation.

The almond-tree, *Prunus communis* (synonyms, *Prunus amygdalus* and *Amygdalus communis*) is native to Central Asia westward into the Near East, which probably accounts for its presence as a cultivated plant at a relatively early date, both west and east of this habitat. In surveying the sources of wild plants which might be useful as economic plants in the U.S.S.R., Soviet botanists found, in the mountain regions of Transcaucasia and Central Asia, wild almonds scarcely inferior to many cultivated varieties; and I myself have observed that the almond-trees of Ayacata in Grand Canary, although derived from trees transplanted there from Spain centuries ago, are hardly distinguishable from wild almond-trees.

Nuts, having hard shells, are very easy to export and import. Almonds were familiar to the Athenians long before the tree itself was introduced into Greece; and the Romans too, at least until imperial times, seem to have known the almond only as a foreign import, for which they borrowed the Greek name *amigdalē*. That name is not the only evidence that the Romans, and therefore the rest of Europe, had almonds from the Greeks; for although the agronomist Columella calls the tree *amygdala*, he calls the nuts it bears *nux Graeca*, Greek nuts. However, all that that proves is that the almond tree was introduced into Greece before it was introduced into Italy.

Turning to the Far East: although not native to either China or Japan, the almond-tree was commonly grown in both countries; and in China, although not in Japan, long before it was known in Europe. It seems quite obvious that here we have two separate domestications of the same plant. Vavilov gives two principal centres of distribution of this plant: the Central Asian one, whence the tree could very easily have been introduced into Chinese, Korean and Japanese horticulture; and the Near Eastern one, whence it reached Europe. But there is an alternative theory: that the almond was originally domesticated in northern India, the Punjab, Baluchistan or the Indus Valley, and that it reached both the eastern and western centres of civilization, and therefore plantation agriculture, from there.

On the subject of the *Prunus* trees in China and Japan, and harking back to the plums, we have noted that the two species which gave rise to the cultivated plums were western natives. Yet it is a fact that plums were of great importance, especially as ornamentals, in Far-Eastern gardens at a very early date, long before any European was growing fruit-trees. That, at least, is true for China; even in Japan, in the seventh century and thereafter, at a period when only plants of ritual significance could be introduced into gardens, the plum was among the rather small number of plants which were admissible. Special ceremonial parties were arranged to visit the plum blossoms by both daylight and moonlight, and fashionable Japanese ladies had special dresses for visiting the plum-blossom.

But the Orient has its own plums. The one which we call the Japanese Plum, and which is now much grown in South Africa and California, derives from *Prunus salicina*, and is native not to Japan but to China. It was certainly in Japanese gardens earlier than AD 600, and in Chinese gardens probably not later than 1000 BC, although it is difficult to distinguish the blossom, in very early representations, from that of *P. simonii*. It is possible, even probable, that *P. salicina* was the first of all the *Prunus* genus to be domesticated, and it was unquestionably domesticated in China. But it is not the only plum of the very ancient Chinese gardens and orchards: *P. simonii*, known as the Chinese Plum, native of northern China, is a hardier tree. On the grounds that it was almost certainly domesticated in north China and introduced to the south as a cultivar, I suggest that it is not as old in cultivation as the so-called Japanese Plum.

As for the Far-Eastern cherries, the Chinese domesticated two species before 1000 BC; it is impossible to get a more precise date. They are *Prunus tomentosa* and *P. pseudocerasus*, and as the latter is known only as a cultivar and has never been found wild, its domestication must have been very ancient indeed.

4

Cabbages and kings

The commonplaces of our ordinary diet are taken for granted. Cabbages and carrots can be made 'news' only by some whim of gastronomic or dietetic fashion. The common vegetables of our daily meals are artefacts just as a work of sculpture is an artefact, but it never occurs to us to spare a word of praise, a thought of gratitude, for the men who made cabbages or carrots, although they shaped and transformed wild plants into the vegetables and fruit we eat, just as a sculptor shapes a bit of stone, intelligently. The trouble is that we know and can enter into the feelings of the individual artist, but have no knowledge of individual people in the generation after generation of nameless men who made the vegetables we eat. But there is more to it than that. The artist's work pleases the senses we choose to honour above the others; and, we believe, it edifies us. But the men who turned weeds into the things which please our palate and nourish our bodies do not, like the artists, benefit from the ancient illusion that the mind is more honourable than the body. It is a strange state of affairs; for though it may be true that man does not live by bread alone, it is unquestionable that he cannot live without it.

One can get further by looking at the matter from another point of view. Mankind could certainly better have dispensed with kings than with cabbages; but it is the history of kings we strive to recall, the history of the cabbage we neglect. What were its ancestors, how did the noble and regal Cabbage family spread its dominion?

The wild ancestor of this nobility was *Brassica oleracea*, a

European native. It is also found wild in the lands of the eastern Mediterranean, notably in Anatolia where there is a wide variety of wild and cultivated forms. It is not the only wild cabbage; there are related species which may have contributed some genes to the modern cabbage. But who were the makers? Since the species involved are confined to Europe and west Asia, and are more or less maritime, there is little point in looking for the original domesticators of the cabbage outside the Mediterranean basin.

According to an old but still usually reliable authority, De Candolle, the cabbage is not found wild in Greece. But the Greeks knew it as a cultivated vegetable and Theophrastus (372–287 BC) listed three varieties in common use. Pliny (AD 23–79) lists six varieties used in Italy. By the seventeenth century European authorities could name twenty, and by the nineteenth century thirty. This increase in the number of varieties would normally mean that, as the vegetable was more widely distributed in horticulture, local 'races' developed and were, in their turn, made available generally; but in this case there is another and very different possible explanation. If we suppose the cabbage to have been domesticated in western Europe and distributed eastward, then there would be more cultivars in the west than in the east; that they were not actually listed until relatively modern times may simply mean that they were confined to their localities of origin for many centuries. That is pure surmise, but there is some evidence in support of it in nomenclature.

Common names for the cabbage are many and ancient in the European languages, few and modern in the Asian. The English word derives from the old Celtic name *kab* or *kap*, by way of the French intermediate *cabus*. An older English name has equivalents in, again, the Celtic languages: English, *kale*; Irish, *cal*; Breton, *kaol*; but also in the Germanic languages – *Kohl* in German, for example, and *kaal* in Danish. This suggests a common root which is neither Celtic nor Germanic, and the most likely is one of the Latin

names for cabbage (the other is *brassica*), *caul*. *Brassica* also
has derivatives in Celtic and non-Celtic languages: *bresic*,
bresych, and corrupt forms such as *berza*.

A possible explanation is that the *kab* names are older than
the *kale* names: that is, the Celtic peoples had their own
names for the cabbage which, as Europe was conquered by
the Romans, were partially displaced by corrupt forms of the
Latin word. Some such explanation is necessary because
there is evidence that the cabbage was not familiar or even
known at all to the ancient Near-Eastern civilizations. There
is, for example, no reference to the cabbage in the ancient
Hebrew literature, and no name for the cabbage in classical
Hebrew. That fact alone brings the date of domestication to
some time later than 1000 BC. Moreover, the names for
cabbage in the Indian languages are all modern. It is true
that there is a Sanskrit word, *karambha*, which is the name of
a vegetable but not, apparently, the cabbage; and that the
Persian *karamb*, from which is derived, probably, the Greek
krambai, was used to mean cabbage once the Iranians had
cabbages. But all that is probably relatively late.

All of which adds up to one of two possible conclusions:
that the cabbage was domesticated somewhere in western
Europe by the Celts during the first millennium BC, and
introduced into the east from Europe; or that the invading
Celts found the cabbage already domesticated by the
aboriginals – Ligurians, Iberians, whoever they were – and
took it over from them.

So much for the senior branch of the family: what about
the even more distinguished cadet branch? Both brussels
sprouts and cauliflowers and all the broccolis are derivatives
of the cabbage. Brussels sprouts are usually considered to
have originated as a mutant of the Savoy cabbages, and they
are much older in garden cultivation, although only here
and there, than is usually realized. In July 1818 Professor
Jean-Baptiste Van Mons of Louvain University read a paper
to the Royal Horticultural Society of London, in which he

pointed out that *spruyten* are mentioned in the market regulations of some Belgian towns as early as 1213. And Gibault (1912) quotes from the archives of Lille the following from the accounts of Charles the Bold, Duke of Burgundy, in 1472: 'For the wedding of Messire Baudouin de Lannoy and Michielle Denne, one of my said lady's maids: one hundred *sprocq*.'

These *sprocq* (sprouts) were also served at the wedding feast of Alcande de Brederode in 1481. It is all the more curious that brussels sprouts were virtually unknown in France until the end of the eighteenth century and in England until the nineteenth. I have not come across, nor can I think of, any explanation.

The cauliflower was first grown in France in the sixteenth century, in England in the seventeenth. A mutant of cabbage, it was originally known in France, and before that in Italy where the French got their first cauliflower seeds, as 'Cyprus cabbage'. For a long time, in fact, seeds were imported from Cyprus and Malta, and probably also from Sicily, where, as anyone knows who has walked round one of the island's vegetable markets, the cauliflowers are still remarkable for their diversity, brilliant colours and size. Pliny's description of a vegetable called Cypriot Cabbage reads as if he may have been referring to our own sprouting broccoli. The earliest description of what clearly is a cauliflower occurs in a twelfth-century Spanish Arabic treatise on agriculture (*Kitab-al-falaha*) by Ibn-el-Awam, to which we shall have occasion to refer again. He names three kinds of cauliflower or broccoli, and calls it Syrian Cabbage. And since there is a tradition that the Italians, more specifically the Genoese, first had cauliflower seed from the Levant, it is likely that it was in Syria that this cabbage mutant was first noticed, selected, segregated and propagated.

If cabbages have been better friends than kings to ordinary men, spinach has served us better than princes and its history is at least as worthy of attention as theirs. Its wild ancestor *Spinacea oleracea* is found growing from the eastern Mediterranean into Central Asia, so that its natural habitat is that of the most ancient agriculture. Yet it is not ancient in cultivation. It is first mentioned in English in a Herbal published in 1568 by the herbalist Turner, who calls spinach 'an herbe lately found and not long in use'. Presumably he means not long in use in England, for it had certainly been in use in some European countries for centuries before 1568.

The European country where it was first cultivated was Moorish Spain; Christian Spain did not have it until much later. Ibn-al-Awam above-mentioned gives some account of the cultivation of spinach in southern Spain. The Arabic name for it is *isfanadsh*. That word is quite obviously the derivation of the Spanish *espinaca*, which becomes *épinard* in French and (*e*)*spinach* in English. We are safe in concluding that Europe had spinach from Spain, and that it was introduced there by the Moors. But whence did they obtain it?

Language is a help again: philologists tell us that the Arabic *isfanadsh* is a corruption of the Persian *aspanaj*. By our rule, since the Arabs had the word, they had also the plant itself from Iran. There is supporting evidence. Berthold Laufer [1] quotes what he calls 'a tenth-century Arab forgery of an allegedly Nabataean work' — *The Book of Nabataean Agriculture* — which refers to both the cultivated and the wild spinach of the region. This again puts the Arab source of spinach in Iranian territory. But it does not necessarily follow that Iran is the land in which spinach was domesticated, since it is found wild farther east. So it will be as well to have a look at the early history of the plant in China.

The Chinese for spinach is *po-se-t'sai*, which means 'Persian vegetable'. The following is an historical note, again quoted from Laufer:

At the time of the Emperor T'sai Tsun (AD 627–49) in the twenty-first year of the period Cen-Kwan (AD 647) Ni-po-lo (Nepal) sent to the Court the vegetable *po-lin*, the flower

[1] *Sino-Iranica*. Chicago, 1919.

resembling the *hun-lan* (*Carthamus tinctorius*), the fruit like that of the *tsi-li* (*Tribulus terrestris*). Well cooked it is savoury and makes good eating.

Spinach is not native to Nepal; and the *Spinacia tetrandra* grown in India is an introduction from Turkestan or Afghanistan where it is called *schamum*, a corruption of *somin*, a Persian word for spinach. It would seem that spinach was domesticated in Iran, probably not much earlier or later than AD 500.

Green vegetable food such as wild cabbage and spinach was important to man long before it was cultivated, so important that prehistoric hunters probably ate the contents of an animal's stomach before turning to its flesh. Roots too were important to food-gathering communities—as important to man as to that other omnivorous animal, the pig. Of all the roots we still eat, the potato, relatively a newcomer to the Old World but an ancient food in the Americas, is, with the exception of maize, by far the most important of the economic plants introduced from the New World to the Old in the sixteenth century. Together with the tomato and tobacco it transformed the Old World's economy, during the subsequent two centuries, far more effectively than all the gold and silver of Mexico and Peru ever did.

The potato, *Solanum tuberosum*, has had a curious career since its introduction. Except in Ireland and Germany, it was accepted rather reluctantly. It was the ruin of Ireland, for the Irish, having become completely dependent on it, starved to death when it failed them, and have never recovered from that disaster. It was in some ways the making of Prussia. It is, today, second only to bread among the starch foods.

There is no difficulty in discovering the general area of the potato's origin as a cultivated plant. It was unknown anywhere in the Old World before the sixteenth century, and at the time of the discovery of America by Columbus it was equally unknown in North and Central America. Why that

should have been so is far from clear, for maize was common
to both the Americas. The fact remains: the potato was confined in cultivation to the Andean area of South America,
and there it must have originated.

As Dr Redcliffe Salaman (1949) has pointed out, it is very
curious that although Central and North America are as rich
as the Andes in tuber-bearing *Solanums*, and some of these
were and still are eaten by some Mexican, Guatemalan and
Navajo Indians, yet none of them was ever cultivated.
Salaman suggests that some of those peoples may have
reached that stage in their culture when they would have
domesticated the local potatoes, but that when the Spaniards
arrived they destroyed their cultures. But that fails to explain
why the civilized Mexican peoples, who were as advanced as
those of the Andes, and in some respects more advanced, did
not accomplish that domestication.

The region in which the Spaniards found the potato in
cultivation was that of the Inca Empire, that is to say, Peru,
north and central Chile, Colombia, Bolivia and Ecuador.
Like the rest of the Americas, the countries were originally
and over a long period of time peopled from the Old World
by migrants crossing the isthmus which is now the Bering
Strait. During the Old-World Palaeolithic those hunters
pushed their way down America, some stopping and settling
and creating local cultures, others pushing farther south, or
breaking away from existing settlements to move south. As
for the western watershed of the Andes, there is a reason
advanced by Salaman (1949) for believing that it was peopled
by migrants from the eastern side of the sub-continent:

The importance of the question is apparent when we consider the dramatic contrast between the environment by the
rain forest of the Amazon and that of the desert coast of Peru,
one or other of which must have played the part of nursery to
the people. If man came from the west over the sea then he
would have known nothing of the jaguar or the boa, the
potato or the coca plant, till he encountered them as he pene-
trated eastward. In which case we should not expect that the

dread of the former and the use of the latter would be already characteristic elements in the social system of the coast at an early archaeological date as, in fact, they were. The evidence would seem rather to point in the opposite direction, inducing us to accept the theory of the eminent Americanist Tello, that man reached the Peruvian coast from the east.

In Chapter 1 I have said something about the domestication of maize, and it is probable that these people coming from the east carried maize, or at least a primitive pod-corn, with them. But as they began to climb the cordillera it would have been of less and less use to them; not until they were over the heights and on their way down to the coast would they again have been able to grow it. The potato must have been first brought into cultivation while they were crossing the Andean highlands (a process which, from settlement to settlement, may have taken centuries), where the potato is native at very great altitudes as well as lower down the hills. If that be so, then we have the pleasing spectacle of the potato acting as a sort of vector for the diffusion of the even more important maize plant.

The theory goes that South American man, driven westwards and upwards not by the usual causes but by the uneasiness amounting to panic terror and permanent melancholy induced even in civilized Europeans by the terrible *montana*, the haunted forests of tropical South America, emerged above the trees at a very great altitude to find that the food-plants he had brought with him from the lowlands were either stunted or killed outright by the cold of the heights. This happened at such places as the shores of Lake Titicaca, 12,000 feet above sea-level, one of his greatest cultural, artistic and therefore economic centres. The cold and bleakness drove the migrants to seek new food-plants adapted to the climate and the poor soil.

From Colombia in the north to Chile in the south a number of tuberous *Solanums*, including that or those

ancestral to our potatoes, were native high on the spine of the
cordillera. Some, of little use as food, grew just below the
snow-line at about 16,000 feet. Others, native between
10,000 and 12,000 feet or lower, were valuable as food. The
settlers took them into cultivation, and at a very early date
were locally selecting superior and even chance hybrid plants,
and segregating them. They had very hardy, nearly frost-
proof varieties, some of which have, in our own time, been
sought out and used by the Soviet botanists for the breeding
of hardy kinds for their own agriculture. The same botanists
have been able to show that some very ancient cultivars, now
established in the wild, are hybrids. There is, of course, no
question of the very primitive farmers with whom we are
here concerned having deliberately made these hybrids; but
they did have the nous to spot them as better plants, and to
preserve and propagate them. Emergence of local 'races'
would have been favoured by the geographical segregation of
plateau from plateau, valley from valley between the west-
pointing spurs, by high mountains, differences of soil, micro-
climates and exposure.

The frost-resistant potatoes of the *altiplano* made life
possible for the migrants. But they did much more than that.
Their planting and cultivation imposed on the people a
measure of social organization and discipline, out of which
came the rules of a system of primitive socialism. In short, it
created peoples, nations, who, when they descended to the
western watershed of the Andes and finally to the coast, were
of the mettle to resist the relaxing influence of much easier conditions, to respond to the challenge of drought on the littoral,
and to create a great and beautifully ordered civilization.

None of these things would have been possible had not the
mountain people not only domesticated the potato but also
found a way of preserving it as a stored food. By alternate
exposure to frost and sun the potatoes were dried, the end
product being a starch food called *chuno*; and they also found
a way to make a kind of beer by fermenting a mash of potato.

The antiquity of these discoveries is doubtful, but both were probably made about 2,000 years ago.

There is no means of dating the act of domestication with any accuracy. The earliest representation of a potato in ceramics belongs to the period which archaeologists call proto-Chimu. (Chimu became the greatest of the pre-Inca coastal states, with a capital city that was probably the largest in the world at that time.) This pot is dated approximately AD 200. But by that time the potato was so important in the economy and social life of the people, as it was in the neighbouring Nasca State, that it had obviously become a cult-object of great significance. Artist-potters made human and animal figures composed of curiously shaped potatoes; other figures were decorated with potato 'eyes'. There is good evidence that at one time human victims, later animals, were sacrificed to the spirit of the potato.

This sort of thing does not happen in a short time. Two centuries would be a very short time for the potato to travel with migrant settlers moving down ever nearer to the coast; several more would be needed for it to become an object of religious awe as well as of primary economic importance. But the best one can do is to say that the potato was first domesticated on the *altiplano* of the cordillera of the Andes during the first millennium BC, possibly earlier.

The adoption of the potato into the European diet would have been much slower than it was had it not been for the fact that people were used to eating roots native to the Old World. Yet some such roots were hardly more familiar than potatoes on west European tables in the sixteenth century. Carrots are a case in point.

Carrots, as we now know them, have quite a complicated history. In the first place, the orange-coloured carrots with which we are familiar are relatively new, the 'end product' of a long process of selecting mutants. There are four kinds of cultivated carrots (I mean four major classes, quite apart from size- and shape-variants of the common orange carrot of commerce): the purple, the yellow, the white, and last the orange.[1] The yellow carrots used to be the most important as a winter food-vegetable in Europe, but have become rare; the older, purple varieties are still in use all over the East, but are virtually never seen in Europe or America; the white varieties were much used as a cattle-food all over the Old World, but are now seen rarely, and then only in some Asian countries. The other colours all derive from the purple carrot, so that we need deal only with that one.

The purple carrot is first mentioned as being grown in England in the fifteenth century. There is no doubt as to where the English obtained it, for it had been in the market gardens and private vegetable gardens of Holland since well back in the previous century. But they must have reached Holland in that century and not earlier: for, says the anonymous writer of the fourteenth-century *Ménagier de Paris*, 'Garroites sont racines rouges que l'on vent es halles par pongées, et chascune pongée un blanc.' That is, carrots are red roots sold in the markets by the bunch, with one white one to each bunch. If it was necessary to tell the reader what carrots were, it is evident that they were relatively new on the market.

The north European countries had their carrots from Italy, where they were first cultivated very late in the thirteenth century. There is no written record of where they came from, but Ibn-al-Awam says that these purple and white carrots were being commonly grown in Spain, that is, in Moorish Spain, in the twelfth century; so no doubt the first seeds to reach Italy came from Granada or just possibly from Moorish Sicily, that is, the Sicily which had been Moorish until the Norman conquest and had retained Arab customs and ways.

This twelfth-century presence of the carrot in Moorish Spain gives the best clue to our next step backwards in its history. It must have been common to all the lands of the

[1] *See* Banga, 1964.

Dar-al-Islam and have reached Spain from one of the eastern ones. Ibn-al-Awam says that it was being grown in Nabataea during the tenth century; according to Laufer it also reached Iran in the tenth century. Now, in the ninth and tenth centuries the loosely associated Caliphate of Arab emirates included not only Spain but also Pakistan, Afghanistan, Turkestan, Iran, Armenia, Iraq, Arabia and Syria. So it is in one of those countries that we must look for the first, the purple, cultivated carrot.

So wide is the distribution of the wild carrot ancestral to the cultigen, *Daucus carota*, all over the northern hemisphere that we can get no help from it; it could have been first domesticated anywhere from China to France, and certainly in any of the Arab countries named above. Fortunately there is another indication—Vavilov's rule that the primary centre of greatest diversity of cultivars is the primary centre of dissemination. During the 1920s Soviet expeditions collected large amounts of cultivated carrot seed in all the Arab countries. The plants to which they gave rise were studied in experimental centres and it was established that by far the greatest diversity of purple-carrot types came from Afghanistan. I conclude that the carrot was first domesticated in that country; and since the carrot, or rather this carrot, was not known in antiquity, we may guess at a date between the fifth and eighth centuries AD.

This conclusion, however, fails to account for the fact that the Romans ate some kind of carrot, although they do not appear to have had a high opinion of it. Gibault quotes a third-century cookery book by Apicius in which there is a recipe for cooking a vegetable called *carota*; and there is a painting of a bunch of carrots at Herculaneum. Furthermore, Gibault mentions a reference to what seem to be carrots in the capitular *De Villis* of Charlemagne; but at that date there is not much difficulty, since by then carrot seed might have reached the west from one of half a dozen Arab countries. Two possible explanations: the Italians domesticated the carrot before the Afghans did so, and independently; or that the Afghan domestication is pre-Islamic, which seems very unlikely.

The yellow carrot is a colour mutant of the purple; it was made into an individual variety by selection not later than the tenth century. The white and orange carrots are both mutants of the yellow; the white has no importance in our context. As for the orange carrot, ancestor of all the modern carrots, it was first selected in Holland in the seventeenth century. It is clear from a study of Dutch and Flemish paintings from the early seventeenth to the mid-eighteenth century that orange carrots emerge as a variant of the commoner yellow kind. They were preferred by housewives and cooks; established by the force of market demand as an individual, later manifold, variety.

To sum up:

1 *Daucos carota* is first domesticated by the Italians in late Republican or early Imperial times. Fails to establish itself and is lost.

2 *Daucus carota* is domesticated again, in Afghanistan *c*. AD 600, as a purple cultivar.

3 Seed of this cultivar is distributed throughout the Dar-al-Islam during the eighth, ninth and tenth centuries.

4 A yellow mutant of the purple carrot is selected and propagated in the ninth or tenth century in Iran or Syria.

5 Purple and yellow carrot seeds reach southern Spain in the eleventh century. From there they reach Italy in the thirteenth, and from Italy reach all Europe in the fourteenth century.

6 The orange carrot emerges as a mutant in Holland in the seventeenth century and is established as an individual variety.

7 The orange carrot is preferred to the other colours because it retains its colour in cooking, whereas the others cook to a bad colour.

8   The orange carrot is distributed all over the western
    world in the eighteenth century and local types are
    established.

So the carrots with which we are familiar are no earlier in
our commerce than potatoes. On the other hand, by the
seventeenth century some root vegetables were so enormously
ancient in cultivation and common use that their origin is
difficult to trace: garlic, for example, and onions.

The true garlic, *Allium sativum*, has been found unquestionably wild in only one restricted part of the Old World,
the Kirghiz, a mountainous and partly desert region between
Afghanistan, Uzbekistan, Kazakstan, Mongolia and Sin-
kiang. There are places where it is locally naturalized, for
instance in parts of Sicily; and Vavilov gives the Mediterranean basin as a secondary centre for the dissemination of
cultivated forms, so that the plant must have been introduced into that region of ancient civilization at some very
early date. Equally early, it reached China by way of Mongolia. There can be no doubt about the antiquity of the garlic
plant in cultivation.

The evidence quoted by the linguistic authorities to
establish its antiquity is diverse and interesting. For example,
in Chinese the word for garlic, *suan*, is written with a single
sign, and it seems that this nearly always means that the plant
is either native or was very early introduced, for it was there,
present and important, in the youth of the written language.
But we know that garlic is not native to China or even to
Mongolia; it follows that it was introduced, perhaps prehistorically, from south-west Siberia.

The complete absence of archaeological evidence that the
Egyptians had garlic conflicts with Herodotus's statement
that the Egyptians made enormous use of it.[1] But an interesting reason has been suggested for the fact that garlic is nowhere represented in tomb-painting: it may have been held

[1] Unger, 1851.

by the priests to be an unclean plant. There is no direct
evidence for this, but it is a fact that some of the priesthoods
of ancient Greece held garlic to be unclean; for example, no
person who had eaten garlic was allowed to enter the temple
of Cybele. Perhaps the Greeks received this prejudice from
Egypt by way of Crete. Was the Athenian contempt for the
Boeotians as garlic-eaters of religious origin? Or was it due
merely to their disgust at garlic-laden breath, a disgust
which was once shared by the English? Other evidence of
considerable antiquity: garlic (Hebrew *schoum*; Arabic *thoum*)
is mentioned, although only once, in the book of *Numbers*, in
the Bible; there is also a native Sanskrit name, *mahoushouda*.
That takes us into the second millennium BC.

By and large, the most likely place for the earliest domestication of this *Allium* is Central Asia; the most likely people,
those speakers of the proto-Indo-European language about
whom we know so little; and the most likely time, say half-
way through the second millennium BC, but possibly a
thousand years earlier. The theory would be supported by the
derivation, advocated by some philologists, of the Hebrew
schoum from the Sanskrit name.

The onion, *Allium cepa*, is at least as old as, and possibly
older than, garlic in cultivation. Juvenal mocks the Egyptian
devotion to onions in his fifteenth *Satire*:

'Porrum et coepa nefas violare et frangere morsu,
  O sanctes gentes quibus haec nascuntur in horti numina!'
['It is sacrilege to bite the leek or onion,
  O holy nation, in whose gardens divinities spring up!']

This was a sneer at the Egyptians for making a god of the
onion; it is possible that there may have been such a cult,
locally. The Egyptian practice of endowing all living
creatures with souls, and some animals and vegetables with
divinity, was an admirable one, a manifestation of their
feeling that all life is one. Perhaps it accounts for the enormous endurance and stability of their civilization. Be that as

it may, the Egyptians certainly made a staple food of the onion. When Herodotus was there, about 2,500 years ago, there was still a memorial plaque on the Great Pyramid of Cheops at Gizeh, recording that during its building 1,600 talents of silver were spent on onions, leeks and garlic for the workmen.

The Greeks had onions at least as early as 800 BC, and probably earlier, from Crete or Lydia. Even in Roman imperial times there was still a local Cretan variety which was much esteemed. The Cretans doubtless had their onions from Egypt. The Italians carried these oriental onions all over Europe; they were nowhere lost during the so-called Dark Ages, were important in continental Europe from the very early Middle Ages, and were often used to pay rents in kind or peppercorn rents. It is, in short, easy to follow the onion's history forward in time from Egypt, but to follow it backwards from the same place is more difficult.

In the first place, no botanists seem to be sure where *Allium cepa* is native. De Candolle suggested that it was formerly common in the wild over an immense area of Europe and west Asia; but if so, it is surely curious that it has entirely vanished. Perhaps it was so sought after and collected in the wild before the Neolithic revolution that it became rare, and was saved from extinction only by that revolution. Vavilov gives three centres of dissemination of the cultivated plant: Central Asia, with a great number and diversity of cultivars and two closely related wild species, one of which is named after him; the Near East, and the Mediterranean, both secondary centres. One piece of philological evidence for great antiquity in cultivation is that the names for onion in the ancient 'basic' languages are distinct and unconnected; there has been no borrowing late enough to be apparent in Hebrew, Sanskrit, Greek or Chinese.

A thoroughly native name usually implies a native domestication, but given the likelihood that the native species were confined to Iran, it is difficult to believe in four or five independent domestications. So: a probable region of domestication of the onion, Central or west Asia; a probable date for this event, earlier than 3000 BC.

Turnips may be even older in use and in cultivation than garlic and onions, at least in Europe, though much less ancient in Asia. The wild plant is *Brassica campestris*, very closely akin to the cabbages. And the same species seems to have given rise not only to turnips but also to a plant which is grown for its oily seeds—rape. There are Central Asian, Near Eastern and Mediterranean centres of dissemination; but as the wild species are native throughout Europe, the western U.S.S.R. and Siberia, there is considerable difficulty in determining the place and time where these plants were domesticated.

That the wild ancestor of our fleshy-rooted turnips is *Brassica campestris* was demonstrated by experiment when in 1874 a French botanist named Blanchard sowed seeds of this species, sowed the seed of the plants he raised from these in the following year, and, selecting the largest-rooted individuals every year, repeated the work for fourteen years. By that time he had turnips twelve centimetres long and two centimetres in diameter at their stoutest point. Blanchard concluded that, although *B. campestris* was the ancestral turnip, there must at some time have been a fleshy-rooted mutant from which the cultivated turnips derive. But in what circumstances would this have been observed, segregated and propagated? Possibly in a plantation of rape. But if this was so, the event must have been prehistoric, for carbonized turnips have been found in Neolithic sites. Moreover, the nomenclature suggests that the turnip is certainly of European origin, for all the oriental names are modern, the European ones ancient.

Early in the seventeenth century there appeared in the gardens of France, Flanders and England a new root-vegetable to compete with that other newcomer, the potato. It bore many different vernacular names, the principal ones in England being Topinamber and Jerusalem artichoke. This latter root is not an artichoke and it does not come from Jerusalem: 'Jerusalem' is a corrupt pronunciation of Italian *girasol*, for the plant is a sunflower. 'Artichoke' is due to the fact that the root tastes slightly of an older, and European, vegetable, the globe artichoke, which is a thistle. The Latin name which Linnaeus gave to the new plant was *Helianthus tuberosus*.

At first it was very dear in European markets and regarded as a luxury food. Its rate of tuber increase is so enormous that some authors saw in it a sort of manna, a possible way of feeding the poor on the cheap. But its popularity was short-lived. As soon as its extraordinary powers of increase made it cheap, the rich found it insipid; as for the poor, they began to find that not only was it insipid, but also that it was not very nourishing. There was another reason for its decline: the potato.

The Jerusalem artichoke is still cultivated, of course, and there are people who like it; but it is no longer of much economic importance. It came to us from Canada.

In 1534 the French navigator Jacques Cartier explored the bay of St Lawrence and founded a colony at Saint-Croix. Henri Quatre sent another explorer, Champlain, to follow up this venture. Champlain founded Quebec; colonists arrived from France; and—the oldest story in the history of American colonization—were soon starving. Reduced to taking the same measures as the natives in order to stay alive, they are said to have taken to, among other contrivances, digging wild roots to eat. But these roots were certainly not always wild. In 1603 Champlain reported [1] that he had had from the Algonquin Indians roots which tasted like artichokes and which they cultivated in their gardens.

The rate of increase of this plant is so extraordinary that it became common in Europe within two decades. In the 1618

[1] 1830 edn., vol. i, p. 110.

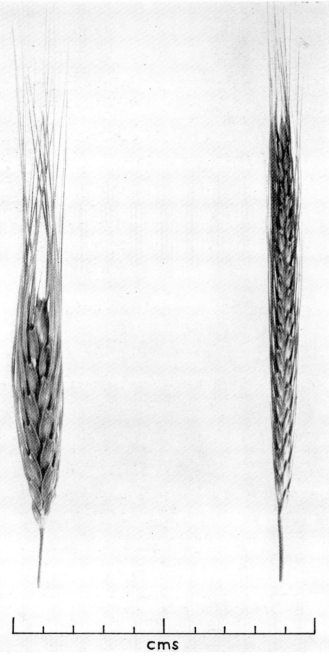

cms

2

1 Wild and cultivated forms of wheat. From left to right: *Triticum boeoticum*, wild einkorn; *T. monococcum*, cultivated einkorn; *T. dicoccoides*, wild emmer; *T. dicoccum*, cultivated emmer. Western civilization in the Old World was founded and built upon exploitation of these grasses, which have given rise to thousands of cultivated varieties in which qualities dormant in natural conditions have been brought into use by hybridization, selection and artificial segregation.

2 Wild and cultivated emmer wheat. In the cultivated kind (*left*) the ripe ears remain intact until the grains are separated by threshing. Neglected by man, the seeds would fail to spread and the 'race' would soon become extinct. In wild emmer (*right*) the individual spikelets serve as disseminators; the whole ear is brittle and separates when ripe so that the seed is spread and the species survives and, in favourable conditions, multiplies.

3 Maize, being the staple on which all the South and Central American civilizations were built, and which later sustained the Inca Empire, was treated as sacred, and became a subject for plastic artists and craftsmen. These prehistoric pottery representations are of early forms of this man-made cereal, which is incapable of surviving without man's care.

4 The most probable wild ancestor of maize, which does not exist as a wild plant, is a 'pod-corn'. This prehistoric pottery figure of a pod-corn ear is from the Peruvian Highlands; it has not been reliably dated. Pod-corn has virtually disappeared from the earliest territories of proto-maize cultivation—weeded out over tens of centuries.

5 Maize as gods? Or simply a subject chosen by the potter because it was held in affection as the staple food of all the native American civilizations? Prehistoric Peruvian potters have left us a range of representations of the earliest domesticated crop-plants which tell us more about the forms of proto-maize and potatoes than surviving forms of those plants.

6 Pottery of the prehistoric Peruvian civilizations which were finally united in the Inca Empire included examples decorated with figures of maize cobs which enable us to trace some of the development, chiefly by selection and segregation, of the modern forms of maize from a wild pod-corn.

7 Wild oat, *Avena strigosa*; from James Sowerby's *English Botany* (1808). It is probable that oats were first noticed by prehistoric north European farmers as good candidates for domestication because they occurred as weeds of cultivation among wheat. Wheat and barley are thousands of years older in cultivation than this late-comer to the community of noble grasses.

8 Wall-painting from the tomb of Nakht, Egypt; fifteenth
   century B.C. The wine-vine was introduced into Egypt from the
   north and there developed by selection. The 'arbour' method
   of training has lasted nearly four thousand years.

9 A relief from Nineveh. The wild grape-vine *Vitis vinifera*
   clambers up trees, thus teaching man how to cultivate it. Here it is
   shown supported on a tree; later came forked sticks and pergolas.
   The practice of pruning vines to form low bushy plants was
   probably a Carthaginian invention. Grape-vines trained on living
   trees can still be seen in Italy and some other parts of Europe.

edition of his *Histoire de la Nouvelle-France,* the French colonist Marc Lescarbot could write:

There is also in this land a certain sort of roots as large as small turnips or truffles, very excellent to eat, having an undertaste of cardoons, even more agreeable, which, being planted, multiply as if challenged in such fashion that it is a marvel. . . . We brought some of these roots to France which have so increased that gardens are full of them . . .'

As this helianthus is native from Arkansas to Canada it is impossible to attribute domestication to a particular tribe; nor, since the Hurons, Algonquins and the rest had no writing, is it possible to date that domestication. But we can at least say that we owe Jerusalem artichokes to the Red Indians.

The gathering of leaves and roots in the wild led to the 'remodelling' of the plants we have described, by selection, mutation in cultivation and hybridization. Succulent shoots were another form of wild vegetable food, and in time the same kind of transformation occurred, so that shoots, instead of sprouting into adult, fibrous growths, were held at the tender stage but enormously increased in size. Asparagus is a good example.

It is an interesting fact that although the practice of growing asparagus seems to have been lost in most of Europe as a result of the barbarian invasions and the fall of the Roman Empire, and only to have been resumed very much later by the Spanish Moors who had this vegetable not locally but from Syria where, in the ninth century, it was an important crop, yet the name retained for it in all European languages is not the Arabic *helyoun* but the Latin *asparagus.* One possible explanation is that *Asparagus officinalis* is a not uncommon European native plant, found on both the Mediterranean and Atlantic coasts, including England; and that, even when forgotten as a vegetable, it was gathered in the wild as an officinal herb. This would have meant that the use of it, at least as a medicine, was continuous throughout the Dark Ages and so the Latin name was never lost.

Asparagus is ancient in cultivation. True, the Greeks seem never to have cultivated it, but it was much valued by the Latins long before the Imperial Roman epoch. Cato, in *De re rustica*, gives instructions for its correct cultivation, and his method was still the usual one until the middle of the nineteenth century, when French growers gave up planting asparagus in trenches and grew it on raised beds. In Cato's time asparagus does not seem to have been a luxury, but it was so by Pliny's time; moreover such progress had been made in improving it that the market gardeners who had their asparagus beds in the sandy marshes near Ravenna were producing asparagus so enormous that there were only three shoots to the pound. This feat was not improved on until about 1,500 years later, when growers in the Argenteuil region of France were producing asparagus weighing up to half a pound apiece.

Although the Romans do not seem to have had the cultivated asparagus from the Greeks, they do seem to have learnt the use of the wild plant from them, for the name is from the Greek *asparagos*, which appears to have been used to mean any still tender, still folded, vegetable shoot. From Theophrastus (*c.* 300 BC) it is clear that the Greek use of *A. officinalis* and of two related species was medicinal, not culinary. The question then is, did the Latins domesticate this native, or did they have the cultivars from some other source?

The plant is found in sandy soils about the mouths of rivers from as far south as north Africa to as far north as Siberia. It was native to, among other places, the Nile Delta. When, towards the end of the last century, the French savant M. V. Loret wrote his *Flore pharaonique*, he included asparagus in that work; he had found among tomb-paintings of fruit and vegetables a representation of asparagus, bunched, trimmed and tied for market much as it still is. The painting dates from the time of the Memphis Dynasties, so that it must be about 3000 BC. It seems quite clear that the asparagus was domesticated by the Egyptians more than 5,000 years ago.

Another succulent shoot, celery, is a relative newcomer in cultivation. It will serve our purpose here to glance backwards at its history. The English botanist and naturalist John Ray, writing in 1686, makes it clear that celery was a familiar vegetable in English gardens by the end of the seventeenth century; but go back only half a century to Parkinson's *Paradisus in sole paradisi terrestris* (1629), and celery appears as a rarity, which means that it must have been only recently introduced.

Ray says that the cultivation of celery came from Italy, and that it had spread from there through France. But from French recipes of the seventeenth and eighteenth centuries it is evident that the celery then being cultivated, although doubtless a considerable improvement on the wild plant, was not as burly, had stalks much less crisp and flesh more fibrous, and a smaller 'heart' than modern celery. The improvements we take for granted have been accomplished in cultivation during the past two or three centuries, by selection, and it is clear that seventeenth-century celery was not an ancient cultivar and had, in short, only quite recently been taken into cultivation.

Wild celery is a biennial herb with a strong and not very agreeable scent; the taste is acrid, almost burning, and a piece of the stem when chewed leaves the mouth sore and slightly numb. It grows wild very abundantly, in marshy places near the sea, from Sweden in northern Europe to Algeria in the north of Africa, and as far east as northern India. So it could have been domesticated by the farmers or gardeners of half a dozen of the most ancient civilizations. But in fact it was not, and back beyond seventeenth-century Italy there is not a sign of it as an esculent vegetable. Almost certainly this is because the taste is too strong to be pleasant.

It was cultivated on a small scale by the Romans, but as a culinary condiment, not a vegetable; that is, it was used as we use chopped parsley. That this was so is clear from Pliny, who, using the name *helioselinum* (from the Greek *eleioselinon*), distinguished the wild celery from a cultivar whose leaves were blanched before use, presumably to reduce the acridity, and then used as a condiment. However, this kind of celery was manifestly unimportant from an economic point of view, for celery is not mentioned in Diocletian's price-fixing Edict (Law of the Maximum, AD 301), in which all foods and wines on the Roman market are listed.

Going back now beyond Pliny, it seems that the plant called *selinon*, first in the *Odyssey*, then in Pindar, Aristophanes and other poets, and the *eleioselinon* of Theophrastus both refer to the wild plant. It was used medicinally and also in funeral wreaths. Gibault (1912) even quotes a popular adage, presumably Greek although he does not say so—'Only the celery [1] is lacking'—to describe the dying condition of a sick man. Apparently the Greeks had this funerary use of celery from the Egyptians. But in all this there is no question of cultivation.

It is quite clear, then, that the domestication of celery occurred in Italy. But why did the Italians find it worth while to work with a plant so acrid that all earlier civilized gardeners had rejected it? There are two possible answers: either (i) that the effect on the flavour of blanching the stalks was discovered or better understood, or, (ii) that a mutant with much reduced acridity occurred in some plantations of celery still being grown in the Roman manner, as a kind of parsley. Or, of course, both answers may be correct. Be that as it may, celery as a vegetable for the table and as a salad was domesticated by the Italians during the fifteenth and possibly as early as the fourteenth century.

---

[1] I am not sure that the word used could not have meant parsley.

MUSHROOMS

No doubt many fungi were gathered and eaten by Stone-Age men, but domestication is relatively modern.

Although the ancients were as fond of mushrooms as we are, it seems never to have occurred to them to try growing them artificially, and there is no trace of cultivated mushrooms in the ancient literatures. In fact the first author to refer in any language to mushrooms as a cultivated crop is Olivier de Serres, in his *Théâtre d'Agriculture des Champs* (1600).

In the year 1698 an English traveller named Lister was touring France, and in an account of his journeys shows himself very much impressed by the abundance and regularity of mushrooms on the Paris markets, an abundance and regularity due to cultivation. He calls them 'forced' mushrooms and says that they are harvested from beds in the open from early August to late October; and from covered hot-beds during the winter months. Lister describes how, in the market gardens of the Vaugirard quarter, outside the gates of the city, the mushroom beds are made up with horse-manure covered with fine soil. Lister seems to have known that the mushroom-growers were relying on a 'sowing' of some sort, not on chance; but he did not know what it was they sowed.

Twenty years before Lister's visit to Paris, a botanist known as Marchant *père* to distinguish him from his son, also a botanist, had demonstrated before the *Académie des Sciences* that the white filaments which develop in the soil under mushrooms will, if transplanted into a suitable medium, give rise to more mushrooms. Market gardeners were remarkably quick to take advantage of this discovery, whence the abundance of mushrooms on the Paris markets which so surprised Lister.

But since mushroom culture was older than Marchant's discovery—we have seen that Olivier de Serres mentions it as early as 1600—that is not quite the beginning of the story.

As has happened so often, the origin of progress was chance, seized and used by intelligence. The market gardeners of Paris were accustomed to make up hot-beds for the growing of melons, and from time to time in autumn one of them would get a fine chance crop of mushrooms on such beds— naturally enough, since the favourite medium for *Psalliota* (*Agaricus*) *campestris* is decomposing horse-manure which is what the melon beds were made of, and mushrooms in neighbouring fields would be releasing countless millions of spores. Some of those market gardeners set to work to discover a means of repeating deliberately what had happened by chance. Whether it was one of them who discovered the use of mycellium, or whether the market gardeners employed Marchant to investigate the life cycle of the mushroom, is not clear. But it would be fair to date the domestication, as distinct from occasional cultivation, of the mushroom as the date of Marchant's lecture to the *Académie des Sciences* in 1678.

LEGUMES

We come now to a class of cultivated plants which, although it is convenient to treat them here as table vegetables, are economically more important as field crops and staples, comparable in some respects with the cereals, than as garden crops. These are the pulses, or legumes. The broad bean, the lentil and the pea are Old-World plants and all are prehistoric in cultivation. Prehistoric in native American cultivation, the kidney-beans are relative newcomers to the Old World.

The enormous antiquity of the bean in cultivation is well attested. Even in Europe, remains of beans have been found by archaeologists on Lake-Dweller sites in England (Glastonbury), Switzerland, Lombardy and Savoy.[1] That takes us back only into the Bronze Age, but at Hissarlik Schliemann found carbonized beans in Troy II. Furthermore, beans have

[1] Heer, 1865, p. 22.

been found in twelfth-dynasty tombs in Egypt, taking us back to about 2400 BC in that country.[1]

According to Vavilov we must consider Central Asia as the centre of primary dissemination of 'all the chief legumes such as peas, lentils and beans', but there is a difficulty about this; for one thing, as we shall see, the Egyptians had beans but not peas (or rather, not our peas), and they would hardly have had one but not the other if the source was identical. There is another reason to believe that the great Russian economic botanist may in this case have been mistaken, for in the Mediterranean centre there is a much larger number and diversity of forms than anywhere else. We also have to take into account the original habitat of the ancestral wild plant, *Vicia pliniana*. But first, Vavilov goes on to say that 'many of the cultivated plants of the Mediterranean countries, such as flax, barley, beans and chick peas, are notable for their large seeds and fruits in contrast to the small, seeded forms of Central Asia, their basic place of origin, where most of the dominant genes of the plant are concentrated'. This, of course, is put forward as evidence that the Mediterranean centre is only secondary. Wild plants in nature are shaped by their dominant genes; it is only in cultivation, and with the segregation of local forms arising from mutants or by hybrids, that the recessive genes are given their chance and that those changes in the morphology of plants occur which make them different from the wild ancestors.

Be that as it may, and although primitive cultivated *Vicia* seeds might have been carried half across the world to Egypt 7,000 or 8,000 years ago, it is a fact that the wild bean is found not, at least nowadays, in Central Asia, but only in the Mediterranean basin. *Vicia pliniana* has been found wild in the Algerian highlands; Pliny describes a wild bean found commonly in north Africa in his time; and the French botanist Trabut confirmed this as late as 1900 when he found, in the region called the Sersou, beans growing as a weed of

[1] G. A. Schweinfurth, *Nature*, 1883, p. 134.

fallows, which seemed to be identical with the ones found in carbonized Lake-Dweller middens in Europe. There is a pretty piece of linguistic evidence for a local Mediterranean and even north African domestication of the bean: the Berber name is *ibivu*, and it seems that this is not a Semitic loan word, which it certainly would have been had the bean come to the Berbers from an eastern Mediterranean source.

I do not think we can get any nearer than this: that the bean was domesticated somewhere on the south side of the Mediterranean in the third millennium BC.

Until about 1900 many respectable botanical and other authorities were still convinced that the kidney-beans and their close relatives, such as scarlet runners, could be identified with (or at least affiliated to) a leguminous vegetable, *dolichos*, mentioned by Theophrastus, with what appears to be the *Smilax beraea* of Dioscorides, and also with the *lobos* (an edible legume pod) of Dioscorides and Galen.[1] I shall not here enter into the arguments which proved that our kidney-beans and runner beans have nothing whatever to do with those ancient legumes used by herbalists and physicians. It is enough to say that there is now no doubt that our beans came to us from Central and South America.

First, as to the species: *Phaeseolus coccineus*, origin of the runner beans, and *P. vulgaris*, origin of the kidney-beans, are confined to America in nature and unknown as wild plants in the Old World. From these two species (and just possibly some others) derive not only all those beans other than *Vicia* of which we eat the dried seeds, but also all the beans of which we eat the green pods.

The first European of note to see and describe any of these beans in cultivation was Christopher Columbus himself who, three weeks after his arrival in the Americas, saw fields of them in Cuba. In 1528 Cabeca de Vaca saw beans in cultivation in what is now Florida, and eleven years later De Soto saw them under cultivation with maize and squashes on the

[1] Gibault, 1912.

west bank of the Mississippi. Meanwhile Oviedo had found the same beans being grown in San Domingo and in Nicaragua. Moreover cultivated beans had been carried by then to peoples who were much less advanced than the Central American Indians: Lescarbot saw them in what is now Maine in 1609, and Cartier had found them in Indian gardens about the mouth of the St Lawrence in 1535.

The two most advanced groups of nations in America were those of Mexico and the isthmus of Panama—Maya, Olmec, Toltec, Aztec, etc., and the Inca empire in the Andes; Mexico with Central America and ancient Peru were the two centres of dissemination of cultivated American plants. Cortés, in a letter to Charles V, describes what are unmistakably scarlet runners used in the Aztec city of Tenochtitlan for a dual purpose, ornament and food-cropping. And the same kind of beans, but in great variety, were cultivated by the united nations of the Inca empire, from Chile to Bolivia. So we have to try to decide whether there were two separate domestications, in Mexico or thereabouts, and in Peru; or only one. Vavilov, applying his usual criteria, gives Mexico as the primary centre, Peru as only secondary; but archaeological findings which were not available to him may cause us to reverse this order.

Cultivated *Phaeseolus* have been found on schists belonging to the Early Farmer epoch of culture in Peru, which begins in 2500 BC. Our knowledge of these so-called Early Farmers, the first people in the Americas, as far as we know, to start cultivating their food instead of gathering and hunting it in the wild, is derived from excavation of their middens. In one of these, the Huaca Prieta in the Chicana valley,[1] cultivated beans were found, but no maize; the implication seems to be that beans may have been domesticated before maize. Now, although prehistoric remains of cultivated beans have been found also in Central America and even as far north as Utah, none have yet been found which can be dated as early as those

[1] Bushnell, 1956.

found in Peru. In the present state of our knowledge, the provisional conclusion must be that the genus *Phaeseolus* was first domesticated by Early Farmers in the Andean valleys during the third millennium BC.

The habitat of the wild lentil is unknown. The botanist Engler thought that it must formerly have been wild all over Asia Minor and southern Europe. Vavilov, as I have said, places the primary centre of cultivation in Central Asia on the grounds that there, in the lentil population, are found the most dominant genes. The fact is that nobody has ever found a wild specimen of *Lens esculenta*. There are half a dozen species in the genus, and conceivably this one could have originated as a hybrid. As we now know the genus as a whole, it is a Mediterranean one, not Central Asian; and there are other grounds for thinking that the first cultivation of lentils occurred in the Mediterranean area.

The antiquity of the lentil in cultivation is attested first by three references in the Bible, the first being in Genesis: there can be no doubt about the identity of the references, for the Arabic word still in use for lentils is *adas*, a derivative of the ancient Hebrew *adashum*. Biblical references do not, of course, exclude the possibility of a Central Asian source. By the time the earliest books of the Bible were being written, the civilized communities of northern India, Mesopotamia and Egypt were in touch with each other and long had been; and as I have already explained, the grape-vine, *Vitis vinifera*, reached Phoenicia and Egypt from ancient Armenia. The lentil is much older in cultivation than Genesis.

According to Schweinfurth, balls of lentil porridge containing intact and identifiable beans were found in a number of Egyptian twelfth-dynasty tombs. The Louvre in Paris actually has three red lentils taken from a tomb of the same period (2400–2200 BC) which are identical with a red lentil cultivated until recently in the north of France. Farther east, lentils certainly go back beyond 1500 BC, since there is a Vedic Sanskrit name for them.

The fact is that the lentil has been in cultivation over a very vast area for at least six thousand years, and domestication simply cannot be placed.

Vavilov also says that Central Asia was the primary centre of dissemination of peas, with the Mediterranean as the secondary centre. But *Pisum sativum* appears to be not merely naturalized but genuinely wild in southern Europe, where in cultivation it has given rise to a large number of varieties. Again, cultivation is immensely ancient, and in this case, tracing that cultivation backwards in time, we do find support for his insistence on a Central Asian origin and begin to wonder whether the plant was so anciently naturalized in Italy and Greece that it now appears to be native, although it is not.

That the pea became a crop-plant very early in Greek agricultural civilization is clear: when the arrow shot by Helenus, the son of Priam, bounced off Menelaus's armour, it did so, says Homer, 'as on some wide threshing floor the dark beans and *erebinths* leap from the winnower's fan in a whistling wind'. *Erebinths* are peas. But if you look to Egypt for the Greek source of the cultivar, you fail to find it. The only peas found on Egyptian archaeological sites are not our *Pisum sativum* (they may be *P. elatius*), whereas the carbonized peas found at Hissarlik were easily identified [1] as *P. sativum*. Hissarlik is the ancient Troy, or rather many Troys.[2] It is reasonable to suppose that the Trojans had their peas originally from one of the more anciently civilized communities of the Near East. And that is as far back as we can go. If the most ancient centre of dissemination of this plant really was Central Asia, then surely China would have had peas at least as early as did Europe; but the introduction of the plant from the west into China is historical, on record.[3]

[1] By the archaeologists Virchov and Wittmack.
[2] *See* Schliemann, 1885, p. 368.
[3] In the late sixteenth-century *Pent-sao*.

5

Salad

Before the invention of farming, when men and women gathered their vegetable food in the wild, vegetables were probably eaten raw. At what point did some anciently civilized community begin to cook some of them, while continuing to eat the others raw? That is, make the fundamental distinction between 'vegetables' and 'salads'? We shall never know, and it does not matter. But certainly the distinction was first made a very long time ago, and salad was already salad in ancient Egypt.

In our own time the most important green salad crop is lettuce; for how long has it been so?

It is probable but not certain that *Latuca sativa*, the cultivated lettuce, derives from the wild *Latuca scariola*, but there are such considerable differences between the two chief classes of lettuce, cabbage and cos, that there may be more than a single ancestral species. However, *L. scariola* is at least some guide to the origin of the cultivars; but only a very rough guide, for the species is native over an immense area—all Europe, north Africa, and all west Asia in the temperate zone. At least, then, the lettuce must have been domesticated in the West and not in the Far East, and this is confirmed by one well-established fact, that lettuces were unknown in Chinese horticulture before AD 600, and must therefore have been introduced from the West.[1]

The Greeks cultivated lettuce as a salad, but they are unlikely to have been its first cultivators. It is true that there is no Hebrew or Sanskrit word for the plant, which suggests

[1] *See* Bretschneider, 1871.

that it cannot have been domesticated prehistorically. In the Jewish Diaspora lettuce is one of the bitter herbs of the Passover, but this may be so only in the European Diaspora. Moreover, whereas cultivated lettuce is not bitter unless badly overgrown, wild lettuce is very bitter, and this fact may support the contention that lettuce is not very ancient in cultivation.

Despite all of which, Loret claims [1] that the Egyptians had cultivated lettuce of the cos type (later known to the Romans as Cyprian lettuce) as early as 3000 BC. Now it is true that *L. scariola* is native to both Upper Egypt and to the Nile Delta, so that lettuce could certainly have been domesticated by the Egyptians. But if it was so domesticated, and so early, it is curious that it had not spread to the other great civilized peoples much earlier than, as far as one can ascertain from their literatures, was the case.

Beetroot is nowadays more commonly eaten as a salad than as a cooked vegetable, though economically, as a source of sugar, it is an industrial plant.

Three forms of beet, all derivatives of one species as far as we know, are important in modern economies: the sugar-beet; the salad beet; and the so-called spinach-beet, a form in which the leaves instead of the root have been developed by selection in cultivation. There is no trace of any of them in the ancient proto-civilizations, and there is not even a name for beet in classical Hebrew, Sanskrit or Chinese, let alone in what we know of earlier languages.

There are, however, Greek and Latin names for the plant, and Vavilov noted that it is in the Mediterranean centre of dissemination that there are the greatest number and diversity of varieties of cultivated beets. The same area is within the habitat of the wild plant, *Beta maritima*, an area which extends from the Atlantic eastwards into India, and northwards from the Mediterranean throughout Europe and the Near East. Yet the beet, though it was used, does not

[1] 1890, p. 68.

seem to have been cultivated by the Greeks or Romans; its
medicinal uses are mentioned by Theophrastus, Dioscorides
and Galen, that is, by the herbalists and physicians who used
both leaves and roots; but it is not mentioned by Pliny,
Palladius or Columella, one and probably all of whom would
have had something to say about it had it been in cultivation.
For this reason alone I do not think that De Candolle can
have been right when he placed the domestication of the beet
three or four centuries BC.

The first author to describe a fleshy-rooted beet was the
Venetian Ermolao Barbaro, in his commentary on Dioscorides (1495). In Fuchs's *History of Plants*, published in
1542, there is a figure of a beetroot, and in the first French
translation of that work, published in 1549, there is a note to
the effect that 'the red beet is cultivated chiefly in noblemen's
gardens, for it is not yet known to ordinary gardeners'. It was
not even introduced into Italy until the sixteenth century. It
would appear that the cultivated beet came in the first
instance from Germany.

How early? Not earlier than the fourteenth century; for it
is not mentioned by the greatest of the medieval German
gardeners, Albertus Magnus, in the thirteenth century, or
by the Italian Crescenzi.

We can, then, attribute the domestication of the beet to
German gardeners some time towards the end of the
thirteenth or beginning of the fourteenth century.

The radish is an anciently cultivated salad vegetable. No
other wild species is clearly or obviously ancestral to our
Raphanus sativus. The radish used for medicinal purposes by
the Greeks, and described by Dioscorides, was apparently
Raphanus agria; and some botanists have believed that
another radish cultivated by the Greeks was *Raphanus
maritimus*, which is native along the whole Mediterranean
littoral. The majority of modern botanists think that our
radishes are derived from yet another species, *R. raphanis-
trum*, despite the fact that there are some morphological

differences which are difficult to get over. Other theories are
that the cultivated radishes derive from a chance hybrid, or
from a mutant.

The earliest reference to the radish as a cultivated
vegetable is in a Chinese work, the *Rhya*, published about
1100 BC.[1] This should mean that the radish has been
domesticated in China at least since about 1500 BC. Again,
the variety of Chinese and Japanese radishes is enormous,
and Vavilov mentions Japanese radishes weighing as much
as 36 lb. each; furthermore the wild species are native in
China. All of which could mean that we had the cultivated
radish from China, except that there is evidence that
radishes are as old in cultivation in the West as in the East
or, if Herodotus can be depended on, older. For radishes
(*surmaia*) were among the vegetables named on the tablet on
the Great Pyramid of Cheops (*c.* 2580 BC), commemorating
the enormous sum of money spent on feeding the builders.
Then, too, there is a figure of a radish on a wall of the
temple of Ammon at Karnak in Upper Egypt, begun about
1000 BC. So the radish was domesticated in Egypt more than
five thousand years ago; and either the seeds of the cultivated radishes were carried across the world to China before
1500 BC, or there was an independent and later domestication
in that country.

The tomato is treated in western *cuisine* both as a vegetable
for cooking and as a salad. As it is also the source of bottled
and tubed sauces and sauce-bases, and of a fruit drink, it is
difficult to place it in this book; but as we most commonly use
it as a salad, at least in Britain, it may as well come here.
Since its introduction in the sixteenth century, after a very
slow start, it has become one of the most important economic
plants in the world.

And yet, when it was first brought to the Old World from
Mexico the tomato plant was treated with the deepest distrust. It will be worth glancing briefly at its European career.

[1] Bretschneider, 1892, vol. 2, p. 39.

Seeds must first have reached Spain about 1525, following the completion of Cortés's conquest of Mexico; possibly not quite so early. The first of the European botanists to examine the plant was the Italian Matthiolus, at the newly established botanical garden in Padua. Matthiolus called it *mala insana*, the unwholesome fruit, but on what grounds it is impossible to say since he must have known that it was a food plant in America. Perhaps, however, that is presuming too much, for in French if not Italian nurserymen's catalogues it was listed as an ornamental well into the eighteenth century. At all events, other botanists followed the example of Matthiolus in condemning it as more or less poisonous, although by 1560 there were some tomatoes growing in Italian gardens and the fruits were being used in cooking. The first botanist to classify the newcomer was Tournefort, at the Jardin Royal in Paris (now the Jardin des Plantes). With an ancient Greek poisonous fruit of some sort in mind, he called it *Lycopersicum*. Later, the English botanist Miller amended this to the absurd *Lycopersicon*, wolf-peach; but since by then the Italians, and presumably the Spaniards, were eating the fruit, and as he doubtless knew that the tomato was a food in Mexico and Peru, he added the specific name *esculentum*.

Although the tomato was accepted as a food-plant by southern Europeans in the seventeenth century, it continued to get a bad press, or at the very least an ambiguous one; for those who did not consider the tomato poisonous thought it aphrodisiac, whence the vernacular names *pomme d'amour*, 'love-apple'. As late as 1653 the French botanist Dalechamps wrote:

These apples, as also the whole plant, chill the body, albeit less than does mandragora; wherefore it is dangerous to make use of them. Nevertheless some do eat them cooked, with oil, salt and pepper. They give little nourishment to the body and that little bad and corrupt.[1]

[1] *Histoire des Plantes*, 1653. (My own translation.)

Northern Europeans were much more reluctant than the Italians to eat tomatoes. It was not until the early nineteenth century that English and American gardeners and seedsmen began to take the plant seriously as a crop; and the old distrust of the fruit persisted among elderly villagers in England into the twentieth century.

Now all this was despite the fact that the Mexicans had been eating tomatoes for many centuries. When Alexander von Humboldt examined tomato plants in Mexican gardens early in the nineteenth century, he came to the conclusion that the plant was already ancient in cultivation; indeed from the earliest figure of the plant with fruit in European botanical literature, it is obvious that the fruits, for example, were already as large as they are now. We have, by selection, improved the shape of the fruit and nearly ruined its flavour, but we have not taken the plant any further from the wild species than the people of Central America or Peru (see below) had done. Moreover, that it was from Mexico that we had the plant is not in doubt; the very name we use is a corruption of the Aztec name *tumatl*. Yet it is far from clear that the tomato was domesticated in Mexico. It is true that wild tomatoes are found in that country, but the probability is that they are degenerate garden escapes. The tomato naturalizes very readily in suitable conditions; I have even seen tiny tomato plants, dwarfed by the very poor conditions, growing on the sides of completely barren volcanoes in the Canary Islands, in nothing but rough slag and where there is virtually no rainfall. The seeds pass undamaged through the human, animal and avian digestive tracts, and germinate where dropped, vast numbers of them in sewage farms.

But the true wild habitat of the tomato is not Mexico; it is in Ecuador, the *Esmeraldas* of the Conquistadores, the Quito of the Inca Empire, and the Galapagos Islands. From that fact there can be only one conclusion as to domestication, especially since, at the time of the conquest of Inca Peru, the tomato was ancient in cultivation there as well as in Mexico.

Tomatoes were brought into cultivation by the advanced and very clever farmers of one of the component nations of the Inca Empire, Chimu possibly, or Nasca, or perhaps Quitu in the equatorial north, the last country to be added to the empire before the defeat and murder of the usurper Sapa Inca Atahualpa by Pizarro. From there it would have passed, by way of Mayan Guatemala, into Mexico. It is quite impossible to fix a date for those events, but if we take into account the fact that even the oldest cultivated tomatoes are enormously different from the ancestral species, we are perhaps safe in guessing at a date early in the first millennium BC. For although artificial selection in cultivation works very much faster than natural selection, it is still a long job from the wild plant to the kind of cultivar which is morphologically so different from its ancestor that the latter cannot readily be identified.

Another salad fruit, the cucumber, gives us far more trouble than the tomato, because it is extremely variable, and it is usually impossible to identify vestiges of cucurbitaceous plants with any assurance. As an example of the difficulty of tracing the salad and pickling cucumbers back to their source we may recall that Flinders Petrie found vestiges of some kind of cucumber, which could, however, be pumpkin or a sort of melon, in the Fayum and on sites dating from the twelfth Dynasty.[1] But since the species *Cucumis sativus*, our cucumber, is not, and in all likelihood never has been, native to Egypt or anywhere west of India, it seems probable that those vestiges were of a cucumber-like variety, *agrestis*, of *Cucumis melo* (melon) which is still known as the Egyptian Cucumber. The original habitat of our *C. sativus* is unknown; but a very closely related species, called *C. hardwickii*, is wild in certain parts of north-eastern India and Burma.[2]

If we identify as *C. sativus* the *sikuos* of Theophrastus, the *sikuos hemeros* of Dioscorides, and the cucumbers which

[1] See also Isaiah 1. viii and Numbers 2. v.
[2] Vavilov, 1951.

Pliny says were grown under glass, by a method described by Columella, for the emperor Tiberius who had a passion for them, then they must have reached the west from India not later than 400 BC and probably rather earlier. Now this is not impossible. For example, although this cucumber is not native in the Indus Valley, the civilized people whose great cities were Harrapa and Mohenjo-daro could easily have had cucumbers from the countries to the east of them— Burma, for example, was, according to Vavilov, a centre of dissemination for cucurbits—and passed them on to the Near-Eastern civilized communities of Mesopotamia with which they certainly had trade relations. From Mesopotamia, through Phoenicia, by way of Lydia into Greece, is not a difficult route.

So, then, in all probability our salad cucumbers were first taken into cultivation and improved somewhere in north-eastern India; and by way of confirmation there is a Sanskrit name for this fruit, *soukosa*, which puts the date back to a possible 1500 BC or thereabouts. But it is not likely that the most ancient Hindu cucumbers and those which were, if our speculation is correct, passed westward through the Indus Valley and Mesopotamia into Europe, were exactly like our own; they were probably more like an elongated melon in shape. There is some literary evidence that they were shaped like 'serpents'; Virgil's reference, however, is doubtless to the serpentine growth of the plant. But to cover all the possibilities, it is worth while examining the ancestry of the word *gherkin*.

Gherkin derives from the German word *Gurke*, but in the older written accounts of this small cucumber the word is *Agurke*. This is a corruption of the Russian word *ogurets*, which in turn is derived from the Byzantine Greek *angourion*.[1] But this last word was not used in Byzantium until the early Middle Ages, reaching the city from the east, probably from one of the Iranian countries, together with the

[1] Victor Heyn, 1888, says the word is Persic-Aramaic.

small cucumber it describes. Whether this cucumber was, however, of Iranian origin or came from farther east again, from India, is not clear.

The nomenclature of the salads called both chicory and endive is so confused that to disentangle its history is very difficult. The French apply the word *endive* to the frizzy chicory, which looks like a green shock-wig. The plant in question they call *Cichorium endiva*, and say that the wild plant ancestral to it is the native *Cichorium pumilum*. On the other hand, the English call the same wild native plant *Cichorium intybus*, a name the French use for what they seem to distinguish as another species, while the English use the same name for the cultivated chicory. The true *C. endiva*, according to English authorities, is a native Indian plant; it is not found wild in Europe or the Near East.

I am here concerned with two forms of what is the same plant: the big, rather tough, shock-wig salad we buy as chicory or endive; and the small, tight-hearted, winter-forced salad for which we use the Flemish name *witloof* (in the United States the latter is known as *escarole*).

The name endive derives from the Latin *intybus*, a salad which the Romans appear to have cultivated although it was unknown to the Greeks except as a common wild plant of the littoral. A vegetable or salad called *intiba* must have been of commercial importance in the Roman Empire in the third and fourth centuries, for it appears in the famous price-fixing edict of Diocletian in 301. What is curious is that the Romans should have been using a Greek name (*intybus* or *intiba* comes from the Greek *entubon*) for a cultivar which they seem not to have had from Greece. Perhaps it was domesticated in Greek, rather than Latin, Italy, or in Sicily.

Cultivation of chicory had to be restarted by the western Christian peoples independently, after the fourteenth century; at all events there seems to have been a second and late domestication in France, the cultivar being thereafter introduced into Italy, Germany and England. Blanching of chicory did not begin until the sixteenth century. In the Flemish countries the word *witloof* is older than the salad we call by that name; it means, of course, *white leaf*, and was applied to the blanched frizzy chicory at least as early as the seventeenth century.

Thus there were two domestications, one by the south Italian Greeks perhaps not much earlier than the beginning of our era, another by the northern French or Flemings about the fourteenth or early fifteenth century.

As for what we now distinguish as *witloof*, there is no doubt about its origin. In 1850 the head gardener of the Brussels Botanical Garden, a Monsieur Bresiers, used some mushroom beds in frames to force and blanch chicory, for which purpose he transplanted root-cuttings from an open bed of the salad. The stout roots which he used gave rise not to the usual frizzy heads, but to shoots like the hearts of a small cos lettuce. Bresiers, having obtained this result by accident, found out by experiment in the following years how to obtain it deliberately, but kept this valuable information to himself for the rest of his life. When he died only his widow knew the secret. She told her own gardener how to grow the *witloof*, he told his friend who was gardener to the Moretus family of Merxen, and soon the technique became public knowledge.[1]

A relatively modern domestication of a valuable wild salad is that of watercress. The ancients, the Europeans of the Middle Ages and the modern Europeans until about 1800 simply gathered watercress from wild beds in streams. The people who supplied the markets often had to go fifty miles or more for their supplies, and the cress they sold was usually mixed with such leaves as those of the kingcup and water-marigold.

The *Annals* of what is now the Royal Horticultural Society contain an account of the beginning of watercress

[1] *See* Gibault, 1912.

cultivation.[1] In the winter of 1809-10, during the peace
following Bonaparte's second campaign in Austria, a
Monsieur Cardon, at that time principal director of
finances of the Grand Army hospitals, was at military
H.Q. in Erfurt, then the capital of Upper Thuringia. M.
Cardon went for a walk in the country outside the town,
although the ground was covered with snow. He was very
surprised to see ahead of him long, three- or four-yard-wide
ditches showing a brilliant green surface. Approaching, he
was astonished to find himself in the middle of an immense
plantation of cultivated watercress beds looking like a
beautiful carpet of verdure against the snow-covered ground
all round them. He made inquiries and discovered that
cultivation of watercress had been established for some few
years and that the business belonged to the town of Erfurt,
which let it out to market gardeners for a rent of 60,000
francs a year, which meant that the revenue from the watercress beds was an impressive sum. Back in Paris, Cardon
scoured the whole region round the city for a suitable site; he
had to have flat land and natural springs to create the right
conditions. He found them, after considerable difficulty, in
1811, in the valley of the Nonette, at Saint-Léonard near
Senlis and Chantilly, and so was able to establish watercress
cultivation in France with the aid of two foremen whom he
fetched from Erfurt to oversee the work.

It seems then that we owe the domestication of watercress
to a Thuringian market gardener, and that it does not date
much earlier than 1800.

[1] 1825, vol. xxii, pp. 77–88.

6

Rubber

The modern story of the domestication of *Hevea braziliensis* deserves a chapter to itself. It is difficult to see how modern mechanical road transport, on which an enormous part of the movement of people and goods depends, or the aircraft industry and air transport, or the colossal electrical industry, would have been possible at all without rubber. For if it be true that it was in the first instance the invention of the 'safety' bicycle, then of the motor-car, which stimulated the swift growth of rubber technology and the rubber industry, it is equally true that, to paraphrase Voltaire's witticism about God, had there been no such thing as rubber, it would have been necessary to invent it. Try for a moment to imagine the technology of today without rubber, and you will see what I mean. It is true that more recently we have invented substitute elastic plastics, but even that invention has been due to the pre-existence of rubber as much as to other stimulant causes.

A large number of plants, especially in the families *Euphorbiaceae* and *Moraceae*, some of them huge trees, others shrubs, many of them herbs, yield a latex of sorts, the milky sap which coagulates when heated into an elastic solid or which, by heat treatment with sulphur, can be vulcanized to various degrees of hardness. Some of these have been used on a commercial scale: *Manihot glaziovii*, for example, and *Castilloa elastica*, both *Moraceae*; a Mexican member of the family *Compositae*, *Parthemium argentatum*; a number of the *Euphorbiaceae* native to the Canary Islands; and, more important, another *Moraceae*, *Ficus elastica* which, in the juvenile form, is that popular house plant known as the rubber-plant. This last, at maturity, is an enormous tree and it yields what used to be called indiarubber, whereas the Brazilian *Hevea* yields what used to be called pararubber. It is *Hevea braziliensis* which is incomparably the most valuable of the rubber-yielding plants.

It will probably never be possible to discover how long before the arrival of Europeans in the Americas, in the late fifteenth century, the American Indians of the great Amazonian rain forest discovered rubber; for they were its discoverers, and for all we know may have made their discovery thousands of years ago. Their practice was to cut the bark of the wild *Hevea* or, in their vernacular, *caoutchouc* (or *cahuchu*, a Carib word) and collect the milky sap from the trees in the cleaned-out rind of a gourd. A lump of soft clay was stuck on the end of a stick and modelled into the shape of a ball; this was plunged into the latex, which stuck to it; it was then heated gently over a fire to make the latex coagulate into rubber, and the clay was then washed out, leaving the artisan with a rubber bottle. Just how the discovery was made it is impossible to say; probably by the common process of reasoning from the results of an accident. In much the same way, the Indians made themselves rubber shoes and also balls for games. It was those balls, which bounded much more satisfactorily than any we had in Europe at the time, which first attracted European attention to the remarkable properties of rubber, some time during the sixteenth century.

So the primitive Amazonian Indians were the first men in the world to discover the latex-yielding properties of the *Hevea braziliensis* or *caoutchouc* tree; to discover how to make the latex into rubber; and to manufacture articles made of rubber. But they never attempted to domesticate the tree; they were at too early a stage of culture to do so, and in any case they had a plentiful supply of plants in their forests.

Although some Europeans knew the properties of rubber

in the sixteenth century, it is a curious fact that science
seemed to take no notice of it for two centuries, though there
would have been many uses for it in the eighteenth century.
The first scientific paper to be written on it was read to the
Académie des Sciences in Paris in 1751, and the first use of
rubber by Europeans seems to date from 1770, when small
cubes of indiarubber, about a centimetre or a little more
cubed, were sold for the equivalent of £0.25 each, and used
as erasers. The next use was in the making of waterproof
cloth, but this was unsatisfactory stuff, for the rubber became
tacky and soft in heat. The defect was largely overcome by
one Macintosh, whose name became a synonym for waterproof coats. But not much more use could be made of the
stuff until an American named Goodyear invented what
came to be called 'vulcanization' in 1839. Rubber heat-
treated with various quantities of sulphur (only about 2 per
cent for soft rubber, as much as 40 per cent for hard rubber)
retained its firmness at normal temperatures of heat, and did
not become tacky. Following Goodyear's invention, factories
for manufacture of articles made of rubber began to spring
up in the principal industrial countries. Solid rubber tyres
were first used on road vehicles in 1867. In 1888 Dunlop
invented the pneumatic bicycle tyre, from which the motor-
car tyre was developed.

But for all those purposes the only supply of raw material
was still the wild *caoutchouc* trees of the Brazilian forests, and
the *Ficus elastica* trees of the Malayan forests.

So, then, a large and very rapidly increasing demand for
latex had been created rather suddenly. In Brazil a sort of rub-
ber-rush occurred, with people abandoning other kinds of work
to go into the forests to tap *Hevea* trees. Most of the forest was
and much of it still is more or less impenetrable, so that only
the trees growing along the openings made by rivers were
workable. Meanwhile, as it had been known since 1810 that
the *Ficus elastica* of Malaya yielded good latex, exploitation
of the wild rubber-trees of the Malayan forests was also

profitable. But whereas the *caoutchouc* tree can be tapped and still live, the Malayan rubber-trees were felled to get the latex. As a consequence, the Government of British India became alarmed at the prospect of the species being exterminated within a few years and decided that something must be done.

The credit for deciding to domesticate one of the rubber-plants belongs to an official of the India Office, Clements Markham, who was also a scholar of distinction with a special interest in South American history, having translated and edited some of the early chronicles for the Hakluyt Society. The initiation of the domestication of rubber-trees was not his only service to plantation farming and industry, for his aid was invoked by H. N. Ridley of Singapore to introduce the cocoa-tree to the East from Mexico.

Markham commissioned James Collins to carry out a survey of the world's principal latex-yielding plants, so that the species most suitable as a plantation crop could be chosen. Collins chose the Brazilian *Hevea*, and Markham then asked Sir Joseph Hooker, Director of the Royal Botanic Gardens at Kew, to send a collector to the Amazon basin to collect *Hevea*-seeds. More than one collector was sent, for seeds proved very difficult to germinate. From one parcel of seeds, however, some seedlings were raised and sent to the Botanic Gardens, Calcutta, to a special nursery in Sikkim, and to the Botanic Gardens at Peradeniya in Ceylon, to be nursed to maturity. All of these failed.

One of the reasons for studying the story of the domestication of *Hevea braziliensis* in some detail is that it throws a little light upon the kind of difficulties overcome by men whose names have not come down to us from the remote past, in the domestication and introduction of economic plants into new countries. In the nineteenth century, with such technical advantages as fast steam transport and Wardian cases (which were small portable greenhouses), the task was much easier than it had been in the past.

One recalls, for example, Bligh's difficulties with the
bread-fruit trees in H.M.S. *Bounty*. Yet even with all
the science, all the technology of the mid nineteenth century,
and with government money to finance it, the attempt to
turn the wild *Hevea* into a new cultigen failed several times
before success. That success was due to yet another plant-
collector from Kew.

His name was H. A. Wickham; he was carefully chosen by
Hooker, and he was later knighted for his service in this
mission. His instructions were to go to Brazil and get the
largest possible number of *Hevea*-seeds back to Kew as
quickly as possible. Preceding failures had made it clear that
the viability of the seeds was very short, and that it was
therefore important to have fresh seed. He was successful far
beyond the earlier collectors, gathering no less than 70,000
caoutchouc seeds. There is an absurd story that he then had
to smuggle them out of the country. This is quite untrue;
Wickham had the help and willing co-operation of the Jardim
Botanico at Rio de Janeiro, and of the Brazilian Government.
He also had the kind of drive the job required, for, realizing
the need for haste, he chartered a ship in Rio to get the seeds
back to Kew as fast as possible.

Nevertheless, so quickly did the seeds lose their vitality
that only 4 per cent of them germinated at Kew. Still, that
gave Hooker about 3,000 *Hevea* seedlings, far more than had
ever been seen outside of Brazilian forests until that date
(1876).

Meanwhile the authorities at the Botanic Gardens at Peradeniya near Kandy had prepared a special nursery garden for
the seedlings at Heneratgoda. Sent out in Wardian cases, nearly
two thousand arrived alive and were planted in the nursery.
At the same time—and this turned out to be very important
—a few seedlings were also sent to the Botanic Gardens in
Singapore—a first consignment of fifty which died, and a
second consignment of twenty-two plants which survived.
Eighteen seedlings were also sent to the Dutch Hortus

Bogoriensis in Java, where experimental work with other latex-yielding plants was in hand. One can still see in this magnificent garden, perhaps the finest in the tropics and now the Kebun Raya, a responsibility of the Indonesian Government, the *Hevea manihot*, and other rubber plants which were planted at that time.

Nine of the Singapore seedlings were transplanted to the private garden of the Resident, Sir Hugh Low, at Kuala Kangsar; the rest were planted in the Economic Plants section of the Botanic Gardens, a section which had been started at the insistence of the Government of India as a condition of their taking financial responsibility for the garden. Those Singapore seedlings were important because it was in Singapore that a means of propagating *Hevea* vegetatively, that is to say without having to rely on seed, was first discovered. This brings us to the next man in the story of that domestication, third after Clements Markham and Joseph Hooker—James Murton.

In 1874 Sir Joseph Hooker had been asked to recommend a superintendent for the Singapore Botanic Gardens, for which the Government of India had just accepted responsibility after the Singapore Agri-Horticultural Society, which had started them, had found the financial burden of maintenance too much for its revenue. Hooker sent one of his own men from Kew, the above-mentioned James Murton. Unfortunately I cannot detail Murton's achievements here, for by his work in economic botany in Singapore he conferred more benefits on Malaya, and south-east Asia generally, than did any other man, including all the princes, proconsuls and poohbahs since the memory of man runneth not to the contrary, with one exception — his successor, Ridley. It was Murton who found out by experiment how to grow *Hevea* from cuttings, a discovery which he immediately communicated to other Botanic Gardens working on the problem.

The importance of this discovery was not so much that it made possible an increased rate of propagation, although that too mattered when seeds were hard to come by, but that it made possible the deliberate propagation of the highest-yielding trees. One of the most important acts in the business of domestication of economic plants is this careful selection of the best individuals as providers of propagating material, for it is that selection which leads to the establishment of 'clones' with particular and desirable attributes. (Clone is the botanical name for a group of plants which are morphologically identical because they all derive from a single parent plant from which they have been propagated vegetatively.)

Murton died in 1888 and was succeeded as Director of the Botanic Gardens by an even more remarkable man, Henry Nicholas Ridley. Like Murton's, Ridley's contributions during a very long life to the well-being of the whole of south-east Asia were very numerous. But here we are concerned only with his work on rubber, and before coming to that it will be necessary to take a look at what was happening in Ceylon.

The very beautiful and very useful Botanic Gardens at Peradeniya on the outskirts of Kandy were, at the time in question, under the direction of Henry George Kendrick Thwaites, a remarkable academic botanist but also one of the half-dozen great economic botanists of that period. His work on coffee, his introduction of *Cinchona*, his reintroduction of tea, all of the first significance, were secondary to his work on rubber, which was as great as Murton's and Ridley's at Singapore.

In 1876 Thwaites received 1,919 of the Kew *caoutchouc* seedlings, and, using Murton's method of taking cuttings only from young-seedling growth, he rapidly increased the stock. Four years later he was sending rooted cuttings to planters who were willing to try a few trees of the new crop in Ceylon, where the spread of a serious disease of the coffee-bushes was making them less reluctant to try something new than they might have been. Other cuttings were sent to southern India and to Burma. At first Thwaites's work was more important than Ridley's in the distribution of young rubber-trees, partly because he had the greater number of the original seedlings. In 1881 some of these flowered for the first time, and later that year he was able to gather seed. Three years later really large-scale distribution of seeds and seedlings began, the principal difficulty being to interest the planters in saving themselves from ruin, as their coffee plantations were wiped out by leaf-disease.

While Hooker, Wickham, Murton, Ridley and Thwaites had succeeded in giving practical expression to Markham's vision, and had domesticated a rubber-tree, there were still troublesome technical problems to solve before such domestication could be judged wholly successful. Owing to the method of tapping the rubber-trees which preserved them alive, the quality of latex from cultivated trees was inferior to that coming from the wild rubber-trees of Brazil; an alternative method of tapping yielded excellent latex, but killed the trees within a few seasons. Ridley started a series of tapping experiments at Singapore, as well as a very thorough study of the *Hevea*-tree in cultivation. After many experiments he discovered a new way of tapping – excision and bark-paring, which confined the wounding of the tree to a single cut which, reopened at suitable intervals, yielded more and better latex without harming the tree. Some of Ridley's rubber reached London for the first time in 1881, and manufacturing experts pronounced it excellent. By 1889 latex was produced in Malaya by Ridley's method in commercial quantities. But Ridley continued experimenting, improving tapping techniques and discovering optimum planting distances and methods of cultivation. By the year 1910 Ridley, Thwaites and their helpers had perfected the methods of growing *Hevea braziliensis* in cultivation and made a good start on selecting, segregating and propagating high-yielding cultivars.

There was one other problem which they had had to solve

before domestication of the rubber-tree could be considered complete, and it is a curious one to which I have already referred in passing. Although in Malaya, as well as in Ceylon, the fungus disease of the coffee-bush leaves was ruining planters by wiping out plantations, they were inexplicably reluctant to change over to rubber, and it was only with the greatest difficulty that they were persuaded to do so. Ridley, as if he had not already enough work on his hands, went about urging that *Hevea* had arrived just in time to save the planters from ruin, if only they would acknowledge the fact. He was not only ignored or laughed at by the planters, he was officially reprimanded by his superiors in the government service for 'wasting his time'. Fortunately for the world, and for the prosperity of Malaysia, Ridley was one of those admirable men who know when to ignore orders.

Finally, in 1896, he made a convert, not among the British, who seemed to prefer ruin to the trouble of learning something new, but among the Chinese. A planter named Tan Chay Yan planted forty acres at Bukit Lintang with Ridley's young *Hevea*-trees, and the country's very profitable rubber industry was launched at last. How fitting that when, in 1966, the Singapore Botanic Gardens' orchid-breeders produced a particularly lovely prize-winning *Vanda*, Dr Burkill, Director of the Gardens, called it Tan Chay Yan.

By 1918 the Singapore Botanic Gardens alone had distributed seven million *Hevea* seeds and tens of thousands of seedlings. Peradeniya, or rather Heneratgoda, was working on the same scale. Ridley, by the way, lived to be more than a hundred years old, so that in the middle fifties of this century he was able to see the extraordinary consequences of his work on *Hevea braziliensis*.

The most curious aspect of this story of a modern domestication of an economic plant is that there was just one country where the conditions were exactly right for *Hevea braziliensis* in its new, cultivar shape, but where it refused to flourish— Brazil, its native land. Plantation repeatedly failed there. The reason was that in Brazil the leaves of the trees were attacked by a specific fungus disease which was, and is, a killer. Naturally, the wild *caoutchouc* trees had this pathogen, but being scattered in the wild, mixed with other trees upon which the fungus could not live, the disease was merely chronic and never reached epidemic proportions. But by planting thousands of *Hevea* trees together, in unmixed plantations, the planters unwittingly created optimum conditions for the fungus, with the result that it became a deadly epidemic. Because the tree had been exported from Brazil, not as a young plant but only in the form of seed, the pathogen was not carried overseas.

The great Ford Motors complex of immensely rich companies tried its hand at rubber-growing in Brazil, and even that commercial giant could not stand the losses. But something useful did come out of its work: when whole plantations of *caoutchouc* trees had been wiped out by the pathogen, a few individuals were left surviving and healthy. Thus, resistant individuals were discovered, and resistant clones could be built up by propagating from them. Perhaps Brazil, the homeland of *caoutchouc*, will after all be able to derive some benefit from the work done by Markham, Hooker, Wickham, Murton, Ridley and Thwaites.

7

Chocolate, coffee, tea and maté

The title of this chapter names the four most important infusion drinks in use today. Chocolate (and cocoa) differs from the others in being both food and drink, but all four have in common the quality of being stimulants. Chocolate has an economic and food value which the others do not possess, in that it is the source of the most popular of all confectionery. Of the four, only tea is very ancient in cultivation. Maté is less important than the other three, but it is drunk by tens of millions of people every day; it is much younger as a cultivar than the others.

CHOCOLATE

Chocolate and cocoa are made from seeds of a small evergreen tree called *Theobroma cacao*, native over a fairly wide range of tropical America. The ancient centre of the habitat is probably the Orinoco valley. J. W. Purseglove (1968), quoting Cheesman, places the centre of the original habitat as 'the equatorial slopes of the Andes'. There is a white bean, *Cacao*, apparently native but perhaps naturalized in Trinidad, where the semi-wild *cacao* population displays such a diversity of types that it must have been an ancient centre of cultivars. How far the range of the species extended before interference by man it is impossible to say. Was it formerly native to southern Mexico, or are semi-wild *cacao* populations of the northern part of the isthmus of Panama naturalized cultivars? The point is not uninteresting, because the domestication of this marvellous plant, which Linnaeus so properly called 'food of the gods' (*Theobroma*), must have

been relatively advanced by horticulturists; yet the centre of
the habitat is by no means a centre of ancient civilization, but
only an area marginal to civilizations old enough to interest
us in this context.

Purseglove says that the *cacao* tree has been in cultivation
for 'possibly over two thousand years'. But on what evidence
he makes this statement is not clear. As will appear below, it
is impossible to follow the career of this plant back as far as
that, in cultivation.

We know a good deal about the cultivation of *cacao* in
Aztec Mexico, much less about its cultivation in pre-
Conquest Peru. For the latter there are six authorities for
plantations of *Theobroma*, all of which are valuable since they
are all sixteenth-century writers.[1] Yet no later authority and
none of the archaeologists have anything to say about this,
nor do those writers, such as Garcilaso de la Vega Inca, who
deal with the social life of the royal Incas mention chocolate,
though it was of almost religious importance in Mexico. If
cacao was grown in Peru at all, it must have reached that
country very late, and cannot have had much economic or
social importance at the time of the Conquest. There is in
fact an interesting speculation at this point: the last province
to be added to the Inca Empire before the Conquest was
Quito in the extreme north. Having conquered it, the Sapa
Inca Huayna Capac married its princess and settled in Quito,
governing the Empire from there. If the original habitat of
the *cacao* was the Orinoco valley, it was as near to the
civilized centres of Quito, a country as advanced in culture
as the more southerly states of the Empire, as to those of
Central America. In short, it is at least possible that the Inca
Empire did not have *cacao* until it had conquered Quito in
the fifteenth century, so that the plant was a newcomer in

[1] Xerez, Francisco, *Verdadera relacion de la conquista del Peru y
provincia del Cuzco llamada Nueva Castilla*, in: Barcia, Gonzales,
Historia dores. Madrid. 1749. Montesinos, Fernando, *Annales de
Peru*. Madrid. 1906. Pizarro, Pedro, *Relaciones del descubrimiento y
conquista de los reynos del Peru*. Madrid. 1571.

Peruvian agriculture when the Spaniards arrived on the scene. This would account for the fact that although the Spaniards did see plantations of chocolate trees within the territory of the Empire, yet chocolate had no social importance in that Empire.

The nearest centre of an anciently civilized people to the centre of the habitat of *Theobroma cacao* was that of the Maya Old Empire in Guatemala. A difficulty in deciding the real range of the species in nature is that it very readily naturalizes itself about any region of cultivation wherever the cultivation of the plantation is neglected and the seeds fall to the ground, so that it often appears to be native, e.g. in Jamaica, where in fact it is not. But it must early have been introduced to Central America, and into Mexico, where it seemed to be native by the time Cortés arrived. The earliest date yet identified on any Maya stele is equivalent to our AD 357. The Old Empire was at its greatest between *c.* AD 550 and 800. It seems to me doubtful whether *Theobroma* has been in cultivation for more than a thousand years, or at the most fifteen hundred.

Let us take it the other way round. There is no doubt that chocolate was very important in Aztec Mexico, the country from which the tree was introduced into the tropics of the Old World. This plantation outside its own natural habitat began when the Spaniards started planting *cacao* in the Philippines in 1674; it was an immediate success and there were more plantations in 1680. Ridley (*see* Chapter 6) introduced *Theobroma* into Malaysia in the nineteenth century, using seeds obtained for him in Mexico by Clements Markham. Alexander Moon, first curator of the Botanic Gardens in Ceylon (Peradeniya), had introduced it there in 1835. *Theobroma* seeds reached the Gold Coast— Ghana—in 1901; Ghana is today the world's largest cocoa-producer.

So important was chocolate in the Aztec economy that its 'beans' were even used as currency. Taxes could be paid in ground chocolate: a considerable city might have to send as many as twenty chests of it to the imperial treasury. *Theobroma cacao* was grown in large, irrigated plantations [1] at low altitudes, while at higher altitudes a hardier and inferior species, *T. bicolor*, was grown instead. Chocolate was drunk hot, flavoured with spices including vanilla, a flavouring derived by fermentation from the pods of a native Mexican saprophytic orchid. But the Aztecs had another way of using chocolate: it was whipped with spices, including vanilla, into a froth or *mousse* so stiff as to be almost a solid, which was eaten cold. The Aztecs, and also some of the Spanish chroniclers of their ways who had adopted the chocolate-eating habit, claimed that a single cup of chocolate was so nourishing that it would sustain a man throughout a long day's march.

The quantities of chocolate consumed in the household, admittedly a numerous one, of the Emperor Moctezuma, although well attested,[2] are hard to believe. Every day Moctezuma himself consumed fifty 'jars' of the *mousse* described above, eating it from a golden bowl with a golden spoon; for his household, two thousand 'jars' were prepared daily.

But there is not the least reason to suppose that the Aztecs domesticated *Theobroma*. They were the greatest organizers, but the last heirs of Central American and Mexican civilization, playing to the more creative Olmecs, Toltecs and Maya the role of Romans to Greeks and Etruscans; and in any case, at the time of the Conquest the chocolate-tree was clearly too ancient in cultivation to have been domesticated by those relative newcomers to the mastery of Mexico. It is notable that the tree and its fruit were treated with religious reverence,

[1] Hernandez, Francisco, *Rerum medicarum Novae Hispaniae thesaurus seu plantarum animalium mineralium Mexicanorum historia ex F. Hernandez.* Rome. 1649.
[2] By Bernal Diaz in *Historia de la Conquista de la Nueva-España* (1632), ch. 91; Oviedo in *Historia de las Indias*, 1526; Gomara in his *Cronica*; Cortés in his letters, *et alia*.

a phenomenon which occurs only in the case of plants very ancient in cultivation, plants which can properly be regarded as partners in the creation of great cultures, like the potato in Peru.

It is likely that the *Theobroma*-tree was taken into cultivation for the first time in Guatemala, or farther south, probably in the early days of the Mayan culture, after its seeds had long been in use by people who were not yet practising any form of agriculture. When, following a disaster whose nature is still a matter of controversy,[1] the Maya emigrated to Yucatan where, in association with the Toltec colony, they worked out a new organization and created the so-called New Empire, they no doubt took the *cacao* tree with them; that might have been about AD 900. From Yucatan, cultivation of *Theobroma* would soon have spread to those parts of Mexico where it would grow.

COFFEE

We think of coffee, *Coffea arabica*, as an Arabian plant, but there is no evidence that it is or ever was native to the land after which it is named. Varieties of this species [2] are found wild in two parts of Africa, Ethiopia and Angola. Ethiopia is a centre, independent of the Mediterranean and Near-Eastern centres, of dissemination of cultivated plants, including some of the most ancient wheats.[3] *C. bengalensis*, formerly used also as a source of coffee, is native to India and Malaysia. *C. liberica*, native to Liberia, became quite important in the nineteenth century, when the so-called Arabian coffees were attacked by a deadly fungus disease. There are other species, or sub-species, or varieties or cultivars, all African and all tropical. But it is not in question that the first coffee to be cultivated was *C. arabica*.

The first question is, when did Europe first become

---

[1] Earthquake, war and civil war have been suggested. I believe soil exhaustion to have been the probable cause. *See* Hyams, 1952.

[2] Purseglove, 1968, treats these varieties as mutants of *C. arabica*; other authorities give some of them specific status.

[3] Vavilov, 1951.

acquainted with coffee? Much later than most of us are aware of, and not long after the Arabs first began to drink it. There is no need, in this case, to go back to the ancients or to seek our subject in pre-Christian-era Chinese botanical works. At the beginning of the thirteenth century a physician of Malaga, a Spanish Moor named Ibn Baithar, travelled all over the north-African and Near-Eastern *Dar-al-Islam*, and wrote an account of the manners and customs of the peoples he visited. The fact that he does not mention coffee is very good evidence that it was unknown to the Arabs, let alone Europeans, before the middle of the thirteenth century.[1]

Another Arabic writer, Shehabeddin Ben,[2] travelling in Ethiopia rather more than a century later, says that coffee had been in use there 'from time immemorial'. This does not help us much. What does it mean? That his hosts, who probably had only the vaguest idea of time, told him that coffee had always been in use in their country; in practice this could mean, say, five generations. It is true that Ethiopia had been a more or less civilized country for at least 2,500 years at that time. But if coffee-drinking had really been as ancient as Shehabeddin's hosts told him it was, it is surely very curious that the use of coffee had not spread beyond the frontiers of Ethiopia, considering that Ethiopia had been a big exporter of, for example, incense gums since before the reign of King Solomon in Israel, and in trade relations with all north Africa, the Near East and south-east Europe for about two thousand years. I believe we can safely exclude the hypothesis of an ancient domestication; and perhaps even the use of coffee from berries gathered in the hillside woods of Abyssinia, which doubtless preceded cultivation of the bush, was not very ancient either. It is simply inconceivable that the Abyssinians would, or could, have kept this delectable infusion to themselves for twenty centuries or so.

[1] Sondtheimer's translation of Ibn Baithar is quoted by A. de Candolle, 1884.
[2] Quoted by Ellis, 1774.

The habit of coffee-drinking, later followed by the coffee-bush itself, seems to have started to spread into Muslim countries, beginning with Arabia and reaching Egypt by way of Aden and Mocha, in the late fifteenth century; and into Iran at about the same time. It is not so much the case that there are clear records of this movement, as that the stories and legends about coffee, and how it became known in this or that Muslim country, usually through the intervention of some saint or holy man, belong to this same epoch.

I do not find that Europeans had heard of coffee before the sixteenth century, and rather later than earlier in that century. De Candolle (1884) says: 'Bellus sent l'Écluse some seeds from which the Egyptians extracted the drink *cavé*. At almost the same time Prosper Alpin became acquainted with coffee in Egypt itself...' Nothing has since been discovered to suggest an earlier acquaintance with coffee. Boerhave, one of the remarkable series of great Directors of the Hortus Academicus at Leyden University, says that Nicholas Witsen, Burgermeister of Amsterdam, urged the Governor of Batavia, Van Hoorn, to start planting coffee in the East Indies, which he did, so that coffee plantations were established there before 1690. In Paris coffee-bushes obtained from Leyden were grown in the hothouses of the Jardin du Roi, with the result that the French botanist and naturalist Antoine de Jussieu wrote the first botanical description of the plant in 1713.[1] The Dutch introduced coffee to the Americas by planting the first bushes at Surinam in 1718. A few years later the Governor of Cayenne, De la Motte-Aigron, personally smuggled seeds out of Surinam and raised them in Cayenne. From Cayenne coffee spread into Brazil in 1727. From the Jardin du Roi coffee-plants were sent to Martinique; a single plant survived the journey, but that was enough. From Martinique coffee was introduced into Jamaica, where it gave rise to the cultivar called 'Blue

[1] *Mémoires de l'Académie des Sciences.*

Mountain'.[1] The Dutch were also responsible for introductions into Ceylon and elsewhere, the English for introductions into India and Africa.

So much for the progress of *Coffea arabica* from the fifteenth century onwards. As to its original domestication, all the evidence clearly points not to Arabia but to Ethiopia as the venue; and to no very ancient date, probably not earlier than about AD 1000, and in all likelihood later. As for the species *C. liberica*, it was domesticated by the English in the second half of the nineteenth century, the seeds being collected in Liberia, the plants raised at Kew and from there sent to Ceylon and Singapore for further propagation.

TEA

The story of tea is enormously older than those of *cacao* and coffee. The English were the first Europeans to make any use of it, when a parcel of tea was imported from China in 1657. It is possible, but there seems to be no record of the event, that the Dutch were trying tea even earlier. But until the nineteenth century China and Japan were the only countries where tea was in cultivation. The Dutch introduced it into Java, the English into India and Ceylon.

The man to whom India owes her flourishing business in the growing and exporting of tea was a practical botanist and plant-collector, Robert Fortune, who was born at Berwick in 1812 and died in 1880. Having received his training in the Royal Botanic Gardens, Edinburgh, he went in 1841 to the Horticultural Society's (not 'Royal' until later) garden at Chiswick. In 1843 the Society sent him to collect new ornamental plants for them in China, and it was while he was collecting seed in the great tea-growing region of Ningpo a year later that he conceived the idea of introducing the tea-plant to the hill-country of northern India. This idea seems to have become a preoccupation with Fortune; for although appointed Curator of the famous Chelsea Physic Garden

[1] Purseglove, 1968.

when he returned to England in 1846, he resigned the post two years later in order to undertake the task of establishing tea-growing in India. He succeeded in collecting the seeds and young plants he needed in China and transporting them to Assam. Although neither Fortune nor anyone else realized it, and although tea had never been cultivated in Assam, this was taking coals to Newcastle with a vengeance. The consequences of this introduction are too well known to need repeating here.

Tea is a little older in Ceylon than in India, having been introduced in 1828. But it was unprofitable until Dr Masters discovered the wild tea-plant—*growing in Assam.* Thwaites planted this Assam tea in Ceylon, and thenceforward the industry became very remunerative indeed, helping to save the planters whose coffee plantations had been devastated by the pathogen *Hemilaeia vastatrix.*

Now we can turn back to consider when and where tea was originally domesticated.

Vavilov gives south China as the centre of dissemination of tea-plants. And it is clear that until about AD 800, when tea was introduced into Japan by way of Korea, China was the only great country where tea was cultivated, and perhaps the *only* country, unless there were plantations on its borders in the Indo-Chinese countries. Purseglove suggests the region about the source of the Irrawaddy as the centre of the origin of cultivation. The Japanese believed that tea originally reached China from India. There is a legend [1] that a priest, having come from India to China in AD 519, sat down under a tree to keep the vigil of prayer and fell asleep. To punish himself and to make it impossible for him to commit the same fault again, he sliced off both his eyelids, an act of mortification which was rewarded by God causing two bushes to spring up where the eyelids had fallen; these were the first tea-bushes.

[1] Kaempferer, E., *Amoenitatum exoticarum politico-physico-medi-carum . . . Japonicum,* 1712. Lemgo.

Bretschneider says that the Chinese themselves have never heard of this legend. He mentions also references to tea as a cultivated crop not only in the *Ryah* (or *Rye*) which is dated *c.* 600 BC, but also in the older *Pent-sao*. This makes it clear that tea has been cultivated in China for thousands of years. One might think that there can be no doubt that tea was domesticated in China; but as far as we know the plant has never been native to China proper.

Tea is a *Camellia*: *Camellia thea* (syn. *Camellia sinensis*; *Thea sinensis*). It has been found unquestionably wild in Assam and possibly wild in Burma. But its range was probably wider in the past than it is now, perhaps extending all through the mountainous country between north-eastern India and south-western China into Yunnan. There cannot really be much doubt that tea was domesticated in south-western China in the third millennium BC.

MATÉ

The country in which yerba-maté is grown and drunk on the largest scale is Argentina, which has about 370,000 acres of maté plantations. But even those extensive plantations cannot supply the country's whole demand, since Argentina exports a part of her maté production to Uruguay, Chile, Bolivia, the Lebanon and Syria, so that maté is imported from both Brazil and Paraguay.

The man responsible for this industry was the founder (1892) and first Director-General of the Botanic Garden of Buenos Aires, Carlos Thays, a French immigrant with a passion for the English landscape garden, examples of which he created all over Argentina. But before dealing with him it will be as well to say something about the yerba-maté tree and the origins of making and drinking an infusion of its leaves.

Yerba-maté is a small holly-tree, *Ilex paraguayensis*, native to the forests of Brazil, Paraguay and the extreme north of Argentina. For an indeterminable time—commonly described as 'immemorial', which means nothing—before the discovery of South America by Europeans, the Indian tribes of those forests had gathered the leaves and buds in the wild and made an infusion of them with hot water. I do not myself believe that this practice was very ancient, for had it been so the practice of drinking maté, and the *Ilex* itself, would most probably had been discovered by one or both of the great civilized complexes of Central America and the Andes, whereas neither the pre-Conquest Mexicans nor the ancient Peruvians grew or even knew yerba-maté. The tips of the *Ilex* leaves, and unopened leaf-buds, are first dried. They are then placed in a small, barrel-shaped vessel called by the Spaniards a *bombilla*, and covered with hot water. The infusion is drawn into the mouth through a wooden or metal tube provided with a strainer at the lower extremity. Like both coffee and tea, the yerba-maté leaf contains the drug caffeine, so that the infusion has the same stimulating effect as they do.

The Spanish and Portuguese colonists of South America adopted the practice of drinking maté from the Indians, who had never domesticated the tree, being content to gather its leaves in the wild.

In 1895 Argentina was spending so much on maté imported from Brazil and Paraguay that Carlos Thays realized that a large saving would result from growing the leaf at home; that plantations of maté in Argentina would give the country a new industry; and that the industry could even, perhaps, export a quantity of the leaf, for there was some foreign demand for it. By then *Ilex paraguayensis* had been under cultivation in Paraguay for about a century; Thays was thus able to obtain seeds from an Argentine specialist connected with the Paraguayan plantations, Doctor Honorio Leguizanon. But not even he could tell Thays how to persuade the seeds to germinate in sufficient numbers.

The testa, or woody outer shell of the seed, is so hard and dense that before germination is possible some agency must attack and partly destroy it. From his first parcel of seed, which he left untreated, Carlos Thays obtained only three seedlings. A second batch, treated by being soaked in hot water, did better, and it was not long before Thays was getting 60 per cent germination. By 1910 he was in a position to distribute maté seeds and young plants in commercial quantities.

There were no maté plantations in South America before about 1750; but it was from Paraguayan plantations that Thays was able to obtain seed of the *Ilex* in 1895. Until the first decade of the nineteenth century Paraguay was still nominally a Spanish colony, in fact a province directed and ruled by the Jesuits, who were responsible for the first yerba-maté plantations. There is a story which I heard there touching the way in which the Jesuit agronomists persuaded the seeds of *Ilex paraguayensis* to germinate. Having observed that birds, after eating the berries of this holly, spread it by excreting the seeds, with the testa softened by digestion, they fed berries to their poultry and planted the poultry droppings, with good results. The story may be true.

8

Plants and weavers

According to Vavilov, the cultivated races of flax, *Linum usitatissimum*, were disseminated from four different centres. Races specialized on the one hand for oil-seed, and on the other for fibre to make linen yarn, are numerous in the Central Asian centre, which includes the Punjab, Kashmir, Afghanistan, Tadgikistan, Uzbekistan and Tian-Shan. The two groups of flax races are also numerous in the Near-Eastern centre of dissemination. In the Mediterranean centre, the ancient flaxes examined were all oil-seed kinds, and the same is true for the Abyssianian centre. If we consider the evidence implicit in the concentrations of dominant gene races of the plant, and in the numbers of primitive cultivars concentrated in a given area, then flax could have been domesticated in any one of those four centres. But there are other considerations.

Flax has a vast habitat in nature, including most of Europe, part of Asia and parts of north Africa. Immensely ancient in use, it is almost as old in cultivation, not only in the most ancient centres of proto-civilization but also in pre-historic Europe. Consequently, and because flax readily 'escapes' from the cultivated field into the surrounding wild, it is extremely difficult to be sure where it is native and aboriginal, and where it is wild but naturalized; that is, where the natural distribution of the species has been interfered with by man. In one sense the argument is a bogus one: man is a part of the complex of nature, and a plant is not less 'wild' in a given place for having got there as a consequence of man's activities rather than of the activities of birds or animals, winds or ocean currents. But since we are seeking the origin of the cultivation of flax, we must try to penetrate back into the past to a point in time before man had started to change the habitats of plants by his interference with them.

So old is flax in cultivation, and so much has man's use of it disturbed the ancient wild habits of the plant, that De Candolle (1884) went so far as to say: 'The Common annual flax has not been discovered with absolute certainty in a wild state.' And from the botanical, genetical, historical and philological arguments first advanced by him and subsequently amended and added to by later scientists and scholars, I think we have here a case of at least two and possibly more independent domestications of two or more species of *Linum*, although later domestications may well have been suggested by earlier ones.

No good purpose would be served by discussing, for example, whether the Greeks of the Homeric epoch had linen or not; there is evidence both ways. The point is that if they lacked it, or did not cultivate flax, it was not because the plant and the craft of spinning and weaving linen were not then available: linen is very much more ancient than Greek civilization.

The distribution of linen in antiquity is curious and significant. In 1865 the Swiss palaeontologist Oswald Heer, excavating Neolithic Lake Dwellers' sites in eastern Switzerland, found that the Lake Dwellers had not only woven linen made from a perennial flax, *Linum angustifolium*, but had also cultivated it. Capsules, seeds and, what is more, the whole lower part of a flax plant were extracted from the sediment under examination at Robenhausen. Moreover there is evidence that those Lake Dwellers, who did not yet have the use of metals, seem to have been importing their flax-seed from Italy, because Heer found seeds of a weed called *Silene cretica* mixed up with the flax. This plant does not grow in Switzerland, but was common in flax fields

south of the Alps.[1] Heer could not at the time identify the
Italian source of the flax-seed used by those Stone-Age folk.
But later the dwelling sites of a New-Stone-Age people
living on the peat lands round Lagozza in Lombardy were
excavated (by Sordelli) [2] and it was found that these people
had been cultivating the same flax and weaving linen.

The obvious place to seek the origin of these crafts is in
Egypt, if only because the most ancient mummies found in
Egyptian tombs were wrapped in linen cloth. Vestiges of
linen have been found in Egypt which are about 6,000 years
old. Tomb wall-paintings of *c.* 3000 BC depict not only the
flax plant but also the whole process of making linen. One
need not, therefore, waste time on the Bible references to
linen; by these standards they are relatively modern.

But although the Egyptians had flax under cultivation
perhaps as early as 4000 BC, it is more or less certain that the
plant can never have been native there. For one thing, no
known flax species can survive dry heat, the typical summer
climate of Egypt is fatal to it, and as far back as we can study
the subject flax has always been an annual, winter crop in
Egypt. From the very few seeds of *Linum* found in tombs
there it appears that the flax they used was not *L. angustifolium*, but the annual *L. usitatissimum*.

That a number of very different peoples had linen and flax
at very early dates in their histories, and independently of
each other, is evident from the ancient nomenclature. True,
the Greek *linon*, Latin *linum*, Celtic *lin* obviously have a
common root. But although these Indo-European languages
have a close affinity with Sanskrit, the Sanskrit words are
quite different, *ooma* and *utasi*. The Hebrew word *pischta* has
no connections with either. In the northern European
languages, again, there is a series of names for flax and linen
which cannot be connected with any of the above. Now this
is good evidence of enormous antiquity in cultivation: any

[1] Heer, 1865 and 1872; both are pamphlets.
[2] Sordelli, 1880.

word-borrowing which may have been done as a result of the dissemination of the plant, and the craft of using it, is so ancient that its traces have disappeared.

But if the Egyptians, with flax in cultivation 6,000 years ago, were still not the originators of that cultivation, who were? Heer [1] records the finding of some flax in a tomb at Ur of the Chaldees, which means that it was in use by what was probably the oldest of the proto-civilizations; and that the notion of cultivating flax, and the craft of using it, could have been carried into Egypt by way of the eastern Mediterranean littoral in the fifth millennium BC. And a dissemination westward along the north coast of the Mediterranean and up the river valleys would account for the use of flax and linen in Neolithic Europe.

Flax must surely be the oldest fibre plant in cultivation. Domesticated in Mesopotamia, perhaps in the sixth millennium BC, its use is not much younger than that of wheat. Linen is the oldest tissue still in use by man; how curious that it should still be one of the most beautiful.

HEMP AND THE SCYTHIANS

The second most important yarn derived from the fibres in the stalk of a plant is hemp, *Cannabis sativa*. Today the word *cannabis* suggests not the centuries-old importance of hempen rope and hempen tissue, but the drug variously called hemp, cannabis, bhang, hashish, marijuana, pot, grass, etc. This, however, is due to a fortuitous circumstance, the very belated discovery by west European and American youth of the mildly intoxicating qualities of the hemp-leaf and seed when grown in hot countries; and to the hysterical excitement of the authorities in those parts of the world at the growth of a habit of smoking hemp, a practice which, provided the leaf used be free from such dangerous impurities as opium, is demonstrably less dangerous from the health

[1] Quoting from the *Journal* of the Royal Asiatic Society, vol. xv p. 271.

10 Apricot as depicted in Matthioli's Commentaries on Dioscorides (sixteenth century); he used the name *Armeniaca minor*.
The Greeks had this fruit from Armenia, but it did not reach
north-west Europe until after a much later introduction by the
Arabs.

11 *Rapum sylvestre*, the wild rape as illustrated in Matthioli. Compare with Plate 12.

12 *Rapum rotundum*, a turnip, cultivated, as illustrated in
Matthioli. The enormous development of the root is a product
of long selection and segregation in cultivation.

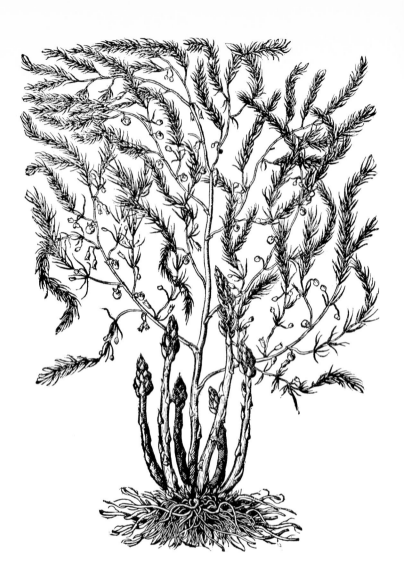

13   Asparagus, as illustrated in Matthioli. Nothing has been altered by centuries of cultivation except the size of the shoots; there has been no hybridization, only selection. Wild asparagus is still gathered and eaten in Andalusia.

14   The same plant as found in England, from Sowerby's *English Botany*, 1808. By selection and rich feeding, Roman and, later, French gardeners produced shoots weighing up to 5 oz. each.

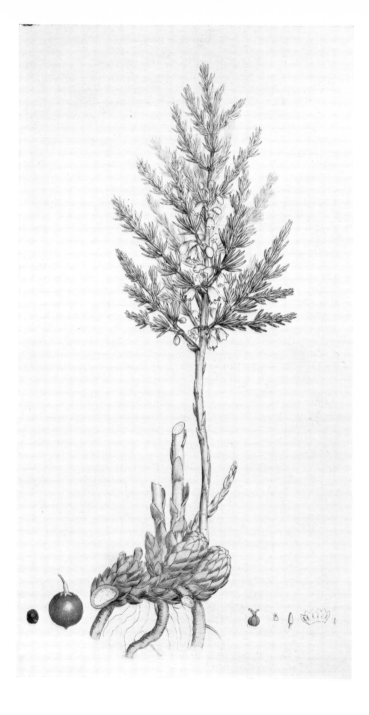

15 Peas as we know them are a product of European domestication. The most ancient civilizations had no knowledge of them.
This representation of a probably wild plant, *Pisum sativum*, is
from Reichenbach's *Icones Florae Germanicae* (1835–55).

16 The cabbage is a native of Great Britain as of all western
Europe. Change in form and habit wrought by long selection
has been enormous. This figure of *Brassica oleracea* is from
Sowerby's *English Botany*.

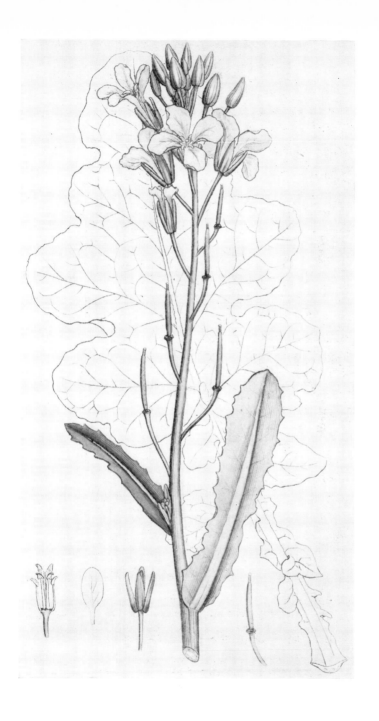

17   Flowerheads of *Cichorum intybus*, chicory. Cultivated forms of
the same plant provide the frizzy-leaved salad (also called
'endive'), and the winter-forced *witloof*.

point of view than the smoking of tobacco. But hemp is much more important as a fibre-plant than as a drug-plant, and when grown in cold countries does not in fact develop the principle which makes it an intoxicant. In the East, where its use as a stimulant has been tolerated for many centuries, it is clearly ancient in cultivation, since the names for it in Oriental languages—*bhang*, *ganga*, *hashish*—are all derivatives of the Sanskrit names *bhanga* and *gangika*.

Hemp has a somewhat confusing history. It is mentioned in the Chinese *Shu-king*, which was written about 500 BC.[1] According to Herodotus it was either unknown or a novelty to the Greeks at about that date; yet the same authority declares it to have been in cultivation by the Scythians at that period. Although by Cato's time it had a Latin name, *cannabis*, the fact that he does not mention it in *De re rustica* ought to mean that it was not cultivated in Italy during his lifetime. Yet the Jews of Republican Roman times had just become acquainted with it as a source of a textile yarn. It is not mentioned by any Latin author until about 120 BC (Lucilius), yet the Sabines were cultivating it much earlier. Although, on the authority of Herodotus, we may accept that the Greeks did not cultivate hemp, yet they were familiar with it as a result of their trading with Scythia, and imported the raw material for their ropes, for their ships and for the manufactured hempen rope; possibly also for sail-cloth, from the Scythians.

Victor Heyn (1888) says: 'The Graeco-Roman name for the plant, originally Median, but also found in the old Indian languages, runs unchanged through all the European languages, in proof of its origin. . . .'

Most of the traces which can still be followed lead us back to the northern shore of the Black Sea and the southern shore of the Caspian. Returning for a moment to Herodotus, for example:

Hemp grows in Scythia; it is very like flax, only that it is a

[1] Bretschneider, 1871.

much coarser and taller plant: some grows wild about the
country, some is produced by cultivation. The Thracians
make garments of it which closely resemble linen; so much so
indeed that if a person has never seen hemp he is sure to
think they are linen; and if he has, unless he is very ex-
perienced in such matters, he will not know which material
they are.[1]

That goes back to the fifth century BC; and the connection
with Russia was maintained, for the import of hempen yarn
by the west-European admiralties for the manufacture of
sailcloth and rigging was still an important trade in the last
century.

So much for the use of hemp as a source of yarn. The
Scythians also used it as an intoxicant, although it is impossible to say whether they discovered its intoxicating properties for themselves or learnt them from some other people.
Here again is Herodotus on the subject:

They make a booth by fixing in the ground three sticks
inclined towards one another, and stretching around them
woollen felts which they arrange so as to fit as close as possible:
inside the booth a dish is placed upon the ground into which
they put a number of red hot stones and then add some hemp
seed . . . immediately it smokes, and gives out such a vapour
as no Grecian vapour-bath can exceed; the Scyths, delighted,
shout for joy. . . .[2]

But had the use and cultivation of hemp reached India and
Europe from the Scythians and Thracians, its history and
nomenclature would have been different. Domesticated in
south Russia or Siberia about 1500 BC, it came into Europe
from the north rather than the south. And it reached India
from the Medes by another route.

What about the habitat of *Cannabis* in the wild? De
Candolle[3] investigated this very thoroughly: *Cannabis
sativa*, he decided, was found unquestionably wild only

[1] Herodotus, iv, 74.
[2] Herodotus, iv, 73, 75.
[3] His monograph on it was published in *Prodromus*, 1869, vol. XVI,
sec. I, p. 30.

south of the Caspian, in Siberia near Irtysch, in the Kirghiz desert beyond Lake Baikal. In short, hemp is a Siberian plant, and it is all the more reasonable to conclude that it was indeed first cultivated somewhere in southern Siberia.

THE TWO COTTONS

Cotton comes from a number of species of plants belonging to the genus *Gossypium* of the family *Malvaceae*, so that it is related to such familiar ornamental plants as hibiscus, holly-hock, and the musk mallow of our own countryside. There were, despite some attempts to prove the contrary, at least two separate and quite independent domestications of *Gossypium*, and I shall have to discuss the Old-World and the New-World cottons separately.

In the Old World two species, divided into a number of 'races' which have emerged locally and are in fact geo-graphical varieties, are in cultivation. *Gossypium herbaceum* is a perennial sub-shrub, that is, a small, perennial, more or less woody, shrub. *G. arboreum* is not, in spite of its specific name, a tree, but a shrub; it was named *arboreum* because it may attain a height of six or seven feet.

In the New World also there are in cultivation two species with local geographical races: *G. barbadense*, a shrub which may attain to nine or ten feet in height, and *G. hirsutum*, another quite tall shrub.

When I say that *G. herbaceum* and *G. arboreum* are the Old-World species, and the other two the New-World species, I mean that they were so before the discovery of America by Columbus. Since then, of course, there have been interchanges of cultivated races of cotton, and the distinction is no longer clear. But we are concerned with the very remote past, so that for our purpose the statement is true.

G. herbaceum, race *africanum*, is native to south central Africa from Angola to Mozambique. As there was neither spinning nor weaving in that part of the world until those arts were introduced from the north very long after the first

spinning and weaving of cotton in Asia and the Mediterranean basin, this cotton shrub must have been brought
north into southern Arabia or Ethiopia by merchants who
were already familiar with cotton made from other races or
other species. The alternative, that it was the first kind of
cotton to be domesticated, is inconceivable; for one would
have to suppose a traveller or merchant who, seeing the
cotton 'lint', had the idea of spinning it, brought the seeds
away with him to Arabia or Ethiopia and started the cultivation of cotton. That, of course, was what was done in the
cases of rubber and, just possibly, *cacao*, but at an epoch of
technical sophistication in both cases; whereas in the case of
cotton we have to go back in time several thousand years. It is
very much more likely that the west African cotton plant
was not used until long after the establishment of cotton
cultivation.

The Indian race of *G. arboreum* may, as Purseglove
suggests, have developed out of *G. herbaceum*. One theory is
that both the race *africanum* and the most primitive known
cultivar, the race *acerifolium*, developed out of an even more
primitive cotton cultivar grown anciently in Ethiopia. But
Vavilov gives his Central Asian centre as the place from which
G. herbaceum cultivars were disseminated. And the oldest
vestiges of Asian cotton cloth as yet discovered, a cotton
which was made from the 'lint' of *G. arboreum* derivatives,
have been found in excavations at Mohenjo-daro, one of the
two great metropolitan centres of the ancient Indus Valley
civilization, and dated *c.* 3000 BC.

Northern perennial *arboreums* spread throughout northern
India, eastwards to Burma, Indonesia and the Philippines,
giving rise to the race *burmanicum*, and westwards across
southern Arabia, the northern Soudan and the southern
borders of the Sahara to West Africa, giving rise to the race
soudanense.[1]

The first people in Africa whom we know to have spun

[1] Purseglove, 1968.

and woven cotton were the citizens of Meroë, a Nubian kingdom which flourished from about 650 BC. But if Ethiopia was the country in which cotton was first cultivated, then, considering the date of the earliest Indus Valley cotton, it must have had cotton in cultivation in the fourth millennium BC. In that case it is inconceivable that cotton would have remained unknown to the Egyptians of the third millennium BC at latest. But there is not a trace of cotton in ancient Egypt even much later than that.

There is only one remaining possibility, an Indian domestication. Wild specimens of *G. arboreum*, race *acerifolium*, have been found in Baluchistan. If it was formerly native there, then it is surely possible that it was first domesticated by the forerunners of the Indus Valley civilized people of the fourth and third millennium BC; if, on the other hand, this small and scattered population of *G. arboreum* originated in plantation escapes, nothing can be argued from their presence. But despite some difficulties with the genetical evidence, it seems to me that the first domesticators of cotton must have been the Indus Valley people, and that it was as a result of their example that the African races of cotton were taken into cultivation very much later.

PERUVIAN EARLY FARMERS

So difficult do some prehistorians find it to admit the simple proposition that men, in a similar situation and under similar environmental pressures, tend to find the same solution to a similar problem, so wedded are they to the idea that every major discovery, invention or device happens only once, that they will perform prodigies of bad reasoning to avoid the conclusion that inventions may be repeated independently. And they do so despite such evidence as that the bicycle, for example, was invented at least twice; that Darwin and Wallace reached the same conclusions about the origin of species almost simultaneously and without communication; or that Leibniz and Newton invented the

method of calculus simultaneously and without communication with each other. It seems to me that all theories which
try to show how the American Indians could have learnt such
arts as agriculture, ceramics, spinning and weaving from the
Old World are as unnecessary as they are far-fetched. The
American Indians were perfectly capable, in due time, of
inventing those crafts for themselves.

But when we come to consider the cotton-plants which
provided them with their raw material there is a circumstance
which forces us to admit a migration, at a remote epoch, of
an Old-World *Gossypium* into the New World. It would be
extremely difficult to give a full explanation of this circumstance to the reader who is not familiar with the terms used by
geneticists, but a simplification is possible and amounts to
this. The two American cotton-plants, *Gossypium barbadense* and *G. hirsutum*, which have been in cultivation
since long before the Columbian discovery of America, both have
genetical attributes which can only be the result of a cross
between an Old-World and a New-World species; for
example between the African *G. herbaceum* and the American
G. raimondi; and between *G. herbaceum* and *G. thurberi*,
respectively.

First it should be said that there is no difficulty in explain-
ing the presence of what geneticists call 'diploid' (genetically
simple) species of the same genus in both the New and the
Old World. Hundreds of genera have representatives in both
Worlds—the grape-vines, *Vitis*, for example, and the roses,
Rosa. An acceptable explanation of this is that the genera
spread from their centre of origin and new species were
formed under the usual evolutionary pressures before the
North American continent was separated by water from
north-east Asia, so that together they formed a single land-
mass; and that since this happened at a time (Tertiary) when
the climate in those latitudes was very much warmer, these
genera included many which would not now be found as far
north as the Bering Strait, from which latitude they retreated

towards the south on both sides of the Pacific as the cold
grew more severe. No, the difficulty is as I have stated it, that
the American cotton races in cultivation before men from the
Old World started in the sixteenth century to interchange the
plants of the two hemispheres have a chromosome composition (are not 'diploids' but 'allopolyploids') which can be
explained only by some such hybridization with Old-World
cottons as I have sketched above.

There is a theory, not very widely accepted but certainly
not to be dismissed, that men from Asia were making the
crossing to America very long before Columbus crossed the
Atlantic; there may be some evidence for this in art-forms
and craft-techniques, but there is virtually none in comparative botany. And if this theory is sound, the surprising
thing is not that some American pre-Columbian cottons have
an Old-World element, but that many more American
species have no such element; and that the most valuable
Old-World crop-plants did not reach America, nor the
American ones Asia, until after the fifteenth century of our
era. Even supposing that Asian men were shipping across to
America in prehistoric times, they were certainly not doing
so as early as 4500 BC, which would have to have been so if we
are to accept the notion that prehistoric man was the means
of getting Old-World cotton to the New World in time for
the genetical phenomenon under discussion to have occurred;
for (see below) cotton was being cultivated in prehistoric
Peru before 2500 BC. And although there are species of cotton
in the Americas which are still diploids, i.e. of pure American
stock, they have not undergone the mutation for 'linting'
which makes the genus a source of fibres capable of being
spun into yarn.

The best and simplest explanation of this mystery is Dr
Purseglove's, that seeds of *G. herbaceum*, race *africanum*,
floated across the Atlantic to South America, germinated and
grew on the eastern coast of the sub-continent, and crossed
with a New-World diploid cotton to produce *G. barbadense*.

There is at least one other plant, the Bottle Gourd, which can only have reached America by that means, so that this event is not unprecedented. And it has been demonstrated that seeds of *Gossypium* remain viable after immersion in sea-water for three years.

So the cotton plants which were domesticated by the American Indians before the arrival of European man had been 'created' for them by a remarkable natural accident. At what period in their prehistory did they take advantage of it?

I have referred in Chapter 4 to the discovery of cultivated beans of the genus *Phaeseolus* during excavation of the Huaca Prieta in the Chicama valley on the coast of Peru. In that same midden accumulated by a people who lived by fishing, gathering shell-fish and wild vegetable foods, but who were already cultivating some plants and are therefore called Early Farmers, the excavator, Dr Junius Bird, found vestiges of a use of cotton so extensive that *Gossypium* must already have been in cultivation. There were pieces of cotton cloth, cotton bags and cotton fishing-nets. There were no spindles; the fibres had been spun by hand, and the fabrics simply twined, although in some cases a weft had been darned in with bone needles. Radiocarbon dating shows some of these cotton articles to have been made *c.* 2500 BC. This is the earliest cotton yet found in the Americas.

The conclusion is that American cotton was domesticated by the Early Farmer people of the Peruvian littoral in the third millennium BC and that its use spread slowly into Central America during the following 2,000 years. A second domestication at a later date in, say, Guatemala, is possible; but the theory of diffusion is much the more likely explanation of the fact that when the Spaniards reached the Americas at the end of the fifteenth century they found that cotton cloth had long been in use by all the civilized and most of the still barbarous nations of American Indians.

9

Athene's gift to sycophants

Three woody fruitful plants are so representative of the Greek and Latin cultures that they have become symbols thereof—the Vine, the Olive and the Fig. So true is this that, were it not for the importance of all three in the Old Testament, parts of which are older than civilization in Greece, it might seem a waste of time to look beyond ancient Greece, or at all events prehistoric Greece, for the origin of their cultivation. But it has already been made clear, in Chapter 2, that viticulture is very much older than Greek civilization, so much older that it was a sophisticated craft before the Greeks were capable of any kind of plantation agriculture; and that, although there may have been wild vines in Greece, the wine-vine of history was introduced there as a cultigen.

The wild fig was probably native in Greece; that will be discussed below. The same is true of the wild olive called oleaster. But the Greeks did not domesticate either of them.

At the present time the olive, *Olea europaea*, is cultivated in all the continents. Its introductions into the Americas, South Africa and Japan are matters of relatively recent history and do not concern us here. The same is probably true for India. In other words, the habitat of the cultivated olive before the great age of European seafaring, conquest and colonization began in the fifteenth century was the Mediterranean basin and the land to the east of it but west of the Caucasus; so the investigation of the tree's history can be confined to that territory.

It is difficult to imagine a country in which the olive-tree

seems to be more immemorially at home and an eternal part
of the scenery than Italy. Italy would not be the Italy we
know and love without the olive-groves, the wild olives on
top of old banks and culverts, the isolated old trees, hollowed
and warped but still vital. Yet the olive was once a new
introduction there, as alien to Italy as were conifers to
England in the eighteenth century.

That the olive was introduced to Italy by Greeks is obvious
from the names *oliva*, *oleum*, which are Greek derivatives.
The only questions, therefore, are, was it introduced as a
domesticated tree, and if so when did that introduction
happen?

Pliny, in his *Natural History*, quoting the annalist
Fenestella, says that at the time of Tarquinius Priscus
(traditionally 616–579 BC) there was not an olive-tree to be
seen in all Italy. This could be unreliable as to the date, but
it does make the point that the olive was an alien. The plant
was introduced there during the following two centuries, for
in a fragment of the fourth-century comic poet Amphis there
is a reference to the olive oil of Thurii. Moreover, two
hundred years after that it is clear from Cato that the olive-
tree and olive oil had long been features of Italian life, and by
the first century BC Italy had become the greatest oil-
producing country in the world. In six centuries *Olea
europaea* had colonized every part of the country where the
climate suited it. The Greeks had also introduced the olive
into their colony of Massilia (Marseilles), whence it spread
along the coast and into the Ligurian region of Italy; so that
as one tide of olive-trees moved up from the south another
was moving down to meet it from the north.

The olives of which Cato wrote towards the end of the third
century BC are called by him Calabrian and Sallentine; both
districts were parts of Magna Graeca. The stepping-stone for
the olive on its way into southern Italy was Sicily, but the
olive is not native there either. On the other hand, the Greeks
may not have had to carry it to Sicily: they may have found it

there when they arrived as colonists; for the Phoenicians were there long before them.

Heyn (1888) suggested that there may be a faint echo of the movement of the olive across the Mediterranean from east to west in the myth of Aristaeus, a very ancient Boeotian, Arcadian and Thessalian divinity whom the Greeks brought with them when they settled in Sicily. He was:

... believed by their descendants to have been the inventor of the olive and of oil. In this myth it is worthy of note that Aristaeus is not said, like Athena, to have *created* the olive tree, but to have *invented* oil or the olive; that he *taught* the preparation of oil, to which belongs the use of the press; and that for this reason he was worshipped by the Sicilians during the olive harvest.

The distinction could be between oleaster and olive; between the creation of wild olive and the inducing of the olive-tree to bear useful fruit. In other words, this myth could, just conceivably, reflect a practical event, the selection of a useful fruitful mutant olive: but that is no more than an interesting speculation.

Aristaeus, according to the myth, had been the divine king of Sardinia before reaching Sicily. Now Sardinia was never Greek, but it had been a Phoenician colony or trading station. Aristaeus had taught agriculture to the Sardinians and had planted trees. Was he, perhaps, a Phoenician? Heyn continues:

From Sardinia he went to Sicily, civilized that island also, and among other rural arts invented the process of gaining oil from olives. Now, as Aristaeus could not hold his power against the new, overpowering and dazzling worship of Apollo and Dionysus (though essentially kindred deities) but sank into the position of their son or tutor, he was evidently one with a Libyo-Phoenician divinity whom the Greek colonists found in Sicily when they came there and adopted as their own ...

The myth of Aristaeus may signify that the olive was planted in Sicily as in Sardinia by men from Tyre and Sidon,

or from the Tyrian or Sidonian colonies in north Africa, and
that the Greek colonists found olive groves round the ancient
Phoenician trading centres when they seized them.

But there is considerable difficulty in reconciling history
(or the nearest one can come to history in this context) and
the probable time-scale of the myth; for if we are to suppose
that the olive reached Sicily before Aristaeus had been displaced by Dionysus, then the date must be very much earlier
than the seventh century BC, during which the westward
movement of the olive seems on historical evidence (see
below) to have occurred.

We have now to work backwards from Greece and try to
discover whether the mainland Greeks could have had the
olive from Phoenicia. Here the distinction between the
cultivated olive and the oleaster must again be emphasized.
There is no question but that oleaster was native to Greece;
in the *Iliad* Pisander's axe, in the *Odyssey* the Cyclops's club
are made of 'olive' wood; and Odysseus built his nuptial bed
on the stump of an 'olive' still rooted in the ground. But it is
clear that these references are not to the fruitful, oil-bearing
olive. The Greeks of the Homeric world were, it is true,
familiar with oil as an unguent, and it was doubtless scented
olive oil; but it was rare, costly and imported from the east.
In the eighth and seventh centuries BC it seems to have been
slowly replacing the animal fats which were used for cosmetic
purposes. There are several apparent references in the
Odyssey which seem to be to the fruitful olive, but Heyn
(1888) demonstrated that in fact they are nothing of the kind.

Hesiod, a poet of this same epoch, the eighth century BC,
would certainly have had something to say about olives had
they then been in cultivation in Greece; his *Works and Days*
is, among much else, a description of the countryman's
working life. He does not mention olives.

All this leads us back to the same conclusion, that the olive
as a fruitful tree and a source of oil was not planted in mainland Greece until the seventh century BC. Herodotus (fifth

century BC) makes the extraordinary statement that '. . . at a time not long past there was not an olive-tree in the world except at Athens'. The same author describes how the Epidaurians, when their crops failed and the Delphic oracle advised them to make statues of Damia and Auxesia out of olive-wood from a *domesticated* olive-tree, they had to ask the Athenians for permission to cut down an olive-tree in Attica, the implication being that there were none to be had anywhere else. Herodotus gives us no date for this. But in the laws which Solon gave Athens at the beginning of the sixth century BC there are provisions touching the cultivation of the olive, very good evidence for the existence of olive groves in Hellas at that time, just as the legislation for the protection of vineyards in the *Leges Anglo-Saxonicae* is good evidence for the existence of vineyards in England during the reign of Alfred the Great. The Athenians themselves explained their monopoly of the olive-tree by claiming that their patroness Athene had created it for their benefit; the original tree which she had created stood in the Citadel and from it were propagated the olive-trees of the Academy, which Sulla cut down to make siege-engines when besieging Athens in 85 BC. There was also a tradition that Pisistratus, the goddess's special favourite, was the first to urge the planting of olive-trees in the ungrateful soil of Attica.

The fact is that that very soil had a great deal to do with the matter; the olive-tree and the fig-tree, as well as the vine, provide means of profitably exploiting thin, limestone soils. So poor were her soils that Athens could not grow enough wheat for her subsistence. Her survival depended on having something to offer in exchange for the wheat she needed: oil was that something. Indeed, the greatness of Athens may be said to have been founded on oil. To 'package' it for export she had to have jars, and thus came to build up a considerable ceramics industry of which her potters also made an art. To carry those jars overseas, she had to have ships, and thus created a great merchant fleet. To protect her merchantmen she had to have warships, and so became a great sea power. Moreover since dependence on trade and seafaring develop the qualities of self-reliance and love of liberty, Athens became the champion of democracy, so that even her political and social system, and therefore her greatness in the fields of philosophy, literature and the arts which develop most nobly in freedom, were indirectly owed to the olive.

But since the cultivated fruitful olive was not older than the seventh century BC in Greece, even in Attica, where *was* it older? In the first place, among the Israelites: the Old Testament makes frequent mention of it (i) as an unguent for anointing the head and body, a practice which still endures vestigially in the coronation rite of sacring, (ii) as a food and (iii) for burning in lamps; which takes us back to about 1000 BC. But the Israelites cannot have brought the olive with them into Canaan after the Egyptian captivity, for the olive was not grown by the Egyptians of that epoch, although they must have been familiar with oil as an import.

Both olive and oleaster are native to the limestone hills near the sea in the eastern Mediterranean. No wild olive with edible fruits is known. The olive of history must have originated as a mutant of wild olive, or of oleaster of which wild olive is another descendant, somewhere in that region of the world, perhaps in Anatolia, perhaps farther south-east in Phoenicia itself. Domestication may date from not much earlier than *c.* 2000 BC. Its subsequent prosperity was in part due to the invention, in the same part of the world and not much later, of the art of grafting. The origin of that art is obscure, but from as far back as we can go its masters were Syrians. This is perhaps significant; a tree which must be propagated vegetatively to be fruitful cannot be easily and widely distributed without grafting.

SYKO-PHANTS

The fig-tree and the abundant use of both fresh and dried figs in the diet are, to our eyes and our imaginations, as representative of Italy as are the olive and the vine. It is as difficult to think of Italy without fig-trees as of Italy without olive-groves and, for another example, the lovely cypress. But the fig is no more native to Italy than is the olive-tree. Nor, for that matter, and perhaps even more disconcertingly, is the cypress native in the countryside of which it seems to us the immemorial symbol. The fact is that the Italy of history is very unlike primeval Italy, the Italy of the first Greek colonies and Etruscan settlements, the Italy of Rome as a mere village of herdsmen. The ubiquitous cypress is not, with due respect to W. J. Bean (1934), 'native to S.E. Europe and Persia'. It was, as pointed out by H. C. De Wit (1967), following Alexander von Humboldt,[1] introduced into Italy; its original habitat was the mountains of Busih, west of Herat, whence it was introduced into Phoenicia, Greece, Sicily and Italy, being increasingly valued for its shipbuilding timber. The island of Cyprus took its name from the tree which grew well there.[2]

As with the cypress, so with the fig. There were already an enormous number of varieties of figs in Pliny's Italy; moreover by that time the fig had naturalized itself and could, as in our own day, be seen growing even out of the cracks in old walls. But figs were common in Italy long before the first century AD. More than two hundred years earlier, whenever Cato sought to remind the Senate of the dangerous nearness of Carthage to Roman Italy, he would hold up a fig, most perishable of fruits, still fresh and unblemished, a Carthaginian fig, and exclaim: 'So near, my lords, is the enemy to our walls!'

But go back still further, and the fig-tree disappears. Like the olive, it came into Italy with Greek colonists who settled Sicily and Calabria between the ninth and the sixth century

[1] *Kosmos*, 1845–62.
[2] 'The cypresses on Lebanon may have been imposing but as they cannot be compared with the giants in the Western region of the Indus, they declare themselves but secondary and derived from the latter.' Heyn, 1888.

BC. It is possible that they may have found the fig, like the olive, already in Sicily, introduced by Phoenicians.

In Greece the fig is as particular to Athens as was the olive. I do not know who nicknamed Plato *philosukos*, fig-lover; but he cannot have been singular in that taste, for so closely were figs associated with Athens that when Xerxes wished to keep ever before himself the mortifying fact that he had not yet conquered the Athenian democracy he had a dish of Attic figs set before him at every meal, figs which he had received not in tribute but had been forced to buy. And the association between Athens and the fig continued into the decadence of Athens, when, in reference to the practice of delation which had become so disgracefully common among Athenians, the Greeks of Corinth and other cities called them fig-informers – *sukophantai*.

Despite all of which, the fig was no more native to Greece than to Italy. There are indeed a number of references to figs and fig-trees in the *Odyssey*. Figs hang above the head of the starving Tantalus in the Underworld; there are fig-trees in the garden of Alcinous; and Laertes is described as a planter of figs. Heyn (1888) argued that these passages are late additions to the ancient text, and in one case 'awkwardly foisted into the really antique description of the palace of Alcinous in order to bring in the *gardens* of the Phaeacian king'. In the earlier *Iliad* there is one mention of figs, but as growing near Troy, not in Greece. This is what one would expect if the following arguments are sound. Hesiod, whose didactic poem deals with all country matters, never heard of figs; the first reliable evidence for the cultivation of figs within Hellas is to be found in the works of the lyric and satiric poet Archilocus (? seventh century BC), who names figs as one of the products of his native island of Paros.

Like the olive, the fig reached Greece from the east; the only question is, whereabouts in the east did it start its westward movement as a cultivated plant?

Figs and fig-trees are as commonplace in the Old Testament as are wine and vine, olives and oil. Moreover they were common in Lydia and so important to the Lydians that the councillors who advised King Croesus not to invade Persia pointed out that the Persians did not even have figs or wine; but if Herodotus is to be relied on they were misinformed, for he says that the Persians did grow figs.[1] So fig-growing was common in Asia Minor at least for some centuries before it was introduced, by way of the islands, into mainland Greece.

What about Egypt? Purseglove (1968) says the Egyptians were growing figs before 4000 BC, but gives no authority for this statement. The Egyptians had *a* fig very early — *Ficus sycamorus* from Ethiopia — but I cannot find that they cultivated *F. carica* at such a remote date, although if (see below) this species spread eastward from the Canary Isles after being exterminated elsewhere during the post-Quaternary Ice Age, then they certainly might have done.

Modern authorities, including De Wit, follow De Candolle in defining the original habitat of the wild fig as the middle and southern parts of the Mediterranean basin from Syria to the Canary Islands and eastwards to Persia or Afghanistan.

Fig-trees have been common in all the Canary Islands, from Fuerteventura in the east to La Palma and La Gomera and El Hierro in the west, since as far back as we have any knowledge of them. This fact introduces the possibility of an explanation of the distribution of the cultivated fig entirely different from the one we have been following, and it is worth a short digression.

Although the islands have been known, at least by hearsay, tradition and in legend, since Homer's day, and were identified as the Elysian Fields, the first reliable reports of their geography, people and flora were gathered by a properly organized expedition sent there by King Juba II of Mauretania during the reign of the Emperor Augustus, a few years

[1] Herodotus, i, 71.

before the birth of Christ. Juba's men reported an abundance
of figs. I do not regard this as necessarily good evidence that
the fig was native there. There can be no doubt whatso-
ever that the Carthaginians discovered the Canaries during
their west African ventures and had been landing in the
islands for many centuries before that date, and figs were
doubtless among their provisions. De Candolle himself
admits that the fig naturalizes itself so readily in suitable
conditions of soil and climate that the presence of wild figs
does not mean that they were always indigenous there. It is
notable that the seeds of figs pass unharmed through the
human digestive tract and give rise to trees of both sexes, figs
and caprifigs. There seems to me, therefore, no difficulty in
admitting that the fig may well have been introduced to the
Canary Islands from north Africa, wittingly or unwittingly,
by Carthaginian seamen, the Carthaginians having originally
introduced figs from their eastern Mediterranean homeland.
It is more difficult to understand how the fig-wasp, *Blasto-
phaega psenes*, essential to the fertilization of all but a very few
cultivars which are parthenocarpic, might have been introduced. Early introductions of fig-growing to California failed
for want of that insect, which had to be deliberately taken
there before the Californian growers started to get fruit. But
I suppose a few insects might have been carried there with
the figs themselves. For the antiquity of figs in north Africa
and the Canary Islands, De Candolle cites the fact that some
Touaregs, and the old Guanche people of the Islands, used
related pre-Arabic words—*tagrourt* (Berber) and *taharemenen*
(Guanche)—for fig. But after all, Carthage was founded
traditionally *c.* 814 BC. No: all the apparent evidence for figs
as native in the Canary Islands could be overcome and the
original habitat confined to the eastern Mediterranean were
it not for a remarkable discovery which was made by the
botanist Planchon in the third quarter of the nineteenth
century.

Planchon found leaves and fruit of *Ficus carica*, our fig,

associated with foliage of the tree *Laurus canariensis* and
with teeth of *Elephas primogenius* in the Quaternary tufa
about Montpellier.[1] It is clear that *Ficus carica* was a member
of the Quaternary flora of Europe, when a large part of the
European forest consisted of *Laurus canariensis*. The next Ice
Age presumably wiped out this sub-tropical flora completely,
except in the Canary Islands where there are still considerable
forests of *Laurus canariensis*. Of course, we do not actually
know for a fact that *Ficus carica* was wiped out *everywhere*
except in the Canary Islands. But it may have been, in which
case it must have been from the Canary Islands that it was
able to repopulate first north Africa and finally the eastern
Mediterranean when the cold had retreated and the climate
was once more propitious. It by no means follows, however,
that the movement of improved, domesticated figs followed
the same route, from west to east, as did the wild fig. In all
probability the wild fig had repopulated the 'fertile crescent'
long before any community of men was sufficiently advanced
to undertake the domestication of plants. Yet the possibility
cannot be absolutely dismissed that the fig was domesticated
at the western end of the Mediterranean, although it is
extremely unlikely since we do know that the civilized arts
were for the most part disseminated outwards from Asia
Minor, east and west, after farming was first invented.

The likelihood remains that even if the species *Ficus carica*
moved from west to east in the period of milder climate
following the post-Quaternary Ice Age, its derivative, the
cultivated fig, moved east to west from Asia Minor. And in
Asia Minor, I believe, the fig must first have been cultivated.
It is true that figs have been found, occasionally and
apparently wild, in India, but they are much more likely to
have been naturalized than really native. Had *Ficus carica*

[1] Planchon, *Études sur les tufs de Montpellier*, p. 63. De Candolle
(1884) also quotes De Saporta, *La flore de tufs quaternaires en
Provence*, in 'Comptes rendus de la 32ᵉ session du Congrès Scienti-
fique de la France, *Bull. Soc. Géolog.*, 1873–4, p. 442. De Saporta
made the same discovery in the Ayglades tufa near Marseilles.

been indigenous to India, it is very unlikely that it would have remained unknown in China, as it was, according to Bretschneider,[1] until introduced there from Persia in the eighth century AD.

It is in Asia Minor that the fig is found in the greatest variety of cultivars and where it flourishes as it does nowhere else quite so fruitfully. Surely it was from Asia Minor that it spread as a cultigen into Greece and north Africa; thence into Italy and Gaul, Germany and Britain, Iran, India and China; and from western Europe into the Americas, South Africa and Australasia.

[1] Bretschneider, 1871.

10

Apples, pears and quinces

The world's potential sources of Occidental orchard fruits
are concentrated in the Near East, the native home of the
grape, pear, cherry, pomegranate, walnut, quince, almond
and fig. The first orchards were undoubtedly located in the
Near East. In Georgia and Armenia one can still observe all
phases of the evolution of fruit-growing, from wild groves
consisting almost wholly of wild fruit-trees, through tran-
sitional methods, to methods approaching those of modern
fruit-growing, including grafting of the better wild varieties
on the less valuable forms of fruit-trees.[1]

The great Russian scientist also gave the Near East as the
centre of dissemination of cultivated varieties of all three
fruits which are the subject of this chapter. Yet perhaps the
truth is, after all, hardly so simple as that.

The species from which our cultivated apples derive is
called *Pyrus malus* or *Malus communis*. Wild in England, it is
fairly easy to find an occasional specimen in an old hedgerow
or isolated coppice. In habit, leaf and flower it looks very
much like a cultivated apple-tree; but the habit is shrubby
rather than arboreal, and the fruit is much smaller. It is
native throughout temperate Europe, Anatolia, the country
immediately south of the Caucasus, in parts of Iran and
possibly in the hill-country of north-western India. Wild
apple trees found in India may, however, be orchard
'escapes', although rather ancient ones; indeed they almost
certainly are so, since such specimens are rare and isolated.

It would be reasonable to suppose that this tree was first

[1] Vavilov, 1951.

cultivated in, say, Anatolia, or at all events in some part of the wild habitat as near as possible to one of the most ancient centres of civilization, where farming and plantation agriculture were invented and improved before they even began in Europe. And no doubt it was so; but in this case that is not the whole story of the domestication.

First, a passage of De Candolle which has not been rendered out of date by any subsequent work, or even by genetical analysis, is enlightening:

The country in which the apple appears to be most indigenous is the region lying between Trebizond and Ghilan. The variety which there grows wild has leaves downy on the underside, short peduncles and sweet fruit, like *Malus communis* in France described by Boreau. This indicates that its prehistoric area extended from the Caspian Sea nearly to Europe. Piddington gives in his *Index* a Sanskrit name for the apple, but Adolfe Pictet unforms us that this name *seba* is Hindustani and comes from the Persian *seb, sef*. The absence of an earlier name in India argues that the now common cultivation of the apple in Kashmir and Thibet, and especially that in the North-West and Central provinces of India, is not very ancient. The tree was probably known only to the Western Aryans.

This people had in all probability a name of which the root was *ab, af, av, ob*, as this root occurs in several European names of Aryan origin. Pictet gives *aball, ubhall* in Erse; *afal* in Kymric; *aval* in Armorican; *aphal* in Old High German; *appel* in Old English; *apli* in Scandinavian; *obolys* in Lithuanian; *iabluko* in ancient Slav; *iabloko* in Russian. It would appear from this that the western Aryans, finding the apple wild or already naturalized in the north of Europe, kept the name under which they had known it. The Greeks had *mailea* or *maila*, the Latins *malus, malum*, words whose origin according to Pictet is very uncertain. The Albanians, descendants of Pelasgians, have *molé*. Theophrastus mentions wild and cultivated *maila*. Lastly the Basques (ancient Iberians) have an entirely different name, *sagara*, which implies its existence in Europe prior to the Aryan invasions.[1]

[1] De Candolle, 1884.

Few modern scientists would use words such as 'Aryan' in this context. De Candolle is referring to the immigrants who settled Europe from the East and whose point of departure in Central Asia is still uncertain: Celts and Teutons, for example; people who spoke one of the Indo-European languages and whose eastern cousins conquered India and spoke Sanskrit.

The cultivation of apples is certainly old among the Celts, De Candolle's speakers of Erse, Kymric and Armorican, Irish, Welsh and Breton. In the poem *Avallenau*, by Merrdin the Caledonian (sixth century AD), there is a curious description of what is more like an orchard than a wood of apple-trees:

. . . and to no one has been exhibited at one hour of dawn what was shown to Merrdin before he became aged, namely seven score and seven delicious apple-trees of equal age, length and size, which sprang from the bosom of mercy. They are guarded by one maid with crisped locks. Her name is Olwedd with the luminous teeth.[1]

One is reminded of the wood of wild apple-trees which the French botanist Bourgeau saw near Trebizond,[2] and of what Vavilov has to say about the immensely ancient orchards of Georgia and Armenia.

Montalembert [3] says that when St Brieuc, accompanied by all his monks, was driven out of Cornwall by the Saxons, they set about planting an orchard as soon as they arrived safely in Brittany. From the same early period there are stories of Breton orchards many miles in extent, and in the ancient North Welsh code of laws, the *Dwll Gwnedd*, there are laws

[1] Davies, 1809. There is a pleasing though doubtless fortuitous analogue between this passage and the verse in the prehistoric Babylonian Gilgamesh epic in which the hero Gilgamesh comes upon the mystical vineyard in the domain of the sun, which is also guarded by a maid, Siduri, the divine Taverner. *See* Hyams, 1965.
[2] Boissier, E. P., *Flora Orientalis*, Geneva and Basle. 1867–84.
[3] Quoting the *Liber Landavensis* in *Les Moines de l'Occident*, 1860–1877.

governing the prices of apple-trees. A typical price-fixing provision reads:

> . . . a graft, fourpence, without augmentation until the kalends of winter after it is grafted. Thenceforward an increase of two pence is added every season until it shall bear fruit and then it is three score pence in value, and so it graduates in value as a cow's calf.[1]

There are similar provisions for controlling the commerce in apple-trees in other ancient Welsh legal codes such as *Dwll Dyfedd* and the *Dwll Gwent*.

All this is relatively late, dating from little more than a thousand years ago; but it does imply the antiquity of apple-growing among the Welsh and Bretons, who may quite possibly have taken over this craft from the more anciently established peoples of western Europe, when they flowed into Europe from the east. For there is good evidence for apple-cultivation in Europe in prehistoric, even Neolithic times.

The Lake-Dweller peoples of Lombardy, Savoy and Switzerland probably cultivated apples. Modern archaeologists and prehistorians very much dislike the generalizations which were common among nineteenth-century scholars touching these Lake Dwellers. For it has since become clear that prehistoric dwellings built on piles over water or marsh are far from being peculiar to one people, region or period; in Europe they may be as old as Neolithic or as recent as Bronze Age. However, the German palaeontologist Heer found carbonized slices of apple of two distinct varieties, associated with the other leavings of people who still had no metal of any kind and were using stone tools, that is, people at the Neolithic stage. This, in Lombardy, Savoy and parts of Switzerland, implies a date somewhere between 3000 and 2000 BC. The apples had been sliced and dried for winter storage. One kind had a longitudinal diameter of

[1] Dwll Gwnedd, in R. Hogg, *Herefordshire Pomona*, 1859.

about 2 cms. and a slightly larger latitudinal diameter; the other kind was larger, about 3 by 3·6 cms.[1]

It is possible, no doubt, that those apples had been gathered for winter storage from wild apple-trees. Heer and De Candolle thought that the supply was so abundant that this seemed doubtful, and they considered cultivation more likely. But they seem to have overlooked the possibility of whole woods of wild apple-trees, such as those which the Soviet botanists working with Vavilov found in Georgia in the nineteen-twenties. But if the apples (and pears) of Europe were not actually domesticated and planted in Neolithic times, they were on the way to that state, as we shall see.

This is not to say that the domesticated apple moved from west to east, for what European man could do round about 1500 BC, Anatolian man could certainly have done very much earlier. And as Europe, starting with Greece and Italy, began consciously and deliberately (not just accidentally) to learn from the more advanced peoples of Asia Minor, to fight them and to trade with them, older cultivars, improved races of fruit-trees, including apples and pears, were introduced into Europe. This fact, on the other hand, by no means implies that the European cultivars were superseded; there was cross-fertilization between the oriental and occidental kinds, and out of that hybridization came still more and better apples. Between 5,000 and 6,000 years of selecting superior mutants and hybrid seedlings have elapsed since the time when it was hard to tell a cultivated apple from a wild one, and this accounts for the enormous number (about 10,000 [2]) of cultivars which are or have been in cultivation, as well as for the great increase in the size and quality of fruits. Although

[1] As late as the second half of the last century an apple corresponding to this one and called *Campaner* was still to be found in German orchards. It seems to be the 'Golden Knob' of my own childhood garden. An English wild apple-tree which I found beside a stream on the skirts of Dartmoor in 1962 bore fruit measuring 2 by 2 cms.

[2] Ten thousand names. But many varieties have more than one name and some a score or more. One can be sure only that there are several thousand varieties.

it deals not with a fruit-tree but with a root vegetable, here is
a relevant passage from Vavilov (1940):

The world's *chef d'œuvre* of plant-breeding is to be found on
the island of Sakurajima in southern Japan: a radish one *pud*
in weight [15 to 17 kgs. or about 34 lb.]. On the same island,
under conditions similar to those in which it thrives, are a
wild radish and a cultivated radish, each related to the same
botanical species, which form only small roots. It would be
vain then to ask how the wonderful giant had been produced;
no one knows, not even the professor of plant-breeding who
lives on the neighbouring island of Kagoshima. But one thing
is certain, the giant forms were the consequence of skilful
selection of extreme variants by unknown breeders many
ages ago . . .

The same is true of fruit trees; time and intelligent interference transform the wild plant into a cultivated form so
enormously different from the wild one that only a botanist
can see that the second is the descendant of the first. So it is
with the cultivated apples: the genetical potential of the wild
Malus, which lived in Anatolia and Europe 5,000 years ago,
has been most marvellously realized.

What is true of apples is true also of pears. The principal
centre of dissemination of cultivated pear varieties is again
the Near East. But *Pyrus communis* is found wild all over
temperate Europe, western Asia, southern Caucasus and in
parts of Iran. Isolated trees and even small coppices of wild
pear have been found as far east as northern India. It is
probable, however, that these were not truly native but were
naturalized, for there is no Sanskrit word for pear; and since
the hill country of northern India is very suitable for pears,
the explanation cannot be identical with that for the want of a
Hebrew name for the fruit—to wit, that pears will not grow
in hot, dry climates. Two other species of pears have given
rise to cultivated varieties or enter into their composition:
Pyrus nivalis, the snow pear of the eastern Alps, and *P.
amygdalus* of southern Europe. The Chinese sand-pear is a
late-comer and of no interest in our context.

Dr De Wit hints at an interesting idea touching the means whereby fruit-trees, including the European apples and the pears which have been found mingled with apple vestiges on Lake-Dweller sites, became domesticated, though in much smaller quantities. Enlarging on that hint we are led to something like the following conclusions. At first the people of those settlements simply gathered and ate the wild fruits; apple- and pear-trees sprang from the seeds which were scattered in rubbish and excrement, or spat out, in the neighbourhood of the village, and thus the first orchards were planted unintentionally. But the ascent of man since the dawn of his reasoning power has been to a great extent a tale of taking intelligent advantage of accidental discoveries: the vestiges of fruit found on Bronze-Age sites show a marked improvement, notably in size, over the fruit found on Neolithic sites, which can only mean that deliberate selection had been at work. Trees bearing the best fruit were preserved and propagated from, while the poorer ones were felled. This shows selection at work before the trees were actually taken into orchard cultivation. The process was progressive because, given this measure of segregation of improved forms, seedlings would tend to include an increasing number surpassing the parent trees in desirable attributes. If this imaginative reconstruction of what happened be true, and it is surely plausible, then apple- and pear-trees were not deliberately taken into cultivation, but rather drifted into it. Domestication is seen as a long, slow process, and only in the final stages are superior cultivars carefully chosen and planted in an orderly fashion.

The pears found sliced and dried for winter storage, and accidentally preserved by carbonization,[1] on Lake-Dweller sites at Robenhausen in Switzerland and Bardello (Lago di Varese) in Lombardy, are very like modern wild pears and so

[1] Carbonization preserves the structure of the fruit and actually makes it easier to study. It should also make radio-carbon dating possible, but as far as I know this has not been attempted.

belong to the first stages of domestication and to the Neo-lithic stage in culture. De Candolle also advances one piece of evidence for the pre-Celtic existence of pears in west Europe: the two Basque names for pear, *undarea* and *madaria*, have no analogue with any European or Asiatic name; and the Basques are believed to be a remnant of a pre-Celtic Iberian population of Spain and parts of France. Since there are Basque words for pear, it seems likely that the Basque people either cultivated pears, or at least gathered wild pears, before the arrival of the Celts in western Europe.

As in the case of apples, so in that of pears, there was an earlier domestication in Asia Minor, probably Anatolia, doubtless along the same slow lines. Much later, in historical times, the eastern pears were introduced into European horticulture by the Romans, and contributed some of their superior attributes, the product of a very long career of selection, to the breeding of still better cultivars in which the qualities of the eastern and western races of cultivated pears were combined. Both apples and pears, then, have been in cultivation for about 6,000 years, and both are, as we have them, the product of a (?) fourth-millennium BC domestica-tion in Anatolia and a (?) third-millennium BC domestication in Europe.

The quince, *Cydonia vulgaris*, gets its generic name from the Greek vernacular term for the fruit, *Cydonian apple*. On the grounds that the ripe quince is strikingly golden, whereas the apple is not, and also that the fruit had religious signifi-cance and ritualistic uses, some authors have argued that the 'golden apples' of the Hesperides (and the golden apple used by Atlanta to cheat her way to victory in the famous running race) were really quinces. Maybe so; what is certain is that the quince was not anciently native to Greece, although it has been found growing wild there because it readily naturalizes in a suitable climate and in suitable soil. It is first mentioned in classical literature by Alcman in the mid seventh century BC. But it seems to me that the quince must have been familiar to the Greeks before that time; for it appears that Solon (640–558 BC), the great law-maker, was only reviving an ancient rite, not inventing a new one, when he decreed that brides must eat a Cydonian apple, thus dedicating themselves to Aphrodite, before entering the nuptial chamber. On the other hand there is a possible explanation which avoids the need to suppose a much more ancient familiarity with this fruit in Greece: Attica had very ancient connections with Crete, implicit in the Theseus legend; and perhaps the eating of Cydonian apples by brides was originally a Minoan-Mycenaean rite.

If so, it was probably older than the builders of Knossos in Cretan culture. Crete was the land of the Cydonians, a race of men more ancient in the island than any other. Their city was called Cydonia, and it may possibly have been the oldest city in Crete. Was the quince, the Cydonian apple, first domesticated by these people whose name the Greeks gave it? And if so, must not the quince have been native to the island?

True, Vavilov gives the Near East as the centre from which the quinces as cultivated plants were disseminated, reaching the whole of Europe by way of Greece, Italy and France. True also that *Cydonia vulgaris* has been found wild and unquestionably native only in Turkestan, in northern Iran close to the Caspian, in the country south of the Caucasus, and in Anatolia; it has occasionally been found wild else-where, but only very doubtfully native. On the other hand it is more than possible that in the remote past its Ana-tolian habitat extended through the islands of Rhodes and Karpathos into Crete. In fact this is quite likely.

On the whole, however, it is probable that quince was first cultivated by the mainland people, perhaps in the fourth millennium BC, and taken by colonists into Crete as a culti-vated plant. An even earlier domestication farther east is by no means impossible. From Crete the quince was taken into Attica and the Peloponnese some time about or after 1000

BC; by the sixth century it had reached Sicily, for the Italiot poet Ibycus of Rhegium has a line describing 'Cydonian apples in well-watered gardens'.[1] Not later than the third century BC the fruit had reached Rome, for Cato discusses it in *De re rustica*. From Rome it reached the rest of western Europe during the following two or three centuries. Its zenith in gastronomy was the Middle Ages, and it has remained popular in eastern Europe and Asia Minor. As its importance as a cooked fruit and a source of jellies and marmalades (marmalade is from *marmelo*, Portuguese for a quince preserve) declined, the quince was given a new lease of usefulness in cultivation when, succeeding hawthorn, it became (as it still remains) a most important root-stock for the grafting of pears.

[1] Quoted by Heyn, 1888.

11

The Phoenix kind

The Arabs have a saying: 'The king of the Oasis bathes his feet in water and his head in Heaven's fire.'

In the north we are not conscious of palms as plants of economic importance. We know vaguely that among the stately family of palms are some of the most useful of all plants; but because we rarely see them growing they do not at once come to mind as the subjects of plantations whose crops support tens of millions of people.

Yet very few plants have contributed more to the civilization, comfort and advancement of mankind than has the date-palm, *Phoenix dactylifera*. It was quite possibly the first of all fruit trees to be cultivated, and its fruits, its wood and its magnificent leaves have been staples of life for many millions of men for many thousands of years. Strabo, in his *Geography*, refers to a hymn, which he calls Persian— Plutarch somewhere refers to it as Babylonian—in which are celebrated the 360 uses of the date-palm. (The number is apparently a mystical one.) Mahomet is said to have taught his disciples: 'Honour the date-palm, for she is your aunt on your father's side; she is made of the same stuff as Adam, and is the only tree that is artificially fructified.' [1] Here he refers to the fact that among palms as among men there are male and female of the species, and that it was the practice to place branches of the male inflorescence in the crown of the female palm when it was in flower.

Nor is the manifold usefulness of the date-palm its only distinction. Its beauty, its slender grace, impressed poets

[1] Quoted by Heyn, 1888.

remote from each other both in time and in culture. Solomon praises his love with the words, 'This thy stature is like to a palm-tree', while Homer puts into the mouth of Odysseus on first beholding Nausicaa: 'I gaze, and I adore. Thus seems the palm . . .'

It would take us away from our theme to tell here what the date-palm meant to the Greeks; suffice to say that they were familiar with it first at Delos, where it was dedicated to the Delian Apollo and known as the Tree of Light or of Day. Moreover for a short time, very much later, when the Arab dominion extended into southern Europe, there were groves of date-palms in Greece, Sicily, Italy and Spain. It often happens that a people expanding into new territory will insist on taking with them a favourite plant, which is part of their homeland scene and which contributes to their preferred diet, and will contrive to make it grow in conditions that do not really suit it. But the palm cannot be relied upon to bear and ripen fruit in the relatively mild climate of southern Europe, and has long since retreated into the blazing heat congenial to it.

We have now to try to work backwards from the present-day habitat of the cultivated date-palm in order to discover where it came from in the first place. The modern range is from the Indus Valley in the east to the Canary Islands and Cape Verde Islands in the west, between latitudes 15° and 30° N. It has been transplanted to the equivalent latitudes in the southern hemisphere; but that is of no interest in our context, for it is unquestionably a plant of the northern hemisphere. The present range, then, in the northern hemisphere does not differ materially from its ancient habitat.

Phoenix dactylifera is a cultivated species, and no wild plant (I mean truly wild and not a plantation 'escape') has ever been found, so far as we know, since the dawn of civilization.

There are about a dozen species of *Phoenix*, but not every

individual plant can be ascribed to a particular species. Where the habitats of two species meet there is a belt of palms produced by hybridization and belonging rightly to neither; for, since all the *Phoenix* palms have the same number of chromosomes (2n = 36), all are interfertile; and all flower in the same hot, dry conditions, except *Phoenix sylvestris*, which flowers in hot, wet conditions. The date-palm can be distinguished from the other *Phoenix* palms because it is the tallest, attaining a height of eighty feet; and it lives for more than a century. But since it has never been found wild it has been supposed to be, in origin, a hybrid between two lesser species or a descendant of a *P. sylvestris* mutant.[1] This theory has been criticized by Professor Corner, who emphasizes, among other characters which clearly distinguish the date-palm from *P. sylvestris*, that which has made its fortune as an historical economic plant: the suckering habit which renders it so easy to propagate. For thousands of years this palm has been selected for suckering, and the question is whether this process has eliminated an older, non-suckering fruitful palm. The fruit of *P. sylvestris* is much inferior to that of the date-palm, but the difference may also be due to selection over an immense period of time. A fact of importance is that seeds of *P. sylvestris* have been found in Egyptian deposits dating from 1400 BC, which means that the species was there, available to man as soon as he had grown to be capable of intelligent exploitation of plants,[2] in one of the lands where civilization based on agriculture was founded.

It has also been suggested that the progenitor of the date-palm may have been *Phoenix reclinata*, an African wild palm which has the suckering habit and bears fruit which, although disagreeable straight from the palm, becomes sweet and palatable after immersion in water for some hours. Professor Corner says: 'One would like to know more about the

[1] For all the botanical information and conclusions in this chapter I am indebted to Corner, 1966.
[2] Swingle, W. T. 1904.

hybrids between *P. sylvestris* and *P. reclinata*'; the date-palm might well be a descendant of such a hybrid.

Since, then, there are no truly wild date-palms, and the progenitors have not been identified with certainty; and since also date-palms very readily spring up in suitable soils and climates from casually dropped seeds, we can obtain no guidance as to the venue of domestication from knowledge of a wild habitat. *One* of the principal centres of the cultivated date-palm must be the original habitat; but which one?

The Greeks knew the date-palm from their dealings with the Phoenicians and accordingly named it the Phoenician Tree—*Phoenix*. [1] But it does not absolutely follow that the Canaanites or the Phoenicians, the people of Tyre and Sidon, were the first cultivators. Nor is it of much use to us that the date-palm was important in some ancient Jewish rituals – the Feast of Tabernacles, for example – because the origin of the cultivation of this palm is very much older than the oldest Hebrew writings. We can be fairly sure that the Israelites had their knowledge and use of the palm from their predecessors in Palestine. Its importance to the Phoenicians is unquestionable: representations of it appear on Tyrian and Sidonian *stelae* and other objects, and also on those of their colonial offshoots in north Africa, including Carthage. We are, I think, safe in saying that even if the oldest date-palms were African rather than Asian, the Phoenician north-African colonies had their palms from their eastern homeland.

Although we cannot identify a proto-date-palm, we do know that the chief centre of the *Phoenix* palms is India,[2] and that *P. sylvestris*, a possible progenitor of the date-palm, is an

[1] *phoenix* in Greek means purple or crimson. The connection here is with the famous Tyrian dye produced from the shell-fish *Murex*. *See* Corner, 1966; Heyn, 1888; and, for a reversal of this derivation in which Phoenicia and the Phoenicians are named after the palm instead of the palm after them, F. C. Movers in *Die Phönizier*, vol. 1, 1841.

[2] Corner, 1966.

Indian native. Yet, oddly enough, we have to dismiss the idea that the palm might first have been cultivated in India, for the very good reason that there is no Sanskrit name for it. As for China, another primal centre of horticulture and agriculture, the first introduction of the date-palm into that country happened well within historical times, having been made in the third century AD, from Iran. We are thus left with three centres of ancient civilization where the domestication might have been accomplished: Mesopotamia, Phoenicia and Egypt.

As a rule, in this inquiry, we have been able to get useful hints from the nomenclature of cultivated plants; but in this case nomenclature is almost as unhelpful as botanical geography. De Candolle, using all the best linguistic authorities and philological indices of his day (and there has since been little revision in that field), found that 'the number of Persian, Arabic and Berber names is almost incredible'.[1] The most ancient Hebrew name, *tamar*, and the most ancient Egyptian name, *beq*, are totally unconnected, from which we may infer that the first contact of the Hebrews with the date-palm was not in Egypt and therefore antedates the Captivity. The significance of this multiplicity of unconnected names, showing a minimum of name-borrowing or none at all, is that even the most ancient peoples of whom we have any knowledge, within the range of the cultivated palms, must have named the palm and its fruits for themselves. And that really does take us back into the darkness where we have to grope for clues.

It may be significant that the extreme western names, the Berber, for example, are apparently older than the extreme eastern names, such as the Hindi or Punjabi.

I am not greatly impressed by De Candolle's point that Pliny mentions the date-palm as growing in the Canary Islands. In the first place, the Guanches (Canarians) were still in the early Neolithic phase of culture even in 1401 when

[1] De Candolle, 1884.

Jean de Béthencourt began the European conquest of the Islands and found figs but no dates, an important product of the Islands. In the second place, Pliny probably based his statement on the account sent to the Emperor Augustus of Juba II's scientific expedition to the archipelago some decades before the *Natural History* was written. King Juba's observers probably took the magnificent *Phoenix canariensis* for the date-palm, which it does indeed resemble. Even if there really were date-palms in the Canary Islands, and Juba's people were not mistaken, the Carthaginians had been visiting the islands for many centuries before that time and might easily have introduced them, accidentally or on purpose. The fact, again, that Herodotus saw date-palms in 'Libya' (north Africa west of Egypt) in the fifth century BC, is not really helpful. Carthage had been founded three centuries earlier, Utica *c.* 1100 BC, and Carthaginian exploration of the west African coast began not later than 600 BC.

The area where the date-palm was of prime importance, and where irrigation could have been used earliest to 'bathe its feet in water', was the whole region between Euphrates and Nile. I am inclined to believe that the first cultivation was nearer to the Euphrates than to the Nile. The fact that King David (*c.* 1000 BC) did not include the palm in the list of trees to be planted in his garden is not significant: only at Jericho did the date-palm flourish in Palestine. The earliest paintings on Egyptian monuments include representations of the date-palm, but Mesopotamian plantation agriculture was at least as early as, and probably earlier than, the Egyptian. Whether the first cultivators of the palm were Egyptian or Asian, it cannot be much less than 8,000 years since that cultivation began, and the date-palm is doubtless as ancient a partner as the grape-vine in man's business of making himself comfortable on this planet.

COCOS

The origin of the coconut palm, *Cocos nucifera*, one of the world's most valuable economic plants, is still a mystery. It is probably true to say that we know less about the origin of this generous provider of oil, timber, fibres, wine and milk than about any other useful tree. To quote Professor Corner again: 'The problem is that all through the Old World it is cultivated. There is no island or shore where its presence is not due directly or indirectly to its having been planted by man.' That problem is complicated by the fact that, because the big nuts float and the fibre-covered woody shell completely protects the embryo, the seed can be carried great distances by ocean currents, so that for thousands of years the palm has probably been colonizing new littorals without any direct help from us.

It is easy, however, to eliminate some of its present habitats as possible places of origin. For example, the introduction of the coconut palm to Brazil and the West Indies in the sixteenth century, and to west Africa in the seventeenth, is a matter of history. Missionaries introduced it into Guiana and the Portuguese authorities into Guinea. De Candolle also eliminates Madagascar, the Seychelles and, with less assurance, Zanzibar. We are left with the Pacific Ocean islands and, if De Candolle is wrong, some Indian Ocean Islands and the west coast of tropical America.

Here is an interesting passage from De Candolle (1884):

The navigators Dampier and Vancouver found it at the beginning of the seventeenth century forming woods in the islands near Panama, not on the mainland, and in the isle of Cocos, situated at three hundred miles from the continent in the Pacific. At that time these islands were uninhabited. Later, the coconut palm was found on the western coast from Mexico to Peru but usually authors do not say it was wild excepting Seeman however who saw this palm both wild and cultivated on the isthmus of Panama. According to Hernandez, in the sixteenth century the Mexicans called it *coyolli*, a word which does not seem to be native.

Oviedo writing in 1526 in the first years of the conquest of Mexico, says that the cocoa-nut palm was abundant on the coast of the Pacific in the province of the Cacique Chiman, and he clearly describes the species. This does not prove the tree to be wild.

If there were any evidence that the Peruvians of the Inca Empire or their pre-imperial predecessors made use of the coconut-palm, then all the arguments which follow would have to be reviewed, as they would also if there were evidence for any considerable use of the palm by the Aztecs. There is none, however, and we can dismiss the idea that this palm could have been domesticated by one of the civilized native American peoples, this despite the fact that there is one good argument in favour of an American origin: all the *Cocos* palms (with the probable exception of *C. nucifera*, see below) are American natives.

Arguments favouring an Asian origin are numerous. (i) The only ocean current whose position is such that it flows between places where climate and soil suit the coconut on both sides of the Pacific sets from Asia to America. (ii) Ancient Asian peoples were bolder navigators than the people of the American Indian cultures, and one or more of their boats, carrying coconuts as provisions, might well have been cast up near Panama as a result of a storm. (iii) The habitat of the coconut-palm is much vaster in Asia than in America, and whereas there are few varieties in America, in Asia there is a large number of varieties. (iv) We know for certain that the coconut palm was a sixteenth-century intro-duction to the east coast of tropical America, and yet at the latitude of the isthmus of Panama the Atlantic and Pacific coasts are only about fifty miles apart. (v) Uses made of this palm are much more numerous and more varied in Asia than in America. (vi) Common names for the coconut-palm are many and original in Asia, few and mostly of European origin in America. (vii) There is no evidence that any use whatever was made of coconuts or that they were ever culti-vated by the American Indians before the sixteenth century. (viii) There are Sanskrit names for the coconut-palm, which means that it must have been known and used in India before

1000 BC. (ix) The Arabic, Persian and Tahitian names for the palm are Sanskrit derivatives. (x) The three roots, other than Sanskrit, from which derive the Malaysian, Indonesian, Chinese, Philippino and Madagascan vernacular names for the coconut tree are all Asiatic, implying the great antiquity of this palm both in use and in cultivation in Asia.

Professor Corner agrees with De Candolle that *Cocos nucifera* originated in the Indo-Pacific area; and to the rest of the arguments in favour of this hypothesis he adds a particularly interesting one:

. . . and I would add that since the palm suffers so much from depredation of young foliage and fruit by monkeys, bears, squirrels and rats, it could not have been native to the continent of Asia, that is from Borneo westwards. Its survival until the coming of primitive man must have been outside the range of these intelligent mammals, eastward in the ancient Pacific . . .[1]

It may be that *Cocos nucifera* started its journey from island to island, or rather, perhaps, became isolated, group from group, as an ancient continent became no more than a few groups of islands. Maybe, under the influence first of changing environments and later of man's interference, it evolved into the plant with which we are now familiar. For small fossil coconuts, measuring only 3·5 – 2·5 cms., have been found, together with pollen grains closely resembling those of the present-day coconut palms, in Tertiary deposits on North Island, New Zealand.[2] This proto-coconut-palm may have been the ancestor of the plant which was first taken into man's service not less than five thousand years ago.

[1] Corner, 1966.

[2] Berry, E. W., 'Cocos and Phymatocaryon in the Pliocene of New Zealand'. *American Journal of Science*, series 5, 12, 181. 1926.

BETEL, AND SOME OTHERS

The late Professor J. B. S. Haldane, on being asked what
betel-chewing was like, rolled his eyes up to Heaven and
continued chewing . . .[1]

As a general rule the stimulating or narcotic drugs derived
from plants such as tobacco, tea, coffee, cannabis, coca and
poppy have spread all over the world from their points of
origin. Alcohol is universal, and so today are many other
drugs. The relatively restricted zone of the betel-chewing
habit, the mastication with other ingredients of the nut of an
Areca-palm, was explained by the late Dr I. H. Burkhill,
Director of the Singapore Botanic Gardens and father of the
present Director, by the fact that betel-chewing calls for a
number of ingredients, so that the habit cannot be transplanted unless all of them can be provided for.

The Areca-palm which bears the betel-nut is cultivated all
over India and Burma, in Malaysia and Thailand and in
Ceylon. No unquestionably wild palm of the species has ever
been found. Corner believes that it may have originated in
central Malaysia, and, as to its origin in use and cultivation,
he refers to an old tradition of the pandan-eating people of
the Gilbert and Ellice Islands, who trace their origin from
red-mouthed ancestors. The betel-chewing habit dyes the
mouth bright red, including the teeth. The people in question
are identified as betel-eating Malays, sea-rovers from the
Molucca or Sulu Islands.[2]

Another palm ancient in cultivation and of particular
interest is the Palmyra palm, *Borassus flabellifer*, whose
centre is India, where its use, and probably its cultivation,
are doubtless older than the Aryans in that country. There is
an old Tamil (pre-Aryan) poem, the *Tala Vilasam* of

[1] Corner, 1966.
[2] Grimble, A., 'The Migrations of a Pandanus People'. *Journal of
the Polynesian Society*, 42, mem. 12, 1–84. 1933/40.

Arumachalam,[1] written in praise of this palm and naming 801 uses. It is the source of palm-toddy, the fermented sap of the big inflorescence, and a large palm may yield as much as twenty litres in a day. The juice is fermented to make the toddy which is distilled to make arrack; or it may be dehydrated to make the syrupy sugar called jaggary. The palmyra fruits are eaten both raw and cooked; the flowers yield good honey, the trunks of old palms good timber; the stem fibres make excellent rope; the leaves are used for thatching and a score of other purposes.

But perhaps the noblest use of this noble and generous provider is as a source of what is claimed to be the earliest writing material.

The dry leaflets are ready ruled and the softer tissue between them was lightly inscribed with a stylus or, maybe in the first place, with a palm thorn. The leaflet was held in the left hand and with the right forearm rigid, the leaflet was pushed to the left between finger and thumb. Thence flowed the horizontal circles, dots and dashes from left to right which distinguishes Sanskrit from the vertical flow of Chinese painting on unyielding bamboo rotated to the right. No table was needed and the peripatetic philosopher could at once inscribe his meditations. . . . The leaflets were bound in books which had to be wider than long. The maximum width of two feet for a line is given by the spacing of the veins and the maximum length of two inches by the breadth of the leaflet. Hence come 'folio' and 'leaf'. And palm leaflets are still in use for letter writing.[2]

The Sanskrit-speaking and writing people of Central Asia, who used to be called Aryans until the Nazis so debased the word as to make it almost worthless, began their migration into India in 1500 BC. There they found an ancient Dravidian

[1] *See* Blatter, 1926. He draws on Ferguson, W., *The Palmyra Palm, embracing extracts from nearly every author who has noticed the tree,* a very rare monograph published in Colombo in 1850.

[2] Corner, 1966, drawing on Blatter and Ferguson. Blatter, 1926, says: 'Pliny says expressly that the most ancient way of writing was upon the leaf of the Palm-tree, an assertion with all the weight of evidence in its favour.'

culture, and no doubt learned from the Dravidians the art of writing on palm-leaves. In any case, the Palmyra palm must have been new to them; its range did not extend beyond India in the north. So the first people to cultivate the Palmyra palm must have been Dravidians; domestication of *Borassus flabellifer* may well belong to the third millennium BC, and may be still older.

The Palmyra palm was not the only one to supply writing 'paper'. The Talipot palm, *Corypha umbraculifera*, has been cultivated in Ceylon, formerly for this among other purposes, for so long that its origin is lost. It, like the date-palm, coconut-palm and betel *Areca*, is unknown in the wild.

Next to the coconut-palm as a source of palm-oil is a palm native to Africa, *Elaesis guineensis*. Here we have an instance of the ancient pattern—a very long period of harvesting the 'crop' in the wild before any attempt at domestication—extending into our own times. The African villagers, who had for centuries gathered the fruits of the wild palms in order to extract the oil, never attempted to cultivate the palm. Even after the first European contacts with these people, when palm-oil became an object of export trade (*c.* 1810), the oil continued for half a century to flow from palms in the wild. It was not until 1860 that Europeans began to plant the palm. Since then it has been extending its range and colonizing suitable parts of America and Asia. It has one marked advantage over the coconut-palm: it can be grown inland, whereas the coconut-palm will not grow away from the sea.

At the other extreme of the time-scale the doum-palm, *Hyphaena thebaica*, is perhaps as ancient in cultivation as the date-palm itself, although, unlike the latter, confined to Egypt.

Like most trees of ancient Egypt, the doum-palm was considered sacred. It was a symbol of male strength. Several representations showing how the palm was worshipped by a man kneeling under the tree are known from different tombs

at Thebes. The god of science, Thout, was represented in
ancient Egypt by the Ibis and the Baboon. As baboons frequently fed on doum nuts and lived in the crown of the
palms, the doum became Thout's special tree . . . often the
baboon and the doum-palm are pictured together . . . as a
rule the baboons are seen climbing the trees and gathering
the fruits.[1]

This palm has been cultivated in Egypt for at least 5,000
years and probably much longer, at first, say in the fourth
millennium BC, for the sweet and juicy pulp of its fruits, for
a drug which is extracted from it, for fibres and for timber;
then, later, for the vegetable ivory of the very hard, white
endosperm.

The people of New Guinea, New Britain or the Moluccas
were responsible for the domestication of another palm when
they began to plant instead of merely gathering in the wild:
the sago, *Metroxylon sagus*. When this happened we have as
yet no means of knowing. This palm produces an inflorescence half as big as itself, or at all events well over twelve
feet in height (often more) and much ramified, with countless
flowers. In preparation for the enormous output of energy
which this entails, the palm stores in its trunk a huge reservoir of starch for the inflorescence to draw upon. This starch
is the raw material of sago, and a single palm may yield as
much as 1,000 pounds of starch. It has been estimated that in
terms of food value the yield of an acre of sago palms, at 25
palms to the acre, is 9,000,000 calories or thereabouts,
enough to feed ten people for a year at a fairly high level.
The domesticators of this palm had a good deal to learn
before they could exploit it effectively. The starch reservoir
begins to be drawn upon two or three years before the
inflorescence becomes visible, and they had therefore to
learn the right moment at which to cut down the tree and
take the starch before the flowers did so. They had also to
learn to cut off the terminal bud of the palm in order to

[1] Täckholm and Drav, 1950, vol. 2.

prevent the growth of an inflorescence. Who was the primitive genius who first connected the starch reservoir with the
inflorescence? And when did he or she live? Questions as
unanswerable as 'What song the sirens sang, or what name
Achilles bore when he lived among women'. But it was the
same kind of intelligence which realized that since *M. sagus*
is a suckering palm, it is suitable for plantation, even though
one must cut down the mature palm to get at its food store.

This chapter seems to be full of such unanswerable questions. Why was the sago palm domesticated, whereas the
nipa palm, yielding a syrupy sugar at least as good as the
maple's [1] was not, nor the great *Raphia* palms of Africa which
yield raffia, bast, sugar, wine and a fish poison? A score,
perhaps many score, of other questions could be mentioned.
No family of plants, with the exception of the Grasses, has
contributed more to the comfort of mankind.

---

[1] 'Brown treacly nipa sugar and white aromatic coconut milk from
the grated endosperm poured on sago puddings made from the sago
of Metroxylon make the three-palm-pudding which should
terminate every curry repast.' Corner, 1966. To which I might add
that the pudding is soothing in cases of 'gyppy tummy'.

12

Oranges and lemons

A: *Here, maiden, take these apples.*
Maiden: Beauties, too!
A: *The seeds came lately from the Great King's land.*
Maiden: Nay, from the Hesperides!
A: *Well, they do say they are the 'Golden Apples'.*
Maiden: Only three!
A: *The beautiful is always scarce and dear.*

This fragment from the work of the comic poet Antiphanes (*c.* 388–*c.* 311 BC) is probably the first reference to any kind of citrus fruit in European literature. Alexander's opening up of Central Asia to Europe, and the broadening and increased flow of trade and other exchanges which resulted, were directly responsible for the first arrival of these fruits in Europe; and the first scientific description of a citrus-tree in a European language was written by Theophrastus:

The East and South possess peculiar animals and plants; Media and Persia among other things the so-called Median or Persian apple-tree. It has leaves like those of the andrachle [1] and sharp thorns; the apples are not eaten but smell sweet, as do the leaves also; if the fruit be laid among clothes it protects them from moths; if anyone has taken poison, it is an antidote; if you boil it and squeeze out the flesh into your mouth and swallow it, it improves the breath; the pips are planted in carefully dug beds and watered every four or five days; when the plants are grown they are moved in the spring to a soft, damp and not too light soil. The tree bears fruit all the year round, and is adorned with blossom, ripe fruit and unripe, all at the same time; those blossoms that have a kind of spindle in the centre are fruitful, the others not; the tree is

[1] Probably *Arbutus unido* or *A. andrachne.*

also planted in earthenware vessels with holes in them, as palms are.

The tree thus described is neither the orange nor the lemon nor the grapefruit nor the tangerine, but the citron, *Citrus medica*.

Scientific authors have as yet little to tell us about the origin of the *Citrus* fruits. Purseglove says that the cultivated species are believed to be native to the tropical and sub-tropical regions of south-east Asia.[1] Vavilov (1951) gives China as a principal centre from which cultivated citrus were disseminated; but he also says that India '. . . is undoubtedly the birthplace of . . . numerous citrus plants, e.g. the orange, lemon and some species of tangerine'; and that 'certain citrus fruits' were native to south-east Asia.

Literary sources are more revealing.

Pliny makes it quite clear that the Italians of his day knew little or nothing about citrus fruits in his time; attempts had been made to grow the Median Apple, that is the citron, in pots under cover, but they had failed. Not until the fourth century is there a reliable account of citrus growing in Italy. [2] This account is of citron trees planted against a south wall and protected by mats in winter. But by the fifth century there were some citrus groves in Sardinia, a few round Naples and probably some in Sicily. They were probably the species, or the cultivar, described by Theophrastus,[3] and no doubt they had reached Italy from Persia by way of Greece.

Now let us take the case of the lemon, *Citrus limon*.

When Jacobus de Vitriaco, Bishop of Accon, afterwards of Tusculum and a Cardinal, who died at Rome in 1240, described the wonderful productions of the Holy Land, the *lemon-tree* cannot yet have existed in Europe, for he expressly considers it among the Palestinian plants that were foreign to Europe.[4]

[1] Purseglove, 1968.
[2] Florentius.
[3] Palladius. Fourteen books untitled but known as *De Agricultura*.
[4] Heyn, 1888.

The same author also mentions another Palestinian citrus, which he calls *pomo de Paradiso*. This seems to have been the shaddock, a native of Malaysia; it must have reached Syria and Palestine in the twelfth century by the same route as the lemon and lime (see below). It was, then, from Palestine that, some time in the twelfth or thirteenth century, the lemon, perhaps the lime, from which it was not at first distinguished, and the shaddock were introduced into Italy, the lemon for its acid juice and aromatic rind, and the shaddock by the Jewish communities who could use it, as they used the citron, in their ritual of the Feast of Tabernacles, which required every worshipper to arrive bearing in his hand 'the fruit of a fine tree' or 'a fine fruit'. The large, bright yellow citrus fruits were doubtless chosen from among the others available because of their handsome appearance.

We have next to consider how the citrus fruits, the lemon and shaddock, reached Palestine. The word 'lemon' is simply the Arabic *limûn*; the latter is a Persic loan-word, and the Persian word itself is a corruption of an Indian word.[1] That takes us back to India, and the route of introduction is India–Persia–Syria–Palestine–Italy.

Next for the orange: there are, as will appear, two distinct species, the bitter or Seville Orange, *Citrus aurantium*, and the sweet or China Orange, *C. sinensis*. At this point we are concerned only with *C. aurantium*, because it was not until much later that Europe had any knowledge of the sweet orange.

Victor Heyn quotes from an essay by Silvestre de Sacy on the history of this orange among the Arabs, in which appears a quotation from the work of an Arab authority, Masoudi. Here is my own translation of de Sacy's French rendering of the Arabic:

Masoudi reports in his history that the Orange was brought from India after the year 300 of the Hegira;[2] that it was first

[1] Heyn, 1888.
[2] A.D. 912.

sown at Oman. From there it was taken to Basra in Iraq and to Syria and it became very common at the houses of the inhabitants of Tarsus and other Syrian frontier towns, at Antioch and on the coast of Syria, in Palestine and Egypt. It was not known before then. But it lost much of its suave scent and beautiful colour which it had in India, because it no longer had either the same climate, or the same soil, or any of the conditions peculiar to that country.

That is clear enough: the Seville orange was introduced into the Dar-al-Islam in the tenth century, and in the eleventh the Arabs introduced it into Sicily, whence it reached Italy, and into the Andalusian provinces of Spain. As to who brought it into Italy, it is very much to the point that the First Crusade began in 1096. Masoudi says that the orange came from India, but the introduction may not have been as direct as that. Our word 'orange' is the Spanish or Italian *naranja* or *arancia*—Italian, French and English drop the initial *n*. *Naranja* is from the Arabic *nârang* or *naranf*, which is a corruption of the Persian *nêrang*; which is a corruption of the Hindustani *narungee*, which comes from the Sanskrit *nagrungo*; so it seems probable that the orange, like the lemon, reached Syria by way of Iran and not directly from India.

Gastronomically and commercially, much more important than any other citrus is the sweet orange which flourishes in enormous numbers throughout southern Europe, large parts of Asia, both the Americas and many areas of Australasia. It is one of the three or four most successfully cultivated species of fruit in the history of pomology, and, like the tomato, has taken only three centuries to conquer the world.

When this orange, *Citrus sinensis*, first made its appearance in England it was called the China orange (*cf.* the saying to convey a very long-odds chance, 'All Lombard Street to a China orange'). The Germans too, and after them the Russians, used names which implied a Chinese provenance: *apfelsina* in German and a corruption of it in Russian. Such vernacular names can sometimes be misleading—turkeys do

18   The potato was domesticated by prehistoric South American Indians in the foothills of the Andes. As a staple crop of enormous importance it became a subject for potters and other craftsmen, and probably a cult-object. This Chimu potato pot is in the British Museum.

19 All the beans of the genus *Phaesiolus*, including Scarlet
    Runners (String Beans) and French Beans, are American
    natives, domesticated in prehistoric Mexico and Peru, and
    unknown in Europe until the sixteenth century. This figure
    was drawn for Matthioli very soon after the first introduction
    of the species into Europe.

20 Flax, of enormous antiquity in cultivation, can only have been
    domesticated in one of the proto-civilizations, but was culti-
    vated in prehistoric Europe, first for its oily seeds, only later
    for its fibres. Linen is certainly as old as and perhaps older than
    woollen cloth, and both are much more ancient than cotton and
    silk. This figure of English common flax is from Sowerby.

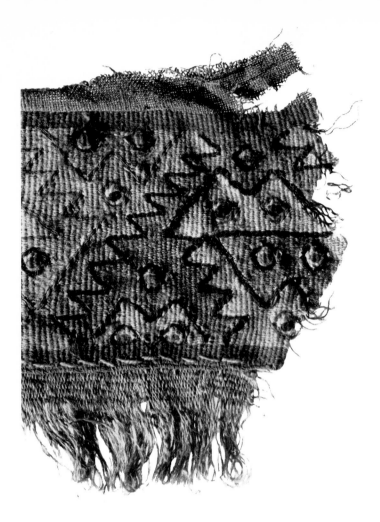

21 Cotton was domesticated independently in two different parts
of the world: south Asia (or possibly Ethiopia), and prehistoric
South America. Although they never invented the loom, the
prehistoric Peruvians wove some of the finest cotton fabrics in
textile history. This fragment (undated) from a prehistoric
Peruvian site is in the British Museum.

22 *Malus sylvestris,* by Stella Ross-Craig.

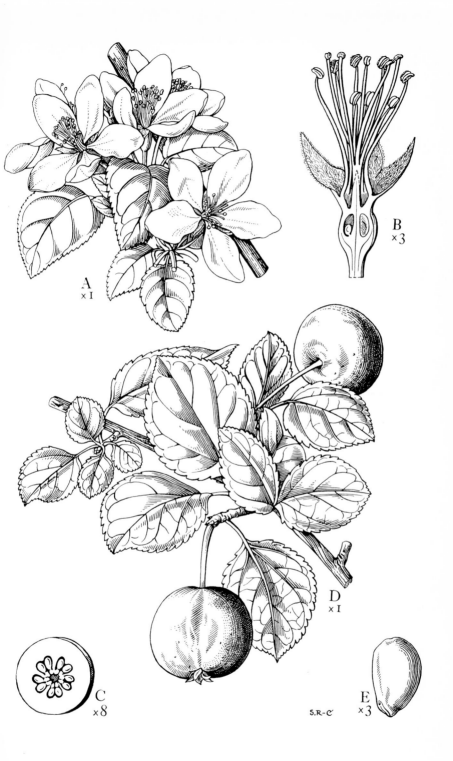

A
×1

B
×3

C
×8

D
×1

E
×3

S.R-C

23, 24 *Malus baccata* and *Malus prunifolia*; from the *Botanical Magazine*. The cultivated apples derive from an unknown number of wild species; domesticated in west Asia but cultivated in prehistoric Europe. The wild apples in Plates 22–24 are all British natives.

25 *Prunus domestica*, wild plum, probably native to west Asia and one of the two species which gave rise to western cultivated plums. From Sowerby.

not come from Turkey—but as a rule they are reliable. Yet the Italian first name for this sweet orange was *portugallo*, which implies that Italy had the fruit from Portugal; moreover the same name occurs in half a dozen other languages.

The Portuguese are, in fact, usually credited with the first introduction of the sweet orange, from south China, where they had established trading posts early in the sixteenth century: Vasco da Gama reached Chinese waters about 1518. The introduction is dated 1548, and we have an actual account of it:

They are called in France orange of China because those which we saw for the first time came from there. The first unique orange-tree, from which it is said that all the others came, is still preserved at Lisbon at the house of Count S. Laurent, and it is to the Portuguese that we are obliged for this so excellent fruit.[1]

Heyn refers to an account by Ferrari of the introduction from Portugal into Italy about ten years later. Ferrari calls the sweet orange *Aurantium Olysiponense*, that is Lisbon Orange, and says that it was sent *ad Pios et Barberinos hortos*—to the gardens of the Pii and Barberini. The Pii in question must be Popes Pius IV and V, whose garden, by the time Ferrari wrote his book, had become that of Pope Urban Barberini. The two Popes Pius occupied the papal chair from 1555 to 1572. Incidentally this introduction of a new commodity from the Far East by the leading maritime power was symptomatic of the great economic revolution which was taking place at the time, and which had been greatly stimulated by the fall of Constantinople to the Turks. Trade and communication were shifting from the old land routes to the new sea routes.

There is, however, some doubt whether this really was the first introduction of the sweet orange into Europe. It has been pointed out [2] that when the Florentine chronicler of Vasco da

[1] Le Comte, 1697. (My own translation.)
[2] *See*, e.g. Gallesio in his *Traité du Citrus*.

Gama's first voyage to the Far East remarked that they found all the oranges in those parts to be sweet, he expressed no surprise, and that subsequent European travellers did not consider the sweet oranges of the Far East as anything remarkable. The inference, drawn by Gallesio and applauded by De Candolle, is that the Portuguese were not after all the first to bring *Citrus sinensis* to Europe. There is evidence for at least two plantations of sweet oranges in southern Spain before 1525; still more surprising, Gallesio also unearthed a *statuto* of Fermo, dating probably from 1379 [1] and referring to the cultivation of sweet oranges among other citrus. If this is reliable, the fruit can only have come from Syria or Persia, ultimately perhaps from India, like the other citrus. What is certain is that distribution of the tree to certain latitudes all over the world followed the Portuguese introduction, and that the latter also points clearly to China as the homeland of this fruit.

Up to this point, then, we have the following results: citron, lemon and lime reached Europe from Iran, but ultimately from India; and the sweet orange from China by way of Portugal.

In the middle of the nineteenth century a number of English botanists, including the great Sir Joseph Hooker, found three or four citrus species, including what seem to have been lemons and citrons, and (but see below) some oranges growing unquestionably wild in the foothills of the Himalaya from Garwal to Sikkim, in Burma and elsewhere in northern India. It may be suggested that these trees were naturalized rather than native; but so excellent a judge as De Candolle was satisfied that they were native where Hooker found them, and Hooker himself was in no doubt. Judging by the location of the genus as a whole, the only other plausible homeland would be southern China; but these citrus fruits, with the exception of *Citrus aurantium* (see below), do not

---

[1] Given elsewhere in the same account as 1309, but that looks like a typographical or MS. error.

appear in any ancient Chinese flora or botany, and Bret-schneider (1871) says that the Chinese names for them are written not in simple but in complex characters, and that is in itself evidence for foreign origin.

If the lemon and the citron were native to northern India, it is most probable that it was there that they were domesticated. They have Sanskrit names, and under those names they reached ancient Media (whence the Greek name *medica*). Heyn thought that the Israelites must have first seen some citrus fruits at the time of the Babylonian captivity, and they might have been responsible for taking seed back to Palestine when in 539 BC the conquest of Babylonia by Cyrus enabled the Jews to return home. In that case citron, and perhaps lemon, must have been in Palestine about two centuries before they reached Greece from Media.

We can conclude that citron and lemon were first cultivated in northern India, probably in the second millennium BC, possibly earlier, and certainly not later than 1000 BC.

I have not yet said anything about the grapefruit, *C. paradisi*, sometimes confused with the shaddock, *C. grandis*. The grapefruit, whose commercial success is a modern phenomenon, has never been found wild in India or southern China or Burma, and has never been connected with Iran. In short, it is not one of the ancient citrus fruits in any great cultural centre. Some authorities give its centre of origin as Polynesia and the first European contact with it as in the eighteenth century.

The place where the largest number and greatest diversity of cultivated grapefruit varieties are found is Indonesia, and we have already noted that this is one good way of identifying a place of original cultivation of a genus or a species. But, as it happens, the grapefruit has never been found even questionably wild in Indonesia or Malaysia.[1] Of course, it still may be, but up to now the only places where it has been found undoubtedly wild and clearly native are two, the

[1] De Candolle, 1884, confirmed by Vavilov, 1951.

Friendly Isles and the Fiji Isles. The botanist Adam Forster [1] found *C. paradisi* 'very common' in the Friendly Isles; and of the same plant in the Fiji group Carl Seemann [2] wrote: 'extremely common and covering the banks of rivers'. I think that these two habitats must have been outlying parts of a formerly more extensive range, and that this citrus must once have been native to the greater islands west of those groups. The most likely venue for domestication is Java, which has been so long and intensively cultivated, and is so crowded, that some once wild species may very well have disappeared. Borneo is another possibility; and perhaps one day a botanist may yet find wild *Citrus paradisi* in less crowded Sumatra. It is impossible to estimate a date for domestication.

I want now to return to the bitter orange, *C. aurantium*. Until not so very long ago there were respectable authors still prepared to argue that there was only one species of orange, of which the sweet and sour were simply varieties. But all modern authorities have abandoned that theory and are certain that the species are distinct. One would have thought that those who in the past clung to the opposite points of view might have corrected their error by glancing at the very different histories of the two fruits.

We have traced the bitter orange back to India. But did it, like the lemon and the citron, start its career there or, like its sweet congener, in China? Actually, although Dr Purseglove says that it originated in Cochin China, there is not much doubt that it is an Indian native. It is true that a number of the nineteenth-century English botanists working in India—Roxburgh, Royle, Griffith and others—failed to find wild oranges in India. But Sir Joseph Hooker did find it wild and clearly native in the same territories as the other Indian citrus species, 'from Garwal and Sikkim as far as Khasia'. [3]

---

[1] Forster, 1786.
[2] Seemann, B. C., *Flora Vitiensis*, 1865–73.
[3] Hooker, 1875.

He describes the trees he found perfectly clearly and he is monumentally reliable. I see no difficulty whatever in concluding that the 'Seville' orange was first cultivated in northern India, like several other species. Maybe this domestication was later than that of citron and lemon, for there seems to be no doubt that the introduction into western Asia and thence into Europe was very much later; had the orange been available as a cultivated species in India as early as the other citrus, it is difficult to see why it should not have come west at the same time.

While driving during the month of January from Badroga to Kalimpong in northern Bengal, I saw, beyond the teak woods that flanked the road on both sides, considerable orchards of tangerines or mandarins. They were being picked over by hundreds of workers, for the most part women and boys, and all along one side of the steep alpine road was a long procession of more women and boys, each carrying an enormous poke-shaped sack of tangerines on his or her back, secured by a band round the forehead so that the carrier could throw his weight forward to balance the enormous load.

Is the original *Citrus reticulata* (or *Citrus nobilis*), whose races are tangerine, mandarin, celestine and satsuma, another north-Indian native citrus? Almost certainly not: it has never been found wild there, and it was not even noted as one of India's orchard fruits until the late eighteenth century, when it was planted in Khasia. The countries where it has been found probably wild and native are Vietnam and south-western China, and it is therefore almost certain that domestication was accomplished by the Chinese. Moreover this fruit has an ancient Chinese name, *kan*, and the written character for it is simple. Finally, there are so many varieties of this citrus known in Japan that it must have been introduced to that country not less than a thousand years ago.

13

Stimulants and narcotics

Despite the progress made in the last few decades in synthe-
sizing stimulating and narcotic drugs, the sources of the most
powerful, useful and pernicious drugs of this kind are still
plants. The two most effective pain-killers used, for example,
in cases of severe wounding or incurable cancers, are mor-
phine and heroin. Both are derivatives of opium, and codeine,
used in cases of milder pain such as headache or toothache, is
another. Cocaine, still the best local anaesthetic although its
undesirable side-effects have led to its replacement with a
synthetic, novocaine, is derived from the shrub *Erythroxylon
coca*. Hemp, *Cannabis sativa*, being more important as a fibre
plants than as a drug plant, has been dealt with in Chapter 8;
but nobody needs reminding of its role as pot, grass, bhang,
marijuana, hashish, etc. The number of plants yielding drugs
is very much larger than the number which has been
domesticated. For example, I do not find that *peyotl*, source of
mescalin, was ever cultivated, despite the fact that it was
much used by the Aztecs in their magic and medicine, and
although this cactus, *Lophophora williamsii*, would be no more
difficult than many others of its kind cultivated as ornamentals.
Perhaps there are remote Mexican hillsides where it is cultivated, although as a hallucinant it has been replaced by the
synthetic LSD. Certain plants, such as henbane, formerly
cultivated on a small scale for their medicinal use, but dangerous because very poisonous, have gone out of cultivation.

PAPAVER SOMNIFERA

In the minds of most people who have not had occasion to

study the subject, opium is associated with the Far East. Ask a score of people chosen at random where it comes from, and about fifteen will answer 'China' without hesitation; the other five will say 'India'. It will be best then to begin with a brief account of poppy in the Far East.

In about 1880, when the French botanist Alphonse de Candolle was trying to trace the history of *Papaver somnifera*, he had some correspondence with the great German sino-logue Bretschneider, who was then living in Peking. In a letter dated 18th June 1882 Bretschneider wrote: [1]

It is difficult to fix the exact date at which the Chinese began to smoke opium and to cultivate the poppy which produces it. . . . *P. somniferum* is now extensively cultivated in all the provinces of the Chinese empire and also in Manchuria and Mongolia. Williamson (*Journeys in North China, Manchuria, Mongolia*, 1868, ii, p. 55) saw it cultivated everywhere in Manchuria. He was told that the cultivation of the poppy was twice as profitable as the cultivation of cereals. Potanin, a Russian traveller, who visited northern Mongolia in 1876, saw immense plantations of the poppy in the valley of Kiran. This alarms the Chinese government, and still more the English who dread the competition of native opium.

That certainly reads as if the opium poppy was and always had been a feature of the cultivated landscape of China. The letter continues:

You are probably aware that opium is eaten, not smoked, in India and Persia. The practice of smoking this drug appears to be a Chinese invention, and modern. Nothing proves that the Chinese smoked opium until the middle of the last century. The Jesuit missionaries to China in the 17th and 18th centuries do not mention it; Father d'Incarville alone says that the sale of opium was forbidden because it was used by suicides. Two edicts forbidding the smoking of opium date from before 1730, and another in 1796 speaks of the progress made by the vice in question. Don Sinibaldo di Mas, who in 1858 published a very good book on China, where he had lived many years as Chinese ambassador, says that the

[1] De Candolle, 1884.

Chinese took the practice from the people of Assam, where the custom had long existed.

There are several points much to our purpose in that letter. It would seem that if we associate the Chinese with opium it is because they invented the smoking of the drug and practised this very widely. Then there is that point of the relative profitability of opium and cereal cultivation. This is an old problem: men will always pay more for their pleasures, especially the pleasure of intoxication and oblivion, than for their necessities, and throughout the history of the Roman Republic and Empire governments had repeatedly to check the spread of vineyards into land needed for wheat, for there was no cultivation so profitable as viticulture. From the same letter it is clear that the smoking of opium was an eighteenth- or late seventeenth-century invention in China, and that opium was imported from India. That reference to the English dread of native opium refers to the Indian export trade in the drug, which was immensely profitable and which the English, their India merchants exasperated by the Mandarins' obstruction of that lucrative trade, had forced on the reluctant Chinese Government, by war, in 1839.

An earlier letter from Bretschneider to De Candolle makes it perfectly clear that if we now go back a couple of centuries we find that opium, and not merely the practice of smoking it, is a scarcely known novelty in China:

The author of the *Pent-sao-kang-mou*, who wrote in 1552 and 1578, gives some details concerning *a-fou-yong* . . . [note that this word is not Chinese but a Chinese rendering of the Arabic *ofium*, as *opium* is an English rendering of the same Arabic name] . . . a foreign drug produced by a species of *ying-sou* with red flowers in the country of Tien-fang (Arabia) and recently used as a medicament in China. In the time of the preceding dynasty there had been much talk of the *a-fou-yong*. The Chinese author gives some details relative to the extraction of opium in his [1] native country, but

---

[1] Either this means that the author was not Chinese, or *his* is a misprint for *its*.

he does not say that it is also produced in China nor does he allude to the practice of smoking it. In the *Descriptive Dictionary of the Indian Islands*, by Crawfurd, p. 312, I find the following passage: 'The earliest account we have of the use of opium, not only from the Archipelago, but also from India and China, is by the faithful, intelligent Barbosa.[1] He rates it among the articles brought by the Moorish and Gentile merchants of Western India to exchange for the cargoes of Chinese junks.'

In other words, China was importing what little opium she bought, from India in the sixteenth and presumably in the fifteenth century, but so little was it used that the author of the *Pent-sao-kang-mou* treats it as a scarce foreign novelty. Nor can China have started the cultivation of the opium until the seventeenth century at the very earliest. It is to the point, by the way, that neither *Papaver setigera*, progenitor (see below) of this poppy, nor any related species, is found anywhere in China in the wild state; or, indeed, anywhere within thousands of miles of China.

So we turn to India, whence the Chinese first had their opium thus late in their long history.

It is probable that the cultivation of opium is quite old in India, for there are two Sanskrit names for it. Yet it is not therefore *very* ancient: Sanskrit was still very much alive well into the Middle Ages of our own era. One of those words, *Khaskhasa*, is either derived from, or is the origin of, or comes from the same common root as, the Persian word *chaschash*. We might guess from this that the poppy reached India by way of Iran, rather than that it is native there. The fact is that *Papaver setigera* (see below) is not and never can have been a member of the Indian flora; that therefore *Papaver somnifera*, its derivative, was an introduction into India, as into China, only a good deal earlier in the former country; and that the introduction was probably from Iran.

The ancient Greeks were familiar with an opiate poppy at a fairly early date. Not only do Dioscorides and Theophrastus

[1] Barbosa's work was published in 1516.

both deal with it in their works, but Homer refers to a narcotic poppy; and even the Italians were cultivating it during
the Etruscan (Tarquinian) monarchy in pre-Republican
Rome. Now the fact that the Greeks were cultivating an
opium poppy as early, perhaps, as 800 BC (although one
should note that Hesiod does not know it) is important for
this reason: *Papaver setigera* was cultivated as an oil-seed
plant very early indeed; and botanists consider that the most
probable origin of *P. somnifera*, a plant unknown in the truly
wild state although often naturalized, is either a mutant with
enhanced soporific properties, of *P. setigera*; or the end
product of a long history of selection from *P. setigera* of a race
or strain with those properties. And clearly the opiate
properties of the poppy were emerging and were known to the
Greeks of Homer's day.

The Greeks received a great many of their civilized
practices, their commodities and even their plants from
Crete, or from Egypt directly or by way of Crete, or from
Asia Minor. In this case we can eliminate Egypt and Crete.
Pliny, indeed, says that in his time the Greeks used poppy-
juice and cultivated the poppy as a medicament. But since
there is not a trace of the poppy in ancient Egypt,[1] it seems
likely that the Egyptians had the poppy either from Greece
or from the same source as the Greeks.

What that source may have been is not easy to determine.
The natural habitat of *P. setigera* is vast. It is found on all the
shores of the Mediterranean and on some of the islands,
including Corsica, Cyprus and Sicily; and this means that it
was available to all the southern European, north-African
and eastern Mediterranean peoples.

Heer, to whom I have referred elsewhere in this book,
found capsules of *P. setigera* on Neolithic Swiss Lake-Dweller
sites in quantities such as to imply cultivation, no doubt for
the edible and oily seed. If Neolithic farmers so far from the
centres of advanced culture were growing the poppy, which

[1] Unger, 1851 and 1852.

was not even native to their country, it must obviously have been cultivated earlier in the culturally more advanced lands where it was native, for example in Greece and Anatolia. It seems not improbable that it was somewhere in Anatolia that some pre-Bronze-Age community, growing poppy for oil-seed as food, first discovered the narcotic properties of poppy-juice, and perhaps began the long tale of selection which gave rise to the cultivated species *Papaver somnifera*. Or the community may have been a Greek-speaking one, either in Europe or Asia Minor, possibly even in Crete. But if we opt for the eastern Mediterranean as the place where the poppy originated, how did it get to India and China?

The word used by Dioscorides for opium is *opos*, of which the Arabic *ofium* is a derivative. So the Arabs probably had opium from the Greeks. When, following the Islamic Renaissance of Greek arts and crafts in the eighth and ninth centuries and thereafter, and the growth of Islam after the Prophet's death, the Dar-al-Islam expanded or, rather, exploded eastward, there can be no doubt that Arab physicians carried the use of poppy with them to, among other places, Persia, and that the Arabs introduced the cultivation of the poppy into the whole Iranian land. From there it went to India and, as we have seen, from India to China, still bearing its Arabic name, although the Persians and Indians had their own names for it. As to possible dates, the Arab capture of Ctesiphon began the domination of Islam in Persia in AD 641, long before the extinction of Sanskrit in India.

To sum up: *Papaver setigera*, a native Mediterranean poppy, was cultivated in Europe and Asia Minor, for its oily seeds, in Neolithic times. Quite early, perhaps before 1000 BC, the new, cultivated species, *P. somnifera*, emerged as a consequence of selection by man. From the eastern Mediter-ranean it reached Italy, Egypt and Arabia. The Arabs carried it to the east. It was established in Iran during the eighth and ninth centuries, and from there was carried to India, whence it at last reached China. The speed of growth of commerce in opium, and of the spread of the poppy in cultivation, is a function of the rate of growth of the opium-eating habit, and of the opium-smoking habit which originated in Assam and was communicated to China.

ERYTHROXYLON COCA

Cocaine is a modern drug. When one considers the atrocious consequences of cocaine addiction as we know them, it is astonishing to find De Candolle writing, in 1884:

Now that it is known how to extract the essential part of the coca, and its virtues are recognized as a tonic which gives strength to endure without the drawbacks of alcoholic liquors, it is probable that an attempt will be made to extend its cultivation in America and elsewhere.

One such attempt was, in fact, made in 1870 by Thwaites, Director of the Botanic Gardens of Peradeniya at Kandy in Ceylon. Plantation there was successful, but the Government of India seems to have been informed of the dangers of cocaine earlier than was De Candolle, and Thwaites was ordered to discontinue the experiment.[1]

The earliest contact between Europe and the coca followed Pizarro's conquest (1533) of the Inca Empire after his treacherous murder of the last Sapa Inca, the usurper Atahualpa. Doubtless some of the earliest Spanish colonists tried chewing the coca leaf, and some perhaps became addicted to the practice; but coca itself, as distinct from its alkaloid, cocaine, never became a problem in the Old World. In the Inca Empire its use was rigorously controlled, and it was not until the Spaniards began to use it as a bait or consolation for the enslaved Indians, whom they abused as miners and plantation serfs, that the debilitating effect of coca addiction became apparent.

Coca was, and long had been, in cultivation on a large scale in Peru when the Conquistadors arrived there, so that

[1] Hyams and McQuitty, 1969.

its domestication was of ancient date. The coca plant could
not be grown by the peasants on the piece of land which each
head of household held from the State. It was cultivated in
very large plantations on the land which belonged to the Sun,
that is, on State land which was not ceded for use by the
people but was retained for the production of that common
wealth which filled the State warehouses as provision against
famine. Most of this land of the Sun was worked by a corvée
system, like all other public works in Inca Peru, but the coca
plantations were worked by convict labour. For example,
under Inca Law: '. . . if a provoked man was killed, his pro-
voker was exiled at the Sapa Inca's pleasure to work in the
coca plantations of Antisuyu where the climate was hot,
humid and unwholesome.' [1] The same punishment was
inflicted on convicted thieves and probably on other kinds of
criminals. Antisuyu was that quarter of the Tahuantinsuyu
(the empire) which included the hot, tropical, humid forests
on the eastern side of the cordillera in the north. The coca
plantations were concentrated there because the climate
suited the plant, a fact which De Candolle might have noted
when seeking the original habitat of *Erythroxylon coca*, as he
might likewise have noted that it failed on transplantation
except in the high humidity of the tropics. The punishment
of criminals working in these plantations was not confined to
that inflicted by the climate; the region was also subject to
warlike incursions by fierce, cannibal tribes of forest savages,
until the Sapa Inca Topa Yupanqui mounted and led a
major punitive war against them, and built fortresses to cover
the frontier and protect the precious coca.

The Incas restricted coca growing to the lower parts of a few
mountain valleys of the Eastern Andes, and the harvest was
carefully supervised. Coca gave four crops in fourteen
months, and immense care was taken in its cultivation. As
soon as it was picked, the leaves were taken to the upper
sierra, possibly because the dry atmosphere would better

[1] Hyams, E., and Ordish, G., *The Last of the Incas*. London and
New York, 1963.

preserve it and because it would be more closely under official supervision—as in the bonded warehouses of our day.

The chewing of coca leaves, with a little lime to release the alkaloid, enabled the chewer to do without food and perform immense feats of endurance. It was given to the *chasquis* [1] who would run fifty miles a day quite easily. It was also used by the *qoyas* [2] and the Chosen Women, [3] and there are accounts of women dying if they could not get it. . . . The abuse of coca, if not quite rare, was not so common as to constitute a social problem. [4]

That will give some idea of what coca meant to the people of the Tahuantinsuyu of the Incas before the arrival of the Spaniards. But the Incas were late-comers; though chief organizers of the great Andean civilization, they were not its creators. They were, so to speak, the Romans, not the Greeks of that culture; and the coca was certainly not domesticated in their time or under their influence.

Owing to the fact that *Erythroxylon* naturalizes quite easily in the neighbourhood of its plantations, interference by man made it extremely difficult for nineteenth-century botanists to decide its original habitat. As I have suggested, they might have been, but were not, guided by studying the location of the Inca plantations. Also, they were misled by finding wild coca bushes which were in fact plantation escapes. It is now established that the original habitat was a region of north-eastern Peru and Bolivia.

The earliest archaeological evidence we have for the use of coca, and its (possible) cultivation as a crop, comes from the Late Formative or Experimenter Period coastal graves far to the south of the habitat. This Period is dated from *c.* 500 BC to the beginning of the Christian era. But this discovery proves a contemporary trade in coca leaves rather than cultivation in the region, where it must have been impossible,

[1] *Chasquis:* post-runners.
[2] *Qoyas:* princesses.
[3] Chosen Women: vestal virgins dedicated to the Sun.
[4] Hyams, E., and Ordish, G., *The Last of the Incas*, 1963.

even with the kind of irrigation which was being developed at the same time in, for example, the Viru Valley.[1]

It is probable that the properties of coca were discovered accidentally when leaves of the bush were gathered by pre-agricultural hunters and gatherers, as a vegetable food worth trying; and that the coca-chewing habit is older than coca cultivation, although the use of lime to release the alkaloid (exactly as in the case of betel-chewing) implies a measure of sophistication, but may have been a later development.

Now the probable route—we traced it when considering the potato—of the migrants, the so-called Early Farmers who moved out of the hot rain forest east of the Andes, over the mountains and down to the coast, was in the latitude of Lake Titicaca, round which there were settlements of those people. East of that region, in country through which the migrants must have passed, or from which they actually came, is the very centre of the original habitat of *Erythroxylon coca*. Whether or not the Early Farmers actually cultivated coca is an unanswerable question, but it is at least possible that they had discovered the narcotic properties of the plant which they had to abandon as they moved above the frost line. They and their descendants must have obtained their supplies by trade with the forest tribes long before the regions where coca will grow were controlled by the civilized nations that sprang up along the western, dry side of the Andes. This means that domestication of coca cannot be dated much earlier or later than 1000 BC.

TOBACCO

Tobacco, the universal drug of our time, was unknown in the Old World before the second half of the sixteenth century. In the nineteenth century there was controversy about this, and some authors tried to show that tobacco was smoked in Asia before the discovery of America. As a result, other scholars made a thorough investigation of the subject, and notably the

[1] Bushnell, 1956.

German Tiedmann who studied the travel-writings of the Middle Ages.[1] He was able to show there is not in the whole body of that literature a single reference to the smoking, chewing or sniffing of tobacco in any Asiatic country. Nor do travellers in such countries as Turkey and Persia in the period immediately following the discovery of America and as late as 1600 mention tobacco in their accounts of customs and commodities.

The story of tobacco in Asia begins in the seventeenth century: De Candolle quotes an English traveller, Thomas Herbert, who found people smoking tobacco in Persia in 1626. Tiedmann quotes, but does not identify, a traveller who found people smoking in India in 1605; and he also quotes another traveller, Methold, who reported tobacco-smoking from 'Arracan and Pegu' in 1619. Sir Stamford Raffles gives 1601 as the date for the introduction of tobacco into Java.[2] Tiedmann, again, gives evidence for a first intro-duction of tobacco into Japan at the beginning of the seventeenth century, and shows that the first reference to the plant and the smoking-habit in China must be dated about 1700.

In fact there is no doubt that tobacco is an American plant and that the practices of smoking it, chewing it and taking it as snuff are American inventions. And since it was Europeans who discovered America, it is reasonable to expect that tobacco would have been established in Europe before it reached any Asiatic country; such was, in fact, the case. Jean Nicot, French Consul in Lisbon, who introduced tobacco from Portugal into France and whose name is commemorated in the generic name of the plant, first saw tobacco under cultivation in Portugal in 1560.[3] One might have expected it even earlier in Spain, since Spaniards were the first Euro-

[1] *See* Tiedmann, 1854; and Volz, *Beitrage zur Kulturgeschichte*, 1852.
[2] Raffles, S., *History of Java*, 1817.
[3] But Purseglove (1968) says that it was first grown in France from Brazilian seed in 1556.

peans to encounter it; but the Spaniards had Haiti in which to start tobacco plantation, and did so in 1530, so that it was 1559 before tobacco-growing started in the mother country. Hawkins brought tobacco from Florida to England in 1565.

When the Europeans first reached America at the end of the fifteenth century they did not need to attain the great urban centres before encountering tobacco; smoking was universal among Indians of all tribes, classes and conditions from Panama in the south to Canada in the north. For some reason tobacco was not used by the peoples of what are now Uruguay and Paraguay, which is curious because in all probability *Nicotiana tabacum* originated in Argentina. The tribes of South America did not smoke tobacco; but it was grown in Peru and used, medicinally, in the form of snuff.[1]

Tobacco was socially important in the great urban centres of Aztec Mexico, rather in the manner of cigar-smoking in Edwardian England. Thus, of dinner parties among the upper classes in Mexico, Father Bernadino de Sahagun says:

When they had all come they were given water for washing the hands, and then the meal was served. Once this was done with, they washed their hands again, and their mouths and then cocoa [*sic*] and pipes were handed about. Lastly the guests were given cloaks and flowers as presents.[2]

This was the custom among the ruling and merchant classes; smoking had not spread to the lower orders of society. The Aztec pipe had no bowl; it was a tube, a hollow cylinder made of reed or earthenware and beautifully decorated. The use and design of those pipes was much older than Aztec civilization. They were filled by a servant with a mixture of tobacco, charcoal and liquidambar.[3] Soustelle says that there was not much smoking of those cigar-like pipes

[1] Garcilaso de la Vega Inca. *The Royal Commentaries of the Incas*, ed. Clements Markham. Hakluyt Society. London. 1910.
[2] Sahagun, *Historia General de la cosas de Nueva España*. Mexico, 1938.
[3] Porter, 1943; and see Bernal Diaz, *Historia de la Conquista de la Nueva-España*, 1632.

between meals and that walking about with a pipe in your hands was a mark of nobility and elegance.[1]

Curious uses were made of tobacco by physicians whose practices were more magical than scientific. When called on to make a diagnosis, they might smoke a pipe themselves or make the patient do so, and in the visions or hallucinations induced by the drug they found the answers they were seeking. One would not have thought that tobacco was strong enough to induce hallucinations; perhaps the Aztec mixture was richer in nicotine. But it is true that more often the much stronger hallucinant *peyotl* was employed, source of the drug mescalin so strongly recommended by Aldous Huxley as a substitute for alcohol. In another and mysterious form of diagnostic magic the physician first rubbed his hands with tobacco, and then 'measured' the patient's left arm with the palm of his right hand.[2]

As I have said, tobacco was not important south of Panama, but the Peruvians used it as snuff. Among some savage tribes it was chewed. So there is no question that the native Americans taught us to smoke, chew and sniff tobacco, and that *Nicotiana* was an American plant.

The native Americans made use of more than one species of this genus. In the north, *N. rustica* was used; it was the first tobacco introduced into England and the first planted (1613) in Virginia, but it was later abandoned for the much superior *N. tabacum*. In Chile a species which De .Candolle calls *N. augustifolia* and the present-day Chileans *tabaco del diablo* was preferred; and De Candolle drily suggested that smokers who really wished to annoy non-smokers with their filthy habit should try this one. But commercially the most important species is *N. tabacum*; it has been so for many centuries, and perhaps in Central America for .thousands of years.

This species is not known in a wild state. As it naturalizes

[1] Soustelle, J., *The Daily Life of the Aztecs*. London, 1964.
[2] Soustelle (1964) quoting Ruis de Alarcon.

easily in the right conditions, it is found apparently wild, but it is a man-made plant, like so many in this book. Modern genetical and cytological studies of the plant have revealed its probable provenance:

There is no well-authenticated record of the occurrence of *N. tabacum* in a wild state, but occasional escapes in a wild state are found. Goodspeed (1954) has shown its demonstrable origin involving progenitors of *N. sylvestris* Speg. & Comes (2n = 24) and a member of the section Tomentosae, probably *N. otophora* Grisebach (2n = 24). It probably originated in north-west Argentina where the parent species are still in contact.[1]

No doubt *N. tabacum* emerged as a chance hybrid in cultivation, was selected and propagated for its superior qualities, and in due course became fixed as a species and also became the only tobacco in cultivation south of Florida and north of Panama. Judging by the age of pipes found on archaeological sites, the practice of smoking is ancient, in any case prehistoric. But because the tobacco smoked may have been of any one of half a dozen species of *Nicotiana*, it is impossible to date the emergence of *N. tabacum* even approximately; one can say only that it was prehistoric.

[1] Purseglove, 1968.

14

The spices, condiments and incenses

Pepper is among the most ancient objects of trade between East and West. True, it is not as important to our comfort as is salt—one can imagine life without pepper—but after salt it is certainly the most important of the major condiments and spices.

Throughout the Middle Ages western Europe was obliged to buy the pepper it needed, for rendering bad meat edible and flavouring savoury preserves, from Arab traders in commodities which had travelled from the East by the overland route or which had been carried by Indian or Arab merchant-seamen, nobody quite knew from where. In either case the peppercorns were sold at an exorbitant price. Wholesalers in Alexandria and Venice made huge fortunes out of the trade; and even such Guilds as the Pepperers of London (from the twelfth century) had, unlike their customers, nothing to complain of. We use the term 'peppercorn rent' as if it meant a nominal rent, but in fact rent paid in peppercorns could be very high.

That pepper came from India and Java. Historians say that one of the forces which drove European seamen like Bartolomeu Diaz, Vasco da Gama and Christopher Columbus to seek sea-routes to the East was the demand for pepper and spices. The Turks unwittingly played into Christan hands by making the old trade-routes unsafe and even impossible; marine architects and shipbuilders played their part too, in creating vessels which could do what the dhows and junks of the Arabs and Chinese could not. With the opening up of the Far East by the Portuguese, the pepper trade passed from

Arab into Portuguese hands, out of which it was, in due course, wrenched by the more ferocious, if no more daring, Dutch merchant-seamen.

The pepper trade was very old: both the Greeks and Romans had used pepper; Theophrastus, Dioscorides and other writers had discussed its medicinal properties. Theophrastus knew two different kinds of pepper, not just the black and white—which are from the same plant, the difference being only a matter of processing—but pepper from two different species of the genus *Piper*. The Greeks must have been importing pepper at least as early as the fifth century BC.

There could be no question of introducing the pepper-plant and growing it at home as a result of becoming used to a supply of pepper. The Greeks can have had only the vaguest idea where the pepper came from; in any case the plant will not grow outside the hottest, most humid, tropics, and this fact alone sets a limit to the locations where we should seek its habitat. Disregarding those tropical regions where it has, to our certain knowledge, been introduced only in this century, or in our own historical epoch, we are left with Borneo and Sumatra, Malaysia, where Marco Polo reported it in 1280. The same author reports pepper from Java, Delhi and Malabar— '. . . a vast abundance of pepper . . .'—and from Guzzerat, as he calls it— '. . . great abundance of ginger, pepper, and indigo . . .' [1]

But *Piper nigrum*, a vine which requires about 100 inches of mean annual rainfall, is not indigenously wild in all those places. Specimens apparently in a wild state have occasionally been found in Burma and Assam, but they were probably the vestiges of some very ancient introduced cultivation of the plant. There is, in fact, only one place in the world where *Piper nigrum* vines are found unquestionably both wild and indigenous—the Ghats of western India in the State of Bombay. There the pepper was taken into cultivation, and

[1] *Travels*.

from there it spread as a cultigen into other parts of India, and, carried by Hindu immigrants, into the Indonesian islands long before the beginning of the Christian era. Pepper was no doubt well established in all the Indonesian islands before 100 BC. As for the date of the original domestication, it was probably not much later than 1000 BC.

RED PEPPER

The Capsicums, from whose dried fruits cayenne or red pepper is ground, were already so widely cultivated, and in places naturalized, in Asia and Africa by the end of the sixteenth century that for a long time botanists believed them to be Old-World plants. Even into the nineteenth century this belief still held, until De Candolle pointed out that, against capsicum as an Old-World genus and even setting aside all other evidence, no capsicum, or red pepper, is mentioned in any ancient Greek, Arabic, Hebrew or old Chinese text; and that no ancient traveller describes such a plant or such a condiment.

The fact is that Christopher Columbus brought home fruits, and therefore seeds, of either *Capsicum annuum*, or *C. frutescens*, to Spain from Haiti in 1493, and that as the seeds long retain their viability, are easily transported by animals, men or birds, those plants spread with surprising swiftness. Moreover because the fierce, hot flavour of those peppers appeals strongly to oriental cooks and gourmets, the cultivation of capsicums also spread rapidly throughout the tropics. Dr Purseglove (1968) says that as early as 1542 three distinct races had emerged in cultivation in India.

C. annuum is an annual sub-shrubby herb and it nowhere occurs in a wild state. Earliest accounts of it are from the West Indies and Brazil, and Brazil was perhaps the land of its ancient wild progenitors. *C. frutescens* is a sub-shrub with a more or less woody stock. Purseglove says that it has been found 'doubtfully wild'. De Candolle (1884) has this to say:

In America where its culture is ancient, it has been several times found wild in forests, apparently indigenous. De Martius brought it from the banks of the Amazon, Poeping from the province of Maynas in Peru, and Blanchet from the province of Bahia. So that its area extends from Bahia to Eastern Peru, which explains its diffusion in South America generally.

Be that as it may, at least one of the capsicums is of very great antiquity in Peruvian cultivation. I have already had occasion to refer to the remains of cultivated vegetables found in the Huaca Prieta, on the coast of Peru. Among them were capsicum peppers; others have been found on other sites, notably at Ancon. These peppers from the Early Farmer epoch date back to between 2000 and 1500 BC. There can be no doubt that the Early Farmers were the first cultivators. What is much less clear is how this tropical plant was carried over the Altiplano and preserved there in the period before the migrants began to move down to the warmer coast.

NUTMEG

Myristica fragrans is an evergreen tree which may attain a height of fifty feet but is usually smaller. It bears pale yellow, waxy, fragrant flowers, followed by a pear-shaped fruit containing the seed, the nutmeg, surrounded by an aril (an outer shell), the mace of commerce. This *Myristica* tree will grow only in well-drained soil, where there is a mean annual rainfall of about 100 inches, and an all-the-year-round temperature which does not fall much below 80°F. In other words, nutmegs grow only in the humid tropics.

In the ordinary, familiar use in cooking and confectionery nutmeg is perfectly harmless; no ancient people seems to have discovered its quality as an hallucinant drug. But anyone who managed to eat four or five grammes of powdered nutmeg, or an equivalent quantity of the so-called nutmeg butter which is obtained by pressing broken nutmeg and mace between hot plates, would suffer symptoms of extreme intoxication accompanied by hallucinations. The alkaloid poison at work is called myristicin, and it is very toxic indeed; there are other alkaloids present, and the nutmeg-eater's violent symptoms, resembling *delirium tremens*, are apt to be followed by death. However, nutmeg and mace used in the ordinary way and in ordinary quantities are, of course, perfectly safe.

The ancient Egyptians, Phoenicians, Greeks and Romans knew nothing of this excellent spice, which seems not to have reached the Mediterranean world until the sixth century AD, when a consignment of it turned up in Constantinople, undoubtedly from India, and a little later small quantities began to reach southern Europe. The trade between India and the Mediterranean was in the hands of Arab and Indian merchant-seamen possessing a body of traditional knowledge of how to use the monsoon winds to make the shortest, fastest crossing of the Arabian Sea. For many centuries Greek and other European seamen had had to make the voyage by the much longer coastwise route, but the Alexandrian Greek merchant-seamen had known about the monsoon winds and how to use them since the publication of *The Periplus of the Erythraean Sea*, *c*. AD 80, in which the observations of an Alexandrian navigator named Hippalus who had discovered the facts about the monsoon from Arab seamen a couple of decades earlier, were used in giving directions to sea captains. Even then the Alexandrians do not seem to have captured much of the spice trade, probably because they did not have the necessary contacts in India and beyond, and could not compete with the Muslim commercial network.

So, for seven or eight centuries Europe was supplied with nutmeg and mace at an exorbitant price by Arabs who were able to keep a monopoly of the trade by the simple process of concealing the source of supply.

But among the incalculably valuable consequences of Vasco da Gama's first voyage to the Far East was the dis-covery of nutmeg trees growing on the islands of Amboina and Banda, in the Moluccas (1512). The secret was out, and the Arab monopoly was quickly broken, to be re-established as a Portuguese monopoly until in the seventeenth century the Dutch took the islands from them by force. Better exponents of capitalism than their predecessors, the Dutch tried to confine *Myristica fragrans* to Amboina by destroying all the trees they could find on neighbouring islands. But alas for private enterprise, the local fruit-pigeons liked *Myristica* fruits and busied themselves dropping seeds all over the archipelago within their range, as they had always done. However, since the nutmeg-tree was extinct on the larger islands, if indeed it had ever been native there, the Dutch had a monopoly for as long as they could keep other Europeans away from the Spice Islands, and to maintain the high price of nutmeg they did not hesitate to burn large quantities of it in Amsterdam (1760).

So, until about 1800 nutmeg-trees were virtually confined in cultivation to two small islands in the Moluccas, with wild plants on neighbouring islands. But in 1776 a Frenchman somehow got hold of some young plants, and *Myristica* was planted in Mauritius. That did not suffice to break the Dutch monopoly, which was maintained until an English botanist of the Honourable East India Company, Christopher Smith by name, visited the Moluccas, collected no fewer than 70,000 nutmeg seedlings and took them to Penang, sending others to Calcutta, Kew Gardens and Ceylon, where his little coppice of nutmeg-trees can still be seen flourishing in the Peradeniya garden at Kandy. Since then nutmeg and mace have been cheaper.

The original cultivators must have been Indonesians. The late arrival of this spice in the Mediterranean markets suggests that domestication was not very ancient, a conclusion which seems to me all the more justifiable when one considers the rather different history of cloves, which, although they came from exactly the same place, reached the Mediterranean markets at least four centuries before nutmeg.

CLOVES

A clove is the dried calyx and flower-bud of a small tree called *Eugenia caryophyllus*, formerly known as *Caryophyllus aromaticus*. It is a member of the myrtle family, so many of which are rich in aromatic oils, *Myrtus* itself, for example, and *Eucalyptus*. Until the nineteenth century the world's supply of cloves came from a few islands in the Moluccas, where the tree is native.

When De Candolle wrote that the clove was unknown to the ancient Greeks and Romans, he was correct; but when he wrote that they were unknown to Europeans until the Dutch conquered the Moluccas, he was wrong by about fourteen centuries. The mistake was extraordinary, and indeed incomprehensible, on the part of so careful an author. In fact cloves were currently imported into Alexandria by Arab and Greek merchant-seamen during the second century, and were a commonplace, albeit a very dear one, in all the principal ports and *entrepôts* of the Mediterranean by the fourth century. They were a familiar luxury throughout Europe by AD 800.

All that happened when the Dutch seized Amboina was the nutmeg story all over again, including destruction of clove-trees to maintain the monopoly and force up the price. Then the French managed to smuggle seeds out of the island of Ceram in 1770 (a special secret expedition was mounted to do the job), and clove-trees were raised in Mauritius and Réunion. By the end of the eighteenth century there were young plantations in the West Indies. And early in the nineteenth century Christopher Smith of the East India Company accomplished for cloves what he had accomplished for nutmeg, by taking an enormous number of seedlings from the Moluccas to Penang.

Also early in the nineteenth century, an Arab Zanzibari managed to smuggle out plants to Zanzibar, where the Sultan Said bin Said, of the Omani royal family long dominant in east Africa, forced all landowners to plant clove-trees on pain of having their estates confiscated. As a result Zanzibar became and has remained the world's principal source of this spice.

Such is the story of the domestication and dissemination of *Eugenia* west and south, a combined operation. The clove-trees on the islands of Ternate, Tidore, Mutir, Makyan and Bachian were indigenes; only those on Amboina and Ceram (Indonesia) were planted, and that brings us to the other half of the story, which concerns the Far East.

There, and in India, the history of the clove is very much more ancient. De Candolle compounded his mistake about the earliest European use of cloves by doubting the antiquity of the Sanskrit word for them, *luvunga*, on the ground that had the clove been known in India early enough to have an ancient Sanskrit name, it must have reached the Mediterranean earlier than (as he thought) was the case. But the Chinese were importing cloves from the islands at least as early as the fourth century BC, and Sanskrit does not even begin its great 'classic' period until 200 BC. The Chinese and Indians both used cloves to check dental decay, toothache (as we still use oil of cloves) and halitosis. In the third century BC they were used by Court officials in China to sweeten the breath when speaking to the Emperor.[1] Clove has for many centuries been one ingredient of the betel-chewer's cud. Finally, cloves were considered aphrodisiac in China and India, and in Persia which had them from India.

It was, in fact, the large and growing demand for cloves from China in the third century BC that led to the original domestication of *Eugenia caryophyllus*, by the deliberate planting of clove-trees on Amboina and Ceram.

CINNAMON

The wood, leaves, seeds, bark and roots of trees belonging to the genus *Cinnamomum* all contain aromatic oils, and as a

[1] Purseglove, 1968.

consequence various parts of the trees have been in use and commerce in the East for many centuries.

In Europe during the Middle Ages, before the fourteenth century, a commodity known as cinnamon was imported from the Far East by way of the Mediterranean. This was cassia bark, the bark of *Cinnamonum cassia*, a tree native to Burma and south-eastern China. Then, in the fourteenth century, Europe began to import real cinnamon, that is Ceylon cinnamon. The change came about more gradually than that statement suggests, and the reason for it was that the trade from Ceylon had fallen into the hands of Arab merchants in the course of the long and unsuccessful attempt to convert the island to Islam; and these merchants were active in building up their commerce with a Europe slowly becoming recivilized after the collapse of post-Roman civilization.

The cinnamon of commerce is in the form of dried bark from young branches of *Cinnamonum zeylanicum*. This, being cut in strips and those strips rolling up in the course of sun-drying, takes the form of quills. The tree is native to the forests of Ceylon. In our present context its most interesting aspect is the extraordinary belatedness of domestication. For centuries, perhaps amounting to thousands of years, the practice was to seek cinnamon-trees in the wild woods at the end of the rainy season, strip the bark of appropriate branches and dry it in the sun. Even the cinnamon of the Arab export trade which began to reach Europe in the fourteenth century was procured in that way, for the tree was not taken into cultivation by the Sinhalese, nor by the Tamils, nor by the Portuguese who controlled the island from 1505 to 1638.

Even the Dutch, who seized the island from the Portuguese in 1638 and ruled it until the English took it away from them in 1796, did nothing about taking the cinnamon plant into cultivation during the first century of their dominion. But in 1765 a Dutch colonist named De Koke began to raise cinnamon-trees with a view to forming a plantation, in which enterprise he had the strong backing of the island's boss, Governor Falcke. By 1770 the plantation was in production, and thereafter was a triumphant commercial success. That success was followed up under English rule, and before the end of the century there were cinnamon plantations in Burma as well as in southern India, and the plantation of cinnamon soon spread to the West Indies and Brazil.

C. *cassia* and C. *zeylanicum* are not the only valuable members of their genus. C. *camphora* is a big tree whose oil-cells, throughout all the tissues of the plant, contain camphor. It is a native of southern China, southern Japan and Formosa. Despite the fact that trees intended to be cut into chips from which camphor is distilled are not felled until they are sixty years old, a serious commercial disadvantage, the Chinese early established plantations of camphor-trees in Formosa. In the early twentieth century the first overseas plantations were made, in Florida. Although camphor is mentioned in Chinese writings as early as 1000 BC, it is not clear that cultivation can be dated so early. In fact, cultivation probably did not begin until about AD 700.

VANILLA

Of the enormous family *Orchidaceae*, so many of whose members are a delight to man's eye and have, as such, become articles of commerce, only a single species of a single genus is of use to any other of our senses. The orchid *Vanilla planifolia* is a climbing epiphyte: that is to say, springing as a seedling from the ground, it climbs trees, clinging to their bark by means of aerial roots which also draw moisture and nutrients from the moist debris lodged in the bark (not, like a true parasite, from the sap of the tree itself), so that if the plant be severed from its ground-root, it continues to live and even to flourish.

This orchid was widely cultivated throughout the tropics of both New and Old Worlds until the production of synthetic vanillin depressed the trade in real vanilla, but it is native to Mexico, possibly to the country south of Mexico, and perhaps to the West Indies. It was unknown in the Old World before the sixteenth century, when the Spaniards learned its use from the Aztecs and began to plant it in other parts of their tropical empire.

The Aztecs used it chiefly, and lavishly, for flavouring their chocolate drinks and confections; they too may have been the first to use it as a tobacco flavouring. They did not rely on gathering the green fruits of the plant, source of commercial vanilla, in the wild, but cultivated the orchid.[1] There can be no doubt that vanilla was domesticated in Mexico, or at least in Central America. But when? And by whom?

There is no evidence, but I do not believe that vanilla can have been ancient in cultivation when the Spaniards first came across it in Mexico: the techniques involved in growing and processing it are too sophisticated. It can be grown only up living trees, which means that it must be cultivated in association with some arboreal crop-plant which enjoys exactly the same conditions. And the treatment of the green fruits to bring out the flavour and aroma is not perfectly simple. Maybe we owe vanilla to the Olmecs or Toltecs; perhaps to the Aztecs from whom we had it.

SAFFRON

Historically, saffron is more important as a dye than as a flavouring for food. But because I do not propose to deal with dye plants, since they have all been superseded by synthetics, I include saffron here, among the spices where it also belongs.

Authors cannot mention saffron without referring to the old story of the pilgrim from the Holy Land who, in the reign of King Edward III, broke the Arab monopoly in saffron by smuggling a saffron crocus bulb out of Palestine

[1] *See*, e.g. Sahagun in *Historia General de la cosas de Nueva España*, lib. 8, cap. 13 and elsewhere. Mexico, 1938.

into England in a hollow staff. That story is merely another version of the tale of the smuggling of silkworms out of China into Byzantium. Needless, perhaps, to add that it is untrue.

The word saffron – French and German *safran*; Italian *zafferano*; Spanish *azafran* – comes from Arabic *za'faran*, derived from a word meaning 'yellow'. This alone makes it clear that Europe had saffron from an Arab source, but that source was not the Holy Land. The Arabs who conquered the south of Spain and created the Andalusian emirates introduced the crocus into their new country in the ninth century. From Spain the cultivation of the bulb spread to all the Mediterranean countries, and then north into Germany, the Netherlands and Britain, during the Middle Ages. That much is clear; but where did the Arabs get the saffron crocus?

Unfortunately the original habitat of *Crocus sativus* is difficult and perhaps impossible to determine. Forms of it have been found wild by a number of reliable botanists, from Italy in the west to Kurdistan in the east, but not one of them is identical, morphologically, with *Crocus sativus*. It is clear that we have here another case of a man-made plant, a plant which has evolved under man's hand into something different from its wild progenitors. Vavilov is uncertain of its origin in cultivation: he puts it into his Asia Minor list but also into his list of Mediterranean cultivated plants, suggesting that there may be two primary centres. A possible progenitor has been found wild in Greece, others in Asia Minor. That Vavilov may well be right is suggested by Pliny's statement that the saffron crocus was cultivated in Italy but that an imported product was preferred.[1] There may have been two saffron crocuses in cultivation, a primitive one in Italy and a more evolved cultigen in Asia Minor.

Nomenclature is not helpful, if only because the authorities are at loggerheads. Heyn derived the Greek *krokos* from

[1] Book XXI, chap. 6.

the Hebrew *karkom*, and argued that the Greeks bought their
saffron-dyed cloth from some Semitic people. But De
Candolle, with no less than five authorities backing him,[1] says
that *karkom* means carthamin. And he adds that in any case
saffron was not cultivated in Palestine or Arabia, though he
does not say how he knows that they were not cultivated in
those countries in the past.

There is some nice literary evidence for a Near-Eastern
origin of the dye, from which we might argue a Near-Eastern
origin of *C. sativus*. 'You Phrygians,' jeers Romulus in the
Aeneid,[2] 'love garments dyed in saffron and gaudy purple.'
Kings of Babylon and Media and Persia wore saffron-dyed
shoes as part of their regalia; thus, when the Chorus in *The
Persians* of Aeschylus calls the dead Darius from the underworld, it bids him '. . . come with the saffron-dyed eumaris
on thy feet. . . .' True, some of the Greek heroes also wear
saffron; Jason the Argonaut, for example, preparing to plough
the field of Colchis, throws off his saffron cloak. But this was
surely in emulation of Phrygian and Lydian mentors, or such
oriental divinities as Bacchus in his *krotokos*, his saffron
gown.

But especially goddesses, nymphs, queens and vestals are
imagined clad in saffron-yellow garments or such as are
ornamented with that colour. The Attic virgins embroider
with many colours the crocus-dress of Pallas Athene.
Antigone, in despair at the deaths of her mother and her
brothers, lets fall the royal crocus-coloured stolla which
adorned her in the days of her pride and joy; so does Iphige-
nea when preparing to be sacrificed at Aulis. Venus clothes
Medea in her own crocus-woven garment. Andromeda
chained to the rocks (or rather Mnesilochus disguised as
such), has assumed the krokoeis. Helena takes with her from
Mycenae her gold-embroidered palla and crocus-bordered
veil, the gifts of her mother Leda . . . The hair of the maidens
in a myth is commonly of saffron hue . . .[3]

---

[1] Forskal, Delile, Raynier, Schweinfurth and Ascherson.
[2] Book IX, line 614.
[3] Heyn, 1888.

The place whence the best saffron was said to come into Greece and Italy was Cilicia. Heyn thought that the Cilician Corcyrian Hollow and the promontory Korykos were perhaps named after the crocus. Not all the old authorities agreed in giving primacy to Cilicia, but all the places chosen— Cyrene by Theophrastus, Lydia by Virgil, Algae by others— were in Asia Minor. Surely it was from that centre that some time in the second millennium BC, early rather than late, the saffron crocus was brought into cultivation. Was the grower's first purpose to make a dye or a spice? Saffron seems to have made its name as a dye and acquired merit as a spice thereafter.

INCENSE

Two plants have for thousands of years been important as incense.

We do not know the details of the visit of the Queen of Sheba to Solomon, but there can be no doubt that it was an economic mission, the primary purpose of which was to secure an agreement concerning the distribution of frankincense and myrrh that would be beneficial to both parties. It is not improbable that arrangements were made covering the shipping of incense over both land- and sea-routes.[1]

The epoch in question is c. 1000 BC, and by that time incense was already very ancient in religious use. According to J. H. Breasted, myrrh was in use in Egypt during the First Dynasty. For thousands of years, moreover, the incense seems always to have come from the same place: southern Arabia. But, as in the case of the spices, nobody was quite sure exactly where these very expensive substances were grown or who grew them. That ignorance was an outcome of deliberate policy. The Arabs of Dhofar in Oman, who, as we know, controlled the trade,[2] were not only secretive about incense trees, but also invented and spread very discouraging

[1] Gus W. van Beek, 'Frankincense and Myrrh in Ancient South Arabia'. *Journal of the American Oriental Society*, vol. 78, p. 1466. 1958.
[2] Phillips, 1966.

tales about them. One of those tales Herodotus had certainly swallowed when he wrote: 'The trees which bear the frankincense are guarded by winged serpents, small in size and of varied colours, whereof vast numbers hang about every tree.' That was in the fifth century BC. Later authors are just as unsatisfactory: Theophrastus, Strabo, Aristotle were all aware that southern Arabia had become immensely rich on the incense trade, but knew neither the people who gathered the stuff nor the plants which produced it. Centuries later it was still the same when Pliny wrote that the south Arabians were the richest people in the world, and remarked on the subject of Nero's extravagance in burning at Poppea's funeral (AD 66) a quantity of frankincense in excess of Arabia's whole output for one year: 'It is the luxury that is displayed by man even in the paraphernalia of death that has rendered Arabia thus happy.'

Another 1,800 years passed before we gained some scientific knowledge of the subject. H. J. Carter, coasting south Arabia in the survey ship *Palinurus* of the Honourable East India Company, found frankincense trees growing there, and was also able to identify Dhofar as the centre of distribution and cultivation.

The frankincense plant is a shrub, *Boswellia carterii*, rarely as much as eight feet high, with a short trunk, ash-grey branches and tiny leaves; the aromatic gum flows freely from April to June, the hot, dry season. It is native to Dhofar and parts of north-eastern Somaliland and, apparently, nowhere else.

It is not clear that the frankincense tree was ever really domesticated in antiquity; but that depends on what one means by 'domestication'. Ordinarily we take the word to mean deliberate planting and improvement in cultivation. But the exploitation of this tree appears to have been of a different kind until very recently.

The chief responsibility for Dhofar's incense production rests with the Bait Kathir tribe, and each family marks its own frankincense trees. Repeated incisions are made every three or four years, with the young tree producing an odiferous milky *luban*, 'olibanum', of delicate fragrance, which slowly oozes out to dry initially in pearly white beads (called milk-incense by the Chinese). These beads soon become pale yellow and more translucent. After three weeks the air-hardened *luban* globules or tears are harvested by the Bait Kathir, much of it from the Dhofar *najd* directly behind the Qara Mountains. This *nadji* or silver frankincense is the highest quality known, followed by the *shazri* from the Qara Mountains, then the *sha'bi* from the coastal plain. After collection the product is safely stored in dry caves until dispatch to the coast during winter to await the arrival of the wholesale merchants. Along the coastal plain at Khor Rori and Hasik (Murbat and Sadh excepted) the frankincense trees are of a poorer quality and are tapped by the nomads or slaves who own no land, only goats, camels and cattle.[1]

The implication is that these Bait Kathir work the wild trees, and that though certain trees belong to certain families they are not planted and cultivated, are 'domestic' only in being somebody's property. This would seem to have been the pattern for at least 5,000 years; it remained unaltered until the 1950s, when the Sultan of Oman, Said bin Taimur Albu Said, started an agricultural experimental station at Ma'mura, Dhofar. This is coconut country and has been since at least as early as the thirteenth century when a traveller, Ibn-al-Mujawir, noted (*c.* 1221) that there were more coconut-palms than date-palms at Ma'murah. Four hundred frankincense bushes from the Dhofar steppe were transplanted to the Sultan's experimental garden here, and *Boswellia carterii* became, possibly for the first time in its long association with man, a cultivated tree.

The scientific name for myrrh used to be *Balsamodendron myrrha*, but the genus is now *Commiphora*, and three species, *abyssinica*, *molmol* and *schimpferi*, are all used as sources of the gum. They are small trees rather than shrubs and may attain thirty-five feet, although in some places they rarely

[1] Phillips, 1966.

exceed ten feet. They have formidable thorns and are deciduous, remaining leafless during the dry season. The gum is red in colour, bitter in taste and has some analgesic properties. The tree is native to the mountainous regions of south-western Arabia and west-central Somaliland which get the benefit of monsoon rain or, at least, mists. Thus, whereas frankincense grows only in Dhofar, myrrh does, as the ancients believed, come from Arabia Felix.

Myrrh is not only important as an incense; it has medicinal uses and is even used in some toothpastes. Yet I can find no evidence for the true domestication of this tree.

$$15$$

Some tropical fruits

AVOCADO

Persea gratissima or *americana* is quite a big, handsome, broad-leaved evergreen tree which can be found growing wild in forests, beside rivers or fairly near to the seashore, from Mexico and the West Indies down to Brazil. In cultivation it is now universal, not only in the tropics but also in the subtropics and even in such Mediterranean warm temperate climates as California, South Africa and the south of France. Until about 1938 it was usually scarce and dear in north-European markets. Since 1948 it has become common and much cheaper, reflecting the success of commercial plantations in both hemispheres and on both sides of the Equator. Probably it has even naturalized itself in some of these non-American subtropical lands. Yet this vast range is misleading. It was first seen in India early in the nineteenth century; it was growing in the Sunda Isles and on Mauritius as early as 1750; but it was a rare novelty then, and had certainly not been seen anywhere in the Old World before about 1600. Or maybe a few Spanish gardeners were familiar with it before that date, since Clusius, the first scientific botanist to examine it (1601), got his material from a Spanish garden,[1] but says that the tree came from America.

But the range of *Persea gratissima* in the American subtropics and tropics is equally misleading. The huge seeds of avocado germinate easily, and the tree naturalizes readily. It is, for example, now wild in the West Indies; but it is not

[1] Clusius, *Historia*.

indigenous there, for its introduction into Jamaica and the other islands is historical and recorded.[1]

Two centres of intense and advanced cultivation of avocados are known from the earliest writings of the Spaniards and Portuguese in the Americas. When Cortés reached Mexico it was found there, growing in gardens and orchards, and later in the wild. According to one reliable natural historian, it was also cultivated on a large scale by the Palto people of eastern Peru, and was consequently known as *palto* to other Peruvians.[2] Yet it had not spread to other climatically suitable parts of the Inca Empire. This fact suggests to me that it was, in the sixteenth century, of fairly recent introduction into Peru, for nearly all the nations united in that great Empire were admirable farmers and gardeners who would not have so long neglected so excellent a fruit-tree, had it been known to them. Peru cannot therefore have been the centre of origin of avocado cultivation. What about Mexico?

Our name for this fruit is a corrupt version of an Aztec word, *ahuacatl*. Hence the Spanish *aguacate* and our own word *avocado*. It was evidently from Mexico that the Europeans made the introduction of *Persea*, first to the islands of the Caribbean, then to the Canary Islands and Madeira, and thence into south Europe and Asia. It seems likely that cultivation of avocado originated in Mexico itself or in the Isthmus, and that this domestication was accomplished by one of the civilized pre-Aztec peoples of that part of America.

PAPAW

This is another of the fruit-plants which naturalize so easily that, becoming wild soon after introduction into a new habitat, they are apt to be mistaken for indigenes. Thus, until the publication of P. Browne's *Botany of the Congo* in 1848 and Alphonse de Candolle's *Géographie botanique raisonnée* in

[1] Browne, P., *The Civil and Natural History of Jamaica*, p.2 14. London. 1789.
[2] Acosta, 1598, p. 176.

1855, botanists were describing *Carica papaya* as an Old-World plant. Browne and De Candolle showed that it was not, and there is now no need to argue the point; papaw is an American fruit tree which was totally unknown anywhere in the Old World until *c.* 1550. Yet less than a century later it was thoroughly and abundantly established from India to Malaysia and Indonesia, and by 1750 was all over the Pacific Islands, China and East Africa. No wonder it was mistaken for an Asian or African native.

Whereas in the case of the avocado it is easy to prove that, indigenous to the mainland of Mexico, it was introduced to the West Indian islands and South America, there is a good deal of evidence that, at the time of the Discovery, papaw was genuinely native to some of the islands, but introduced as a cultigen to Mexico; and that everywhere on the mainland it was cultivated or, if found wild, naturalized since cultivation began. This, then, is a fruit-plant domesticated by the Caribs. True, it is found wild in Brazil, but as far as I can discover only in what was once Carib territory. Perhaps if we could retrace exactly the migrations of that remarkable people, we should find them marked by surviving populations of papaw trees.

BREADFRUIT

Perhaps no introduction of a plant from one region of the world to another has ever received such resounding publicity as that of the breadfruit tree, *Artocarpus altilis*, from the South Seas into Jamaica and other West Indian islands.

When the West-Indian planters learned, from the accounts of such travellers in the South Pacific as Captain Cook and Sir Joseph Banks, of a remarkable tree which bore as its fruit an excellent substitute for bread, virtually a whole food, they saw in it the possibility of feeding their wretched slaves on the cheap. At their request, made in the form of a petition to King George III, Banks was required by the British Government to arrange for the introduction of this wonderful tree into the British West Indies. A ship was commissioned, specially fitted as a plant-carrier, named *Bounty* (one wonders what the slaves would have said to that) and placed in command of Lieutenant William Bligh, R.N.

The rest of the story is well known but will bear repeating. Bligh sailed from Tahiti in April 1789 with more than 1,000 breadfruit plants, and a few other Tahitian plants, in 837 pots, boxes and tubs. He had had to wait in Tahiti while the expedition's gardener rooted the breadfruit cuttings, for the tree, being an ancient cultigen, did not come true from seed. Bligh's destination was Jamaica, but three weeks after sailing, and being then off the Friendly Isles, the famous mutiny broke out, provoked by his ill treatment of officers and men. It resulted in Bligh's heroic voyage, with eighteen men in an open boat, 3,618 miles to Timor. By the time he reached England in March 1790 the mutiny, together with that feat of seamanship and endurance, had made breadfruit the most famous plant in the world.

Bligh was commissioned to try again in 1792. This time he succeeded in introducing breadfruit trees to St Vincent, whence they were introduced to Jamaica, and from there into the rest of the American and Old-World tropics where conditions were suitable.

I have said that this *Artocarpus* was ancient in cultivation; but only in Polynesia. It had reached Malaysia before, though not long before, 1750, and its introduction into the rest of south-east Asia is on record as having taken place in the nineteenth century. It is nowhere found wild, except on the islands where it was discovered in cultivation, and even there it seemed to be a man-made plant, descendant of two or more other species of its genus. Surely De Candolle was mistaken in saying that it was probably a native of Java; this is a tree domesticated originally by Polynesians, and since no people before the advent of steam made more remarkable ocean voyages, its distribution through the islands is not difficult to explain.

BANANA (*Musa sapientum*)

The origin of the banana in cultivation has been a subject of great botanical and geographical controversy. It is the only tropical fruit which has become a world staple food, eaten in enormous quantities far beyond its range, partly because, given ships which can make the journey from plantations to northern markets in a few days, it is relatively easy to carry without spoiling; partly because it is a more substantial food than the familiar temperate zone fruits.

It was long believed that bananas must be native to America. This was due to three facts: (i) Prescott, the great American historian of the native American civilizations, followed the usually reliable Garcilaso de la Vega Inca in saying that bananas were a staple food of the people in the warm and temperate regions of the Inca Empire before the arrival of the Spaniards; (ii) Father Joseph Acosta also says that bananas were cultivated in Peru before the arrival of Europeans [1]; and (iii) the opinion of Alexander von Humboldt, who had seen bananas cultivated by American Indian tribes apparently cut off from all contact with the outside world. Botanists were thus driven to conclude that there were American as well as Asiatic species of *Musa*, and that there had perhaps been separate Old- and New-World domestications of this fruit-plant, which, by the way and despite its size, is not a tree but an herbaceous perennial.

Of the antiquity of banana in Asia there never was any doubt; for not only do ancient Greek and Latin, and less ancient Arabic, authors make references to it as a remarkable fruit-tree growing in India, but Pliny was able to tell us exactly when the Greeks first met with bananas — during Alexander's expedition into and beyond the Punjab. Yet it is unlikely to have been so very ancient there either, for food-plants really ancient in India were always known to the peoples of Syria and Egypt. Bananas grow perfectly well in

[1] Acosta, 1608, p. 250.

Egypt, to which they were introduced well within historical times; they were unknown in ancient Egypt, nor do they occur in any old Hebrew writings. On the whole it seems probable that the banana had not been introduced into India before 1000 BC, and probably not until some centuries later.

The theory that there was a banana species native to tropical America received a serious blow when in 1814 the French botanist Desvaux showed that all forty-four known varieties of *Musa sapientum* (Asiatic, African and American), cultivated for their fruits, belonged to a single species.[1] This opinion was reinforced four years later by an English botanist, R. Brown,[2] who made a comparative study of Congo and American bananas; the local races of bananas in America might be different, there was only a single species in cultivation. Moreover, it was pointed out that at least one very early introduction of bananas from the Canary Islands into San Domingo was on record: by Father Tomas de Berlagas in 1515. Again, neither Columbus nor Cortés nor any of the earliest writers on the subject of American plants had mentioned seeing bananas wild or cultivated anywhere in the Americas.

It seemed clear, then, that the banana was not a native American plant. Still, the difficulty is not entirely removed. Although Humboldt's observations can easily be explained away, the downright assertions of Garcilaso and Acosta remain. There is a theory that bananas might have accidentally reached the tropical west coast of South America from Asia or the Pacific islands, before, but not long before, the arrival of the Spaniards. I say 'not long before', because the conflicting accounts can be reconciled only if we suppose that the bananas had not, when Columbus arrived, had time to spread to the east coast. But even if that is what happened, and it is rather unlikely, that still means that the bananas came from Asia.

[1] *Journal of Botany*, quoted by De Candolle, 1884.
[2] Brown, R., *Plants of the Congo*, p. 51. 1818.

Up to now, then, we have India as apparently the oldest homeland of the cultivated banana, but not its native land. It is not and never has been found wild there, and was introduced at all events before, though we do not know how long before, 300 BC. The banana as we know it, *Musa (paradisiaca) sapientum*, in all its races, is not, however, found wild anywhere else either; it is yet another man-made plant. In this case the probable progenitors are known: they are believed to be *Musa acuminata* and *M. balbisiana*.[1] The native habitat of both is fairly restricted—Malaysia and Indonesia. Now Vavilov notes the Malay Archipelago and Indo-China (also the Philippines) as centres of dissemination of the largest number of cultivars. So it must have been in south-east Asia, probably between 1500 and 1000 BC, that bananas, taken into cultivation, gave rise to the cultigen which, selected, propagated and distributed east and west, has finally conquered the entire tropical and subtropical world and has made millions of men dependent on it to such an extent that it is almost possible to use the word symbiosis to describe the relationship between certain peoples and certain races of *Musa sapientum*.

PINEAPPLE

This is another plant which spread so swiftly throughout the tropics of the Old World that some botanists took it for a native of Asia. But there is here nothing like the confusion which bedevils the history of the banana, and there was never any real doubt that it is an American plant introduced after AD 1500 into the Old World. It was unknown to all the ancient authors from China in the east to Greece in the west, and there is no native Asiatic name for it in any language. In any case, the pineapple plant is a Bromeliad; of that family, *Bromeliaceae*, the forty-six genera and 1,700 species are confined, with the possible exception of a single species, to the Americas.

[1] De Wit, 1967.

The first European of note ever to set eyes on a pineapple was Christopher Columbus, in 1493, when he saw it in cultivation on Guadalupe. The first scientist to examine parts of the plant was Clusius, in 1599; his material came from an African source, but that was a century after the Discovery, and the pineapple had had time to migrate from Brazil, no doubt in Portuguese hands.

The principal centre of cultivation at the time of the Discovery was Mexico, and there the fruit was ancient in cultivation, since the fruits were seedless or nearly so. But although the plant is said to have been found wild in Mexico, it is almost certainly not native there: some plants produce fruits with a few seeds, and cases of naturalization are known, so it could have been naturalized in Mexico too.

Although the pineapple was cultivated by the Aztecs in, and probably for a long time before, 1500, and doubtless by their predecessors in Mexico, and in the Caribbean islands, we seem not to have had it from there. For whereas we still use the Mexican names for tomato and chocolate, we do not use the Aztec name, *matzatl*, for pineapple. The scientific *Ananas* (*sativus*) is a Portuguese corruption of a Brazilian Indian name, *nanas*. The vernacular name is from the Spanish *pinas* which was given to the fruit because it looks rather like a pine-cone.[1]

The great majority of the Bromeliads are native in northern South America, Central America and the extreme south of the United States. *Ananas sativus* is native to a region bounded by Colombia in the south-west to Guatemala in the north-east. Seeking an anciently civilized people within those boundaries, one would guess that we may owe this fruit to the Maya.

GUAVA AND CHERIMOYA

Systematic study of plants did not begin until the middle of

---

[1] The decorative 'pineapple' of architecture is in fact the pine-cone, for it long antedates the introduction of the pineapple into Europe.

the sixteenth century. In the following century, the first men with any knowledge of botany who found the plant subsequently named *Psidium guajava* wild in various parts of Asia very naturally took it to be indigenous there. They were mistaken. It is the old story: so easily is the guava spread by fruit-eating birds and animals that within half a century of its first introduction this fruit-tree, whose seeds germinate so readily and which reaches fructification within four years, had become naturalized in half a dozen new habitats. I can give some idea of its ability to establish new colonies if I say that in the Fiji Islands it had to be classified, some time ago, as a noxious weed.[1]

The route of introduction is not difficult to determine: the Spaniards carried it from San Domingo to the Canary Islands; the Portuguese from Brazil to Madeira, then to Africa and the Far East. But whereabouts in America did it come from?

The guava must be quite ancient in cultivation. For one thing, there are four races, a white-fruited, a red-fruited, an oval and a pyriform; and there are permutations and combinations of these four, all found in cultivation in the Americas. When the Spaniards and Portuguese arrived they found this tree not only wild over an immense range from Mexico almost to Patagonia, but in cultivation also in various parts of Mexico, Peru and Brazil. Both the Aztecs and the people of Peru had several cultivars.

The probability is that the wild range was not, originally, nearly so wide, but that following introduction and cultivation in country outside the original habitat, the guava did in America exactly what it was later to do in the tropics of the Old World, colonized new territory. The original habitat must surely have been in that territory where the wild tree was within as easy reach of both the ancient pre-Inca Peruvian and the ancient Central American civilizations. That places the ancient home of *Psidium guajava* in Colom-

[1] Purseglove, 1968.

bia, and its cultivation there can hardly be less than 3,000 years old.

The case of the cherimoya is very similar. This fruit and its congeners, the Custard Apple and the Bullock's Heart, were all among the fruit-trees which the Spanish and Portuguese found both cultivated and, later, wild in their new American empires in the sixteenth century. A native Brazilian Indian name for the cherimoya was *anon*, and of this Linnaeus made *Annonas* for the whole genus. Equally advanced in cultivation as guava in both centres of native American civilization in the sixteenth century, and almost as wide ranging in the wild, the *Annonas* fruits can be traced with a fair degree of assurance to an origin in the extreme north of South America—Colombia, perhaps, or Ecuador—and a prehistoric domestication.

MANGO

If a traveller ignorant of Jamaica's history had landed on the island for the first time a century ago, one of the things he would have noted would have been whole woods of that valuable fruit-tree *Mangifera indica*, the mango. Seeing those woods, he would very naturally have supposed the plant to be indigenous. But in fact this is a striking example of what can happen when an alien plant is introduced into new territory in suitable conditions; for the same traveller, arriving a little more than a century earlier still, would have found no mangoes at all.

The tree was introduced into Jamaica by an accident of war; like the famous 'Ghent' azaleas, it was originally a naval prize. In 1772 the French had decided to introduce the mango into the island of San Domingo (Haiti) but their vessel, carrying young mango trees from Bourbon, was taken by a ship of the British Navy, whose captain had the good sense not to throw the plants overboard but to take them to Jamaica. There they flourished. The population, including the Negro slaves, relished the fruit and, by throwing away the stones wherever they happened to be when eating a mango, inadvertently sowed those woods of *M. indica* which thus became a feature of the island. Jamaica is not the only foreign colony of this Asiatic plant, for today it is wild in the Seychelles, in parts of Africa and in parts of Brazil.

Mango was unknown to any west Asian, European or African people until after the Age of Discovery. Yet it is ancient in cultivation in India and Ceylon, for there is a Sanskrit name. In fact some of its modern names are derived from the Sanskrit *amra*, for example the Sinhalese *ambe*, the Arabic *amb* and some modern Indian names. Also, mangoes are found wild in parts of India and in the woods of Ceylon, but, as I have shown, the tree naturalizes very easily and quickly, and it does not follow that these wild mangoes are indigenous.

The other group of names for this fruit—*mango*, Spanish *manga*, etc.—presumably come from Malayan *mangka*; and whereas the wild mangoes of India and Ceylon are almost certainly naturalized, it is in Malaysia that the species is found wild in such considerable numbers and over such a range as to make it probable that they are native there, and moreover cultivated in by far the greatest number of races and cultivars. There, surely, must have been the mango's origin in cultivation; thence it was carried eastward into China and westward into India, at a date later than the Aryan invasion of India (*c.* 1500 BC).

16

Sugar

Sugarcane, *Saccharum officinarum*, is one of the few economic plants to find its own historian. Well over a century has now passed since the publication of Karl Ritter's outstandingly fine monograph [1] on the plant and its product, and there is still not much to be added to what he discovered. But, as it happens, he reached no conclusion touching the origin of this remarkable plant in cultivation. Alphonse de Candolle, writing nearly forty years after Ritter, drew on him for most of his facts and arguments in the chapter on sugarcane in his *Origin of Cultivated Plants*, but added a hint, which Ritter himself had missed, from an eighteenth-century work by Loureiro (see page 200). Vavilov, using his usual criteria, gives two centres of dissemination of cultivated sugarcanes, India and Indo-Malaya, but nowhere mentions the plant as not merely wild but indigenous.

It is almost as difficult to conceive of life in our century without sugar as without salt. Yet all the great civilizations before our own, from the earliest in Mesopotamia, Egypt and China to the Hellenistic and the American native cultures, did without sugar as we know it. Most of them had some kind of sweetening commodity, though in very small quantities. Honey, for example, was well-nigh universal, and there were the many sugars made by partially dehydrating the sap of certain trees—palm-sugar (jaggary) and maple-sugars. But only in our own western Christian civilization which has now imposed itself, in its final technological phase, on the whole world, and then only since late in the seventeenth century,

[1] Ritter, Karl, 1848.

26 *Pyrus communis*. Like the apples, the wild pears are native to western Europe and were much used by prehistoric man in Europe. But domestication was accomplished in west Asia, and cultivated varieties were introduced to cross with the natives and produce hundreds of distinct cultivars. From Sowerby.

27 The distribution of the palm *Cocos nucifera*, one of the most
valuable economic plants in man's history, is confusing,
probably because the nuts can drift for thousands of miles on
ocean currents and germinate when they are washed ashore in
a suitable climate.

28   Bitter orange, *Citrus aurantium*. All the *Citrus* fruits are native
to and were domesticated in south-east Asia many centuries
before their introduction to the Near East and the western
hemisphere. First came citron, then the lemon and bitter
orange, then the sweet orange and tangerines and grapefruit.

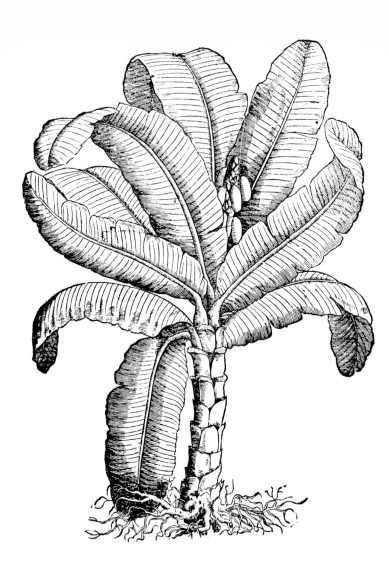

29, 30 When these figures of the banana plant were drawn in the
sixteenth century for Matthioli, the species was believed to be
native to Central America. In fact the genus *Musa* is confined
in nature to south-east Asia and was introduced to America
via the Canary Islands.

31   Matthioli's sixteenth-century figure of a pepper-plant, as first
seen in Europe. Although widely grown all over south-east
Asia since early historical times it is native only to western
India, where it was domesticated and whence it was introduced
into its now much wider habitat.

32 Matthioli's figure of *Fragaria vesca*, the source of strawberries
all over Europe until the eighteenth century. Our much bigger
modern strawberries all derive from an American species
which was introduced from Chilean gardens and, by crossing
with another American species, from the north this time,
yielded 'races' of strawberry plants bearing huge fruit.

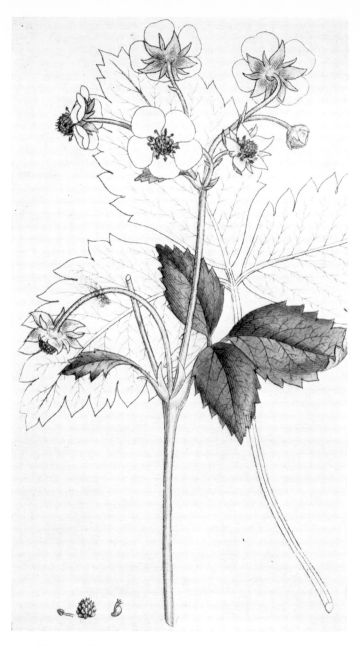

33 *Fragaria elatior.* A less common European wild strawberry cultivated as the 'Hautbois' strawberry. From Sowerby.

has sugar been an ordinary, cheap, daily commodity, used by everyone in large quantities, and the basis of great industries.

The nineteenth–twentieth-century development of beet-root as a source of sugar has, of course, seriously affected the cane-sugar industry in all the tropics and subtropics. But even today more than 55 per cent of the world's sugar comes from sugarcane.

Cane-sugar, the dried sap of *Saccharum officinarum*, first became known in western Europe after the first Crusade (1096–9), that is, as a result of Frankish contact with the Arabs. As it was then known only in very small quantities and as a medicine sold in pharmacies, Linnaeus, although dealing with the subject centuries later, used the specific epithet *officinal* when classifying the plant in his binomial system.

For centuries the consumption of sugar in Europe grew very slowly, even though it fairly soon ceased to be regarded simply as a medicine and was taken into ordinary household use by the rich. By the sixteenth century, however, consumption had become fairly considerable in wealthy households, although not by modern standards. Professor De Wit [1] quotes the interesting example of sugar consumption in the Tucher household in sixteenth-century Nuremburg. Anton Tucher was a rich merchant; his household comprised at least ten people, and their annual consumption of sugar was between twenty and fifty-five pounds, that is, from two to five and a half pounds per head. The present annual consumption of sugar per head in Germany is sixty pounds. Sugar was, of course, far too expensive to be within reach of the ordinary people, even if supplies had been available in sufficient quantity: one pound of sugar cost the equivalent of fifty eggs at the mean annual price of eggs, say £1.25 per pound in our money.

Sugar reaching northern Europe was imported from the

[1] De Wit, 1967.

Mediterranean ports, ultimately from two sources: the Near East (Arabia) and south Spain. At one time there may have been a little coming from Sicily.

Now at the time when the tales of returning Crusaders began to create and slowly build up a demand for cane-sugar in Europe, the Muslim peoples who supplied it had not themselves had it for very long. As we shall see, the Arabs of the Yemen, of Arabia Felix, may have had sugarcane, and had certainly had the use of sugar, for many centuries; but they seem to have kept it to themselves. It was the tremendous explosive expansion of Islam following the death of the Prophet which led to the expansion of sugar production in the West. From southern Arabia the cane was taken to Egypt and established there as early as the seventh century; it reached southern Spain and perhaps Syria in the eighth, and Sicily in the ninth century. Henry the Navigator introduced the cane from Sicily to Madeira in 1503. The Portuguese took it to Brazil, the Spaniards to Mexico, about 1530. It had been established in the Canary Islands almost as early as in Madeira, and from there reached the West Indies (1520), thus beginning the atrocious story of black slavery in the Caribbean.

Cane-sugar was not quite unknown to the ancient Greeks and Italians; like the medieval Europeans they used it medicinally in tiny quantities, but unlike them did not go beyond that stage to use sugar as a household commodity. Theophrastus describes what he curiously calls a 'sweet salt' derived from a reed-like plant. As in the later case of western Europe, this knowledge of sugar resulted from Alexander's invasion of the Punjab (327 BC), where his men made the acquaintance of what they called a solid honey which did not come from bees. The small amount of sugar imported into Greece and Rome came from southern Arabia, either from Arabian plantations or imported from India by Arabian merchants. The Arabs and Dravidians were trading across the sea separating them at a date so early that the mere fact that sugar reached Rome from southern Arabia does not necessarily imply sugar plantations there.

I have not been able to discover when sugarcane was introduced into southern Arabia, but presume the introduction to have resulted from the import trade in sugar: when an importing people conceive the idea that they could grow at home a commodity they are buying overseas, they usually do so sooner or later.

It was once suggested, after sugarcane plants had been found growing wild in the hill country of southern Arabia, that it might be native there. It is, however, inconceivable that if the Arabians of remote antiquity had sugar, the ancient Jews, and for that matter Egyptians, would have remained in ignorance of it, which their literatures reveal to have been the case. Cultivated sugarcane very, very rarely sets any seed when grown in good conditions, but neglected in growth on poor soil, it will do so, as if it 'knew' that in such conditions it could no longer rely on the perennial habit for survival. No doubt the Arabian wild sugarcanes were plantation escapes. And since this *Saccharum* is a perennial grass, there would quite likely be a few vestiges of old, abandoned plantations.

A much more likely homeland for sugarcane is India. There is, in the first place, Vavilov's observation that it is the principal centre of dissemination of cultivated kinds. Then there is the demonstrable fact that the cane has been in cultivation there for an immensely long time. The name *saccharum* has forms in every European language, and it is derived from Sanskrit *sakkara*, meaning sugar. The cane itself in Sanskrit is *ikshu*, which occurs in Bengali and other modern Indian languages, but not in southern India or in the north, in the Indo-Chinese and Indo-Malay regions. These Indo-European, these Sanskrit derivatives, are not the oldest names for sugar in India. There are a number of pre-Aryan names, a fact which suggests that sugar is at any rate older than the Aryans, who arrived in the country *c*. 1500 BC.

And the countries to the north-east of India, as well as the southern Indian provinces, have different, non-Aryan names for sugarcane and sugar, a fact which is significant since it may indicate independent local domestications.

But despite all this excellent evidence for the antiquity of sugarcane in India there is a difficulty in admitting India as the country of origin of sugar cultivation. Not one of the botanists who made a thorough study of the Indian flora during the nineteenth century ever found a single plant of wild sugarcane which was unmistakably indigenous; nor has wild sugarcane since been found in India; nor has it ever been found in Ceylon; nor does it occur in the florae of Malaysia or Indonesia or Polynesia.

Just as Arabia was once suggested as the country of origin of sugarcane, so, later, was China. But Bretschneider was able to show that it was quite unknown in China until well into our own era.[1] He has, he says, been unable to find any allusion to sugarcane in the most ancient Chinese works. The first book to mention it—the *Nan-fang-tsao-mu-chuang*—is a work of the fourth century AD, and Bretschneider quotes from it as follows:

The chê-chê, kan-chê grows in Cochin-China. It is several inches in circumference and resembles the bamboo. The stem, broken in pieces, is eatable and very sweet. The sap which is drawn from it is dried in the sun. After a few days it becomes sugar, which melts in the mouth. In the year [here follows a date equivalent to AD 286] the kingdom of Funan sent sugar as a tribute.

Chê means bamboo, *kan* means sweet. Bretschneider says that the word sugar is rendered by a compound of Chinese characters, and I take that to mean that there was then no simple word for it, in short that it was something new. Funan was an Indian kingdom on the far side of the Ganges. Bretschneider also says that according to another authority

---

[1] Bretschneider, 1871.

an Emperor who reigned from AD 627 to 650 sent a man to Behar in India to find out how to manufacture sugar.

Clearly, he was successful, for when Marco Polo was travelling in the Far East in the late thirteenth century, he found sugar production important in a number of places. The first he mentions is Bengal; but his next reference to sugar is to it in China itself—Kublai Khan levied a tax of $3\frac{1}{2}$ per cent on the abundant sugar production of Kin-sai. Of the city of Un-guen (as his translator writes it), Marco says: [1]

This place is remarkable for a great manufacture of sugar, which is sent from thence to the city of Kanbalu for the supply of the court. Previously to its being brought under the dominion of the great khan, the natives were unacquainted with the art of manufacturing sugar of a fine quality, and boiled it in such an imperfect manner, that when left to cool it remained in the state of a dark-brown paste. But at the time this city became subject to his majesty's government, there happened to be at the court some persons from Babylon who were skilled in the process, and who, being sent thither, instructed the inhabitants in the mode of refining the sugar by means of the ashes of certain woods.[2]

'Babylon' was the European medieval name for Cairo; Kublai Khan's sugar-refining experts were Egyptians. Below this passage is one touching the seaborne export of sugar from the city of Kan-giu. So sugar was abundant in China in the thirteenth century but had been unknown there in the third.

A point of particular interest in the context of this book is that the author of the *Nan-fang-tsao-mu-chuang*, who says that the sugarcane grows in Cochin-China, may mean either that it is cultivated there or that it is wild in that country. Since the Chinese emperor who in the seventh century sent a man abroad to learn how to make sugar had to send him to India, it is probably fair to conclude that he meant to say that sugarcane grew wild in Cochin-China.

[1] *Travels.*
[2] These ashes would have supplied the alkali required to cause the sugar to granulate.

Now it happens that late in the eighteenth century a botanist named Loureiro produced a study of the flora of Cochin-China,[1] which Karl Ritter failed to consult. Among the plants native in the region Loureiro includes *Saccharum officinarum*.[2] I believe that the plant must once have been indigenous in all the country from north-eastern Bengal to Cochin-China, and that it was taken into cultivation in what is now Bengal, perhaps as early as the third and certainly no later than the second millennium BC.

There remains a curious little mystery: why was it that the Indians learnt to cultivate sugarcane and use sugar whereas the Chinese did not, although the wild plant grew readily for both peoples in territory which is equally accessible to both?

[1] Loureiro, *Flora Cochin-Chinensis*, 1790. A revised edition was produced by Wildenow in Berlin in 1793.

[2] The passage reads: *Habitat, et colitur abundantissime in omnibus provinciis regni Cochin-Chinaensis : simul in aliquibus imperii sinensis, sed minori copia.* On this A. de Candolle (1884) comments: 'The word *habitat,* separated by a comma from the rest, is a distinct assertion. . . .'

17

Berries and nuts

The most ancient 'economic' act which any man performs
nowadays is that of going out to gather the berries and nuts of
wild plants. Long before our race had emerged as human,
when our ancestors were still 'hominids' of pre-human type,
and before them when *Homo sapiens* was still potential in
some even less man-like creature, berries and nuts must have
been a part of 'our' diet. In Eurasia and America strawberries, raspberries, blackberries, currants and all kinds of
nuts were gathered in the wild by pre-men and men, and
their families, for tens of thousands of years; so that when
mother organizes a blackberrying expedition, or takes the
children out to gather elderberries to make wine, or when
father gets the car out to take the kids nutting, they are
establishing a sympathetic link with the remotest recogniz-
able ancestors of our race. Yet the curious thing is that the
most obviously valuable berrying plants were not among the
earliest, but among the latest, to be cultivated; nor are nut-
trees very ancient in cultivation. Yet perhaps this is not so
strange; until relatively recently supplies of these fruits and
seeds were so plentiful and accessible in the wild that there
was not much point in cultivating them; except, of course, in
order to improve on nature and produce bigger and better
berries and nuts. Let us take the case of the most popular and
probably the most delicious of all berries.

STRAWBERRIES
The strawberries we grow now are man-made plants; the
tale of their creation is quite a long one but, unlike that of

most of the plants dealt with in this book, does not take us back to remote antiquity.

There is a strawberry, *Fragaria vesca*, which grows wild abundantly all over Europe. Its fruits are not as large even as a blackberry; they have the characteristic strawberry taste, but their texture is dry and they lack the lusciousness of the strawberries of commerce. This berry was well known to the Greeks and Romans but apparently as a medicinal herb only, and it was never taken into cultivation by them, nor was it known to any of the pre-Greek civilizations of the Old World.

Strawberry cultivation begins with the taking of *Fragaria vesca* into gardens, in the first decades of the fourteenth century:

In the accounts of a north French hospital for the year 1324: *Pour fraisiers à planter en la montaigne acatés* [i.e. *achetés*] *à Pierrot Paillet et Aeles Paiele, XIId.* In 1386 a gardener of the French king Charles V set twelve thousand strawberry plants in the royal gardens.[1]

As late as the seventeenth century Olivier de Serres in France, and Parkinson in England, were still recommending gardeners to get their strawberry-plants in the woods, transplant them into the garden, and by care increase the size and quality of the fruit. From time to time mutants with special qualities emerged, were noted, selected, propagated: the modern 'alpine' strawberries, the *fraises des bois*, derive from them.

Another European wild strawberry, *F. elatior*, which is not so common, has slightly larger and more highly flavoured fruits; it was taken into cultivation later and, in its cultivated form, became known and highly prized as the 'Hautbois' strawberry. 'Hautbois' were still grown in most western European countries into the nineteenth century, and only certain genetical difficulties prevent one from asserting that they must be the origin of the musk flavour in some nineteenth-century hybrids. Now, oddly enough, neither of these

[1] Hyams, E., *Strawberry Growing Complete*. London, 1962.

European strawberries, cultivated for about six centuries, has anything whatever to do with the modern strawberry of commerce, which in origin is wholly American.

Fragaria virginiana, a North American wild strawberry with larger fruits than the European species, yet nothing like the size of commercial strawberries, first reached Europe in the seventeenth century, or possibly late in the sixteenth, although the first recorded appearance is in Paris in 1624, when Jean Robin, King Louis XIII's gardener and botanist, planted some in the royal gardens. This species was never cultivated by any American people, or if it was we have no record of the fact. It was introduced into England by the elder Tradescant, and it became valued there for its superior fruits, although its flavour does not compare well with 'Hautbois'. As far as one can determine, there was no crossing between European and American strawberries; there is in fact, a genetical barrier.[1]

Until this point, then, the only improvement produced in strawberries by cultivation was such as can be produced in any wild plant by selecting the best individuals for propagation, and by tilling and manuring their soil. The history of crop improvement is a history of selected superior mutations; or of the bringing together and crossing of species which, for geographical reasons, cannot cross in the wild. Superior mutations are extremely rare occurrences, and in this case no hybridization was possible as a means of unlocking the genetical treasure chest of recessive characters. In time, mutation and segregation would doubtless have produced better strawberries, but in the event something else happened. A French naval officer, happily named Frézier, brought home some plants of a South American strawberry species in about 1780.

Fragaria chiloensis is native to the Island of Chiloë, the islands of Juan Fernandez, the mainland in the region of Valdivia; it has local races up the west coast of North America

[1] The European species are diploids, the American octoploids.

also, as far north as Alaska. Frézier noticed it in Chileño gardens and the mystery is that, while bearing fruit so much larger than any other strawberry, it had had to wait until late in the eighteenth century to be noticed. It is possible that the species was cultivated by the pre-Discovery Peruvians and that the plants which Frézier acquired were anciently cultivated ones, but I have found no real evidence for this. He took them on board his ship, but only five survived the voyage to France. What happened to them is not clear, but it seems that the French botanist Duchesne got hold of two or three of Frézier's plants, or of some other *F. chiloensis* plants. Examination of the flowers showed them to be a dioecious species, in itself evidence that they had not been long in cultivation, and all pistillate (female). Duchesne fertilized the flowers with pollen of *F. virginiana*, obtained fruit and fertile seed, and raised seedlings among which were some very interesting hybrids. One, put into commerce as *Ananas*, was superior in size and flavour to any other strawberry variety then in cultivation.

No doubt Duchesne would have continued this work, had he not been interrupted by the French Revolution. But some of his strawberry plants were sent to England; and with these, and more plants of *F. virginiana* and *F. chiloensis*, a grower named Michael Keens began hybridization. Although he was an unscientific empiricist his results soon surpassed Duchesne's, and in 1821 the ancestor of the modern large-fruited, luscious, high-flavoured strawberries was put into commerce as *Keens' Seedling*.

From our point of view that is the end of the story: strawberries had been 'tamed'. More scientific gardeners than Keens improved on his results, notably T. A. Knight and Thomas Laxton. But Keens was the forerunner.

There is another short chapter to the story of strawberry domestication. The large-fruited strawberries we have been discussing are all varieties with a short summer season of fruit-bearing, say three weeks. In this they differ from some

of the old European strawberries derived from *F. vesca*, the
so-called alpines, whose season is more protracted, often
continuous throughout the summer. The Abbé Thivolet, an
amateur gardener and parish priest of Chenoves in France,
was growing in his garden both some of the new *fraisiers
anglais*, as the French called them, and some of the alpine
varieties; and he was trying to cross them, without realizing
that he was attempting the genetically impossible. He
obtained a seedling which bore the large fruit of a *fraisier
anglais*, but over a season of nearly three months, forming and
ripening successive flushes of fruit. This was propagated and
put into commerce as the variety Saint-Joseph. Light on
what had really happened—a mutation—is thrown on this
event by the similar occurrence of a 'perpetual' strawberry
in the United States.

On 28th September 1898, Samuel Cooper of western New
York, while examining his field of strawberries, noted a plant
with several runners attached, all of which were bearing
blossoms and fruit in all stages of development. The plants
among which these were found were of the Bismarck variety
. . . Mr Cooper set aside these plants which were bearing
fruit in the fall and named the variety *Pan-American*.[1]

Saint-Joseph and *Pan-American* gave rise to the scores of
strawberry varieties which bear their fruit in the autumn, or
which bear fruit continuously from June to October or later.
Strawberry-plants are very sensitive to length of day.
Variety 'A', planted at a latitude which exposes it to a long
day, produces nothing but stolons (runners); moved to a different latitude, it produces nothing but flowers and fruit but
no stolons. At a point somewhere between those two latitudes,
it strikes a balance between flower-bud and stolon-bud.
Variety 'B' behaves in the reverse order. Thus, by shifting
the latitude at which a particular variety is grown, one can
alter its behaviour; or, alternatively, by artificially shortening

[1] Hyams, E., *Strawberry Growing Complete*. London. 1962.

or lengthening the daylight hours. That is the final act of strawberry domestication.

THE RIBES

The name, *Ribes*, of this genus of bushy plants is derived from the Danish word *ribs*, meaning currant, or from a very similar word in one of the other Nordic languages. But this is no guide to the history of the plants; some of them may have been domesticated independently in the north of Europe, in Scandinavia, but they were certainly domesticated elsewhere as well.

The gooseberry (*Ribes grossularia*), so named because the fruits were eaten cooked with roast goose, is indigenous to the whole of Europe. Some authorities insist that it is only naturalized in Britain, but I do not know why; it is as likely to be native in Britain as anywhere else in Europe. It is rare in the south of Europe and west Asia, common in the whole of northern Eurasia.

The plant and fruit do not appear in any early literature; it is evident that neither the Greeks nor the Romans, let alone any more anciently civilized people, had even noticed it, let alone cultivated it. A possible reason is that it might not be thought worth growing by peoples with a plethora of grapes. Where grapes were not easily grown, gooseberries were used for making wine.

This fruit has a curious history in England. In the late eighteenth and early nineteenth centuries it became a sort of cult object to amateur gardeners of the working class in the industrial Midlands and north. Gooseberry clubs were formed, usually based on an inn or public house whose proprietor donated some of the prizes for which members competed with their gooseberries. Miners and factory operatives tended their gooseberry bushes in little cottage gardens, producing single fruits as large as plums and weighing upwards of two or three ounces each.

The fact that there is no record of gooseberry cultivation

in England before the sixteenth century has led some authors to assert that cultivated gooseberries were introduced here from western Asia by way of the Continent. But there is no evidence whatever for gooseberry cultivation in western Asia; nor of introduction from any of the three countries where, apart from England, gooseberries were grown at about the same time: Germany, Holland and France, in that order of importance. Nor is there any evidence for a foreign introduction in the vernacular nomenclature of cultivars. My own belief is that English cottagers domesticated this plant by introducing it from the wild into their gardens, a belief which of course entails another, that the gooseberry is indigenous in Britain; and that there were similar 'folk' domestications in Germany and Holland.

Three other *Ribes* are of some importance in temperate zone horticulture. One of these, the black-currant, is important industrially, in the making not only of jam but also of bottled juices of more or less medicinal standing. The other two can be thought of as one, because the white-currant is only a variety of the red-currant.

The cultivated red-currant seems to be a man-made plant composed of species *Ribes rubrum*, *R. petraeum* and *R. vulgare*. All are Eurasian natives, and at least one is indigenous in England, or if not indigenous, thoroughly naturalized at some early date. At all events, when, in 1557, Thomas Tusser published a list of all the fruits cultivated in England, red-currant was not in it.[1] It does, however, appear in the first edition of Gerard's *Herbal* (1597), as a fruit rare in cultivation and which the author is obliged to describe as unfamiliar.

This fact suggests a recent introduction from Europe, and we know that *Ribes rubrum* was in cultivation in some parts of Europe before it appeared in English gardens. There is indeed some evidence for very early cultivation in Brittany: it is not very clear, but it seems that the Breton name

[1] Tusser, 1557.

kastilez for this fruit is older than any French name, and that vernacular French names in different parts of France imply an alien origin. That is as far as we can get. Maybe the Bretons domesticated this bush during the Middle Ages.

Since the discovery that black-currants are very rich in Vitamin C, and since the German invention of sterilization by filtering through porcelain filters instead of by heat treatment, the black-currant, *Ribes nigrum*, has become commercially important as well as horticulturally popular in northern Europe.

The species is native all over Eurasia, from the extreme west to the river Amur and the Himalayas in the east. It is much commoner in the north than in the south, which may account for its being rather a late-comer among domesticated plants. It was apparently unknown to any of the ancient civilizations, or at all events it is unmentioned by their writers. The fruit has names in some pre-Indo-European languages, yet it is not to be heard of in cultivation until the Middle Ages, and De Wit goes so far as to say that the garden varieties of this *Ribes* were not developed until the eighteenth century.[1] According to one authority it was unknown in France before 1830, and it may even be true; certainly it is not mentioned by sixteenth- and seventeenth-century horticultural writers.[2]

There is a little second-rate evidence that the first cultivators of this currant may have been the Russians and that the fruit was introduced to the rest of Europe by way of Germany.

RASPBERRY

Rubus idaeus is indigenous to all Europe and all Asia including Japan, yet it seems never to have interested any ancient people in either continent. It occurs nowhere in Greek, Latin or Chinese writings. In fact the raspberry did not

[1] De Wit, 1967.
[2] Legrand d'Aussy, P. J. B., *Histoire de la Vie des Français*, 1782.

become of any real importance in Europe and North America until the nineteenth century; but I do not, of course, suggest that it was not cultivated until then.

In John Tradescant's mid-seventeenth-century catalogue a number of raspberry cultivars are listed and by then white as well as red kinds had emerged, which in itself is evidence for some considerable antiquity in cultivation. There are few earlier references to *Raspis* and *Hyndberries*, and the further back we go, the more often is the fruit described as sour, which implies that there had been no selection for improved varieties in cultivation.

This may be one of the fruits which were first cultivated, in European countries including England, by cottagers who took the canes from the wild into their gardens, as they did with the little wild wood strawberries: and that selection and improvement began there before the fruit interested professional nurserymen.

NUTS

Nuts are among the most obvious of wild foods and were surely, like the wild berries, gathered and eaten by pre-human hominids.

One of the first nut-trees to be domesticated was the almond, but about that something has already been said in the chapter on *Prunus*. The Greeks imported almonds as nuts for a considerable time before they had the almond-tree in their own plantations.

The Greek name for chestnut was *Dios balanos*, which can be translated *God's Acorn*. The Latins used a virtual translation of the same word—*Jovis glans*—but they seem later to have transferred the name to the walnut, and still later we used it—*juglans*—as the name for the genus to which the walnuts belong. Where did these two magnificent tree species come from as cultigens? As to their native habitat, chestnut is native right across Europe from the Caspian to Portugal; and in all the sufficiently advanced countries cultivation has for very long consisted in two acts: deliberate planting, and grafting with superior varieties. In the case of chestnuts, the superiority of the scion-variety has always consisted in single-kernel, as against two-kernel, nuts. So the point is to discover where these superior kinds, used as scions, first came from.

There is no doubt where the French and other north-European peoples found their superior chestnuts for planting. The varieties which Olivier de Serres recommends [1] are called 'Toscane' and 'Sardonne'; the first is obvious, and the second refers to the chestnuts which came from Sardis in Asia Minor. In fact we can skip Italy and Greece, for it was from Sardis that all the single-kernel chestnuts came in the first place, so that probably 'Toscane' also was originally an Asian cultivar. But Sardis was not the only origin, nor perhaps the oldest.

Our word chestnut is a corruption of *châtaigne*, which is a gallicization of *castanea*. Why did the Italians, beginning with the Romans, call the chestnuts Castanean? Presumably they came from a place called Castanea, or something like it. Now the poet Nicander, writing in the second century BC, does mention a place called Kastanis famous for its nut-trees. Herodotus, much earlier, and followed by the geographer Strabo, mentions a place, a small seaside town in Magnesia, called Kastanaia, which Theophrastus says was famous for the nuts he calls Euboean, after Euboea, an island off Magnesia. I suppose they might be chestnuts. The Kastanis of Nicander, however, was a much larger and more important place, in the Pontus,[2] and the Greeks imported nuts from somewhere in that part of the world, which they called simply 'Pontic nuts'. These seem to have been mixed nuts of all kinds, including almonds, but perhaps they also included chestnuts. We can conclude that the improved chestnuts reached Greece and the rest of southern Europe from Asia

[1] Serres, O. de, *Le Théâtre d'Agriculture des Champs*, 1600.
[2] Heyn, 1888.

Minor, but there is some evidence that the finest chestnut trees originally came from still farther east.

Then as to the filberts and cobnuts of the hazel kind, the tree is *Corylus avellana*. The epithet forming the specific name means 'of Avella', Avella Vecchia, formerly Roman Abella, being famous for its apples and nuts. The Italians had the tree from the Greeks in the second century BC at the latest, for Cato, in his *De re rustica*, recommends planting these Avellan nuts. They were among those which the Greeks called 'Pontic'; moreover Xenophon says in the *Anabasis* that when he and the Ten Thousand were marching through the land of the Mosynoiki, a Pontic nation, they found large quantities of nuts stored in the food lofts. Since, very much later, this country was celebrated for its fine nuts, it is fairly safe to assume that this *Corylus* was domesticated in Pontus some time before 300 BC.

To go back now to the walnut, *Juglans regia*. This was indigenous in western Asia as far east as Afghanistan, and in eastern Europe, but never in western Europe. The Greeks seem not to have known it, nor is it identifiable in Cato's list of nuts worth planting. On the other hand, the tree had reached Italy before Varro wrote *his* book of the same title, *De re rustica*. It looks as if the walnut reached Italy in Varro's lifetime (116–27 BC). But from where, and where it was first cultivated, it has been impossible to discover: doubtless, from Asia Minor again.

Very different is the story of the peanut, or ground-nut, or monkey-nut, *Arachis hypogaea*, now one of the four most important sources of vegetable oil in the world, and grown on a vast scale in many tropical countries. This is a legume, like the pea (hence the name), but with the odd habit of pushing the seed-pod under the ground to ripen. There are two varieties, and they are cultivated in India, China, Africa, southern U.S.A., Italy and Spain. In his great *Species Plantarum* Linnaeus wrote that this plant 'inhabits Surinam, Brazil and Peru'. But it was so widely grown in Asia before the middle of the eighteenth century, and in Africa too, that botanists considered it to be indigenous in the Old World and decided that China was the country of its origin in cultivation. Some botanists even identified peanuts in Theophrastus, who does allude to a plant called *Arachis* whose name Linnaeus borrowed; and on the ground that Theophrastus said so, asserted that the ancient Egyptians had peanuts.

But the two De Candolles, father in the *Prodromus* and son in several of his monographs, had to go to a great deal of trouble to demonstrate once and for all that peanuts were quite unknown to all the ancient civilizations and that *Arachis hypogaea* had been first introduced by the Portuguese into all the Old-World countries in the sixteenth century, by way of Africa. They were even able to show that this is an introduced plant even in Mexico.

The *Arachis* cultivars have never been found wild anywhere in the world. There are six species which have, and they are all confined to Brazil. Doubtless our ground-nuts are descendants, in cultivation, of two or more of these species. The first 'document' we have of it as a plant in use for food, and almost certainly cultivated, is some *Arachis* seeds found in a prehistoric midden at Ancon, ten miles from the coast of central Peru. It has been dated to *c.* 700 BC.[1] So this would seem to have been one of the many useful plants originally domesticated by the Early Farmer culture of Peru, *c.* 1000 BC.

The pistachio nut has a much briefer history. *Pistachia vera* was distributed from Italy to the places where it will grow in Europe, Africa and America. But it is not an Italian native tree: not only was it introduced, but we even know when, for Pliny says in his *Natural History* that it was introduced from Syria by Vitellius, at the end of the reign of the Emperor Tiberius; and from Italy into Spain by Flavius Pompeius. It was introduced as a cultigen; but as this tree is native to Syria, there is no need to look further for the

[1] Chavin horizon.

place of its domestication, which was probably of no great antiquity.

The cases of plant-domestication presented in this volume have been described as if they were deliberate acts following upon clear conceptions. This is because there are no means of describing briefly the growth of tiny event out of tiny event producing a result which can be seen as a great and significant change only very long after the accomplishment. The domestication of plants, as of animals, should not be seen as a series of deliberate undertakings, but as a slow process of evolution. Many writers now deprecate the use of the term 'Neolithic Revolution'; and, in fact, it is misleading in its suggestion of a sudden waking to agricultural and industrial possibilities after long ages of inertia without change.

Nevertheless, although the earliest plant domestications were the results of accidents such as the throwing away of fruit-kernels from which sprang seedlings, it is surely true that in each case there was a first time when a man or woman, having drawn conclusions from the observation of such accidents, deliberately planted seed, tended seedlings, and expected a harvest. Such acts were the foundation acts of civilization. If you believe that ordered, progressive civilization alone can lead us to understanding of and dominion over the universe, including our own natures and our own potentialities, and that such understanding and such dominion are the only proper destiny of man, then it is to those first domesticators and farmers of plants and animals that we should be grateful for the means to reach that end.

Bibliography

Note: other sources are acknowledged in footnotes to the text.

ACOSTA, J. (1598; 2nd edn, 1608). *Historia naturalia de Indias.*

BANGA, O. (1964). *Origin and distribution of the Western cultivated carrot.* Wageningen.

BEAN, W. J. (1934). *Trees and Shrubs Hardy in the British Isles.* London.

BLATTER, E. (1926). *The Palms of British India and Ceylon.* London.

BRETSCHNEIDER, E. (1871). *On the Study and Value of Chinese Botanical Works.* Foochow.

(1892). *Botanicon Sinicum.* Shanghai.

BROWNE, P. (1848). *Botany of the Congo.* London.

BUSHNELL, G. H. S. (1956). *Peru.* London.

CHAMPLAIN, S. DE (1830 edn). *Voyage de Champlain.* Paris.

CORNER, E. H. J. (1966). *The Natural History of Palms.* London.

DAVIES, E. (1809). *The Mythology and Rites of the English Druids.*

DE CANDOLLE, ALPHONSE (1855). *Géographie botanique raisonnée.* Paris.

(1884). *Origin of Cultivated Plants.*

DE WIT, H. C. (1967). *Plants of the World.* London.

ELLIS, J. (1774). *An Historical Account of Coffee.* London.

FORSTER, J. G. A. (1786). *De plantis esculentis oceani australis.*

GALEN. *De alimentis.*

GIBAULT, G. (1912). *Histoire des légumes.* Paris.

HEER, O. (1865). *Pflanzen der Pfahlbauten.* Zurich.

(1872). *Über der Flachs und die Flachskultur in Altertum.* Zurich.

HERODOTUS. *Histories*. Everyman's Library edition.

HEYN, V. (1888). *The Wanderings of Plants and Animals* (trans. J. S. Stallybrass). London.

HOOKER, J. (1875). *Flora of British India*. London.

HYAMS, E. (1949). *The Grapevine in England*. London.

(1952). *Soil and Civilization*. London.

(1965). *Dionysus*. London.

HYAMS, E. *and* MCQUITTY, W. (1969). *Great Botanical Gardens of the World*. London.

LE COMTE, L., FR. S. J., (1697). *Nouveaux Mémoires sur l'état présent de la Chine*. Paris.

LORET, M. V. (1890). *Flore pharaonique*. 2nd edn. Paris.

NEGRUL, A. M. (1938). *The Genetical Basis of Grape-Breeding*. Commonwealth Bureau of Agriculture, Cambridge.

PARKINSON, J. (1629). *Paradisus in sole paradisi terrestris*.

PHILLIPS, W. (1966). *Unknown Oman*. London.

PLINY. *Natural History*.

POLO, MARCO. *Travels*. Everyman's Library edition.

PORTER, M. H. (1943). *Pipas precortesanas*. Acta Anthropologica, 111, 2. Mexico.

PURSEGLOVE, J. W. (1968). *Tropical Crops: Dicotyledons*. 2 vols. London.

RITTER, K. (1848). *Über die geographische Verbreitung des Zuckerrohrs*.

SALAMAN, R. (1949). *The History and Social Influence of the Potato*. London.

SCHLIEMANN, H. (1885 edn.). *Ilios*.

SORDELLI, G. (1880). *Sulle piante delli torbiera e delle stazione preistorica della Lagozza*.

SWINGLE, W. T. (1904). *The Date Palm*. U.S. Department of Agriculture.

TÄCKHOLM, V., *and* DRAV, M. (1950). *Flora of Egypt*. Cairo.

TIEDMANN, J. (1854). *Geschichte des Tabaks*.

TUSSER, R. (1557). *A Hundreth Points of Good Husbandrie*.

UCKO, P. J. *and* DIMBLEBY, G. W. (1969). *The domestication and exploitation of plants and animals*. London.

UNDERG, F. J. A. (1851). *Die Pflanzen des Alten Aegyptens.*
   Vienna.
   (1852). *Die Pflanzen als Erregungs- und Betäubungsmittel.*
   Vienna.
VARAGNAC, A. (ed.) (1968). *L'Homme avant l'écriture.* Paris.
VAVILOV, N. I. (1940). *The New Systematics.* Oxford.
   (1951). *The Origin, Variation, Immunity and Breeding of
   Cultivated Plants.* New York.

Index